My Adventures as an Expat in Belgium

By Natalie Fowler

Copyright © 2015 by Natalie Fowler

All rights reserved. No part of this publication may be produced distributed or transmitted in any form or by any means, including photocopying, recording, or other electronic or mechanical methods without the prior written permission of the author, except in the case of brief quotations embodied in critical reviews and certain other noncommercial uses permitted by copyright law.

For permission requests, contact the author via the website below.

www.NatalieFowler.com

All photos included in this book come from the author's personal and family collection. Credit for the front cover image belongs to Susan Fowler. Thank you for sharing your passion for photography with us throughout the years and for always bringing your camera with you everywhere.

In a few select instances, names were changed to protect privacy.

MY ADVENTURES AS AN EXPAT IN BELGIUM/Natalie Fowler—
1st Edition
ISBN-13: 978-1548298937

To my husband, John—life with you is an adventure. Thanks for dreaming big, for getting us to Belgium, and for all of your love and support, especially with my various writing projects.

Acknowledgements

Thank you to my family, John of course, but also to Avery, Luke and Isabelle. You make every day an adventure, no matter where we live.

To my literary agent, Terrie Wolf of AKA Literary, LLC, thank you for being you and for believing in me.

To our family, especially our parents and brothers and sisters, for your many visits, care packages and phone calls while we lived so far away.

To all of our visitors, thank you for making us a destination or a stop through onto adventures of your own; we so enjoyed having the chance to show you around our little corner of the world.

To our beloved friends in Belgium and throughout Europe: We miss you terribly, and would love the chance to welcome you in Minnesota. Our door will always be open to you, in the same way way you opened your hearts to us. Maybe one day, we can begin to return your generosity.

To the teachers and staff at Ecole Saint-Joseph d'Ohain. You accepted us into your community and became our surrogate family while we lived so very far away from home. Thank you for your love and support.

To my friends from the American Women's Club of Brussels.

To our friends from Nativity of Our Lord, who held us in your hearts while we embarked on this amazing adventure, and welcomed us back with open arms. Also, thank you to the teachers, staff and friends we made upon our return. Without you, our transition back to Minnesota would have never gone as smoothly as it did.

*To our neighbors in Saint Paul for welcoming us back.
We are so glad our house never sold.*

*To my editor at FATE Magazine, Phyllis Galde, for telling me I needed to attack this project with a brutal edit and publish it myself.
And also for telling me to pick a different font.*

To my soul sister, Jessica Freeburg, for your never-ending love and support, and for helping me reinvent myself upon my return.

To my mother for encouraging me to "do something" with my blog and for teaching me perseverance and resilience. Thank you also, for your help with the brutal edit. To my father, who taught me to face life's challenges with a healthy sense of humor. To my mother-in-law for the many photos you've shared with us and for your help with the cover. To my father-in-law, for keeping an eye on all of us from heaven.

Friday, February 8, 2008
Getting Ready to Go…

The question around here lately seems to be, "What do I do next?" John and I are each working through a dozen different lists of things to do. My lists range from "what goes to storage" to "what to pack for our house hunting trip." Is it too soon to panic? No, considering the days are flying by. Moving day will be here before we know it, and we'll be off on this crazy adventure—f or better or worse. (We're praying it's the former.)

Wednesday, February 27, 2008
House Hunting

We've spent the last two days crisscrossing southern Brussels to look at houses and schools with our relocation agent. It has been a week filled with ups and downs. And while we're exhausted and tired of driving around to appointments, her expertise and assistance were invaluable.

Looking at houses has been interesting. We even looked at a house that had chickens and a coop in the backyard. And when I asked if the chickens came with the house (and it got translated to the landlord) everyone laughed but no one really answered my question. But I was serious, all I could think about when I saw chickens was the bird flu!

We settled on a nice modest row house. But we won't tell Avery about the house we saw that looked like a castle. If he finds out that we turned it down, we will never hear the end of it.

Wednesday, February 27, 2008
Channeling Jason Bourne

I finally understand why I always find myself criticizing Johnny's driving skills whenever he returns from traveling in Europe. It's because when he drives in Europe, he channels Jason Bourne (as in, Matt Damon in the Bourne Identity movies) as a matter of survival. It's actually quite fun because he's really good at driving a 5-speed down these tiny little streets at break-neck speed. (But don't tell him I said that because I yell at him to slow down when he drives too fast.) Although, I'm not so sure I'm looking forward to driving around here myself anytime soon. I think we'll be car shopping for an automatic at the very least.

Tuesday, March 18, 2008
Moving Out…

We moved out two weeks ago. John and I got back from our trip on Saturday, March 1 and it's been a whirlwind ever since. The packers came on Tuesday and it mostly went fine. Except, I did see him take my junk drawer, wrap the contents in paper and dump it into a box. That makes me worry a lot about unpacking. But at least I won't have to think about it for a while, our stuff is shipping by boat.

Avery asked if he could go on the boat along with our furniture. I pictured a cargo ship with a smelly crew of men and said, "No."

Tuesday, March 18, 2008
Funky Town…

After the physical exhaustion of jet-lag (twice in two weeks) followed by packing and moving, we endured the emotional exhaustion of saying goodbye to everyone and everything. It was really, really hard to say goodbye.

I took the boys to say goodbye to the house. When we got into the car, the Skrek II soundtrack was playing the song, Funky Town. The exact line? "Gotta make a move to a town that's right for me..."

Tuesday, March 18, 2008
Looks Like We Made It.

It was a long journey but we made it.

We left on Sunday night on the 8pm flight. For our family members that think we're too far away, we met an American family at the airport, with two young babies, heading back to their home in Qatar.

Everyone did well. The kids slept well on the plane, Johnny and I did not. A really drunk passenger caused a ruckus. But we got to witness the orderliness of the Dutch upon landing when the airport security team safely and efficiently escorted him away.

Thanks to Luke, we cleared customs quickly. We walked up to the passport check point and Johnny announced, "I'll handle everything," but he barely got a word in. The officer took one look at Luke, got a big grin and started asking him the questions. Luke explained that, "He was Luke and he was moving to Belgium with his Mommy, Daddy, big brother Avery and his cat Athena."

We arrived with just enough time for Johnny to run to the store and grab some dinner and groceries for the morning. Meanwhile, the kids watched an Aladdin cartoon in Dutch followed by a Nick Jr. cartoon in French. We were all very happy to tuck into our beds in our cozy little cottage for our first night in our new country.

Friday, March 21, 2008
A Few Things I've Learned This Week…

Mostly, I've learned that I have a lot to learn. But here are some of the more comical lessons from our first week in Belgium:

1. The laundry detergent does not go in the middle slot on the French/Dutch washer, that's for the fabric softener.

2. The green and red bottle under the kitchen sink is actually toilet bowl cleaner for the bathroom upstairs, not dishwasher soap like I thought. (Don't worry, I figured it out before I actually used it on the dishes, although it would probably would have been a better story if I hadn't.)

3. At the grocery store, you need to put a coin in the cart to unlock it from the other carts. No matter how hard you pull on said cart, without said coin it won't move.

4. If you pack toys away, and ship them to yourself in another country, it will feel like Christmas when they arrive.

5. Kids don't care if a cartoon is in French, English, or Dutch. If a cartoon is on, they'll stand there and watch it anyway, even if all of their toys just arrived from the other side of the ocean.

Tuesday, March 25, 2008
Happy Easter!

We had an interesting weekend. Friday night, Luke was up all night with a high fever, leaving us no choice but to find a pediatrician. Johnny navigated the situation really well, finding a doctor our insurance would cover, finding directions to the doctor's house, and calling the doctor and getting new directions in French after he got lost. Then he filled the prescriptions for antibiotics, nose drops and cough syrup AND remembered all of the instructions from the pharmacist, all while taking care of Luke. It was hard for me not to be the one to take Luke to the doctor, but I certainly couldn't have done as well as Johnny did in the situation.

Sunday, everyone was feeling better so we attempted Easter Sunday mass…without much luck. We gave ourselves plenty of time, but the church proved to be really difficult to find, and we never made it. All dressed up with nowhere to go, we drove to La Hulpe to show the boys our new house.

Wednesday, March 26, 2008
A Good Day in Belgium

So far, today has been my favorite day in Belgium. No one has jet lag. No one threw up. No one is running a fever.

We had a successful trip to the grocery store and hopefully, found some good breakfast things for Avery. Breakfast at home used to be Avery's favorite meal and he's really missing his frozen waffles and pancakes. Which is a little ironic, considering we now live in Belgium, where the waffles are world famous.

Luke has been asking for "tak-o-late" for breakfast, lunch and dinner. And then has a fit when I tell him we can't have chocolate for breakfast, or lunch or dinner. But it's safe to say, he is hooked on Belgian chocolate.

The boys are sleeping peacefully and it's raining outside, which makes for a cozy night.

Sunday, March 30, 2008
Three Strikes…

We found the English-speaking church this morning. We parked, excited that we found it with time to spare. As we were getting the kids out of the car, the front doors to the church were thrown open and everyone came out. John and I looked at each other wondering what on earth we were missing. He looked at his phone, and noticed that the clock was an hour off, and that's how we discovered that it was Daylight Savings here in Belgium today.

We headed back to Waterloo, where we knew of a French-speaking catholic church. John thought we might be able to catch its later service. We were hopeful as we pulled into the full parking lot. But as we opened the doors to go in, we were met with a stream of people trying to get out. For the second time today and the third time in a row, we missed mass.

We went into the church anyway, and took a seat to have a few minutes of quiet time. After a couple minutes, I realized that Luke was singing quietly next to me. He started out by singing the "Hallelujah" song from the first Shrek movie (which he calls his "church" song). And then it changed to, "Take me out to the ball game, take me out to the crowd. Buy me some peanuts and cracker jacks, I don't care if I ever get back..."

Monday, March 31, 2008
It's Hockey Night. In Belgium.

Tonight, John has his "tryout" tonight for the Leuven ice hockey team, the Jayhawks. They have a professional team, but Johnny is trying out for the club, not the pro team.

It could be interesting, since he doesn't have a stick. When we discovered that the packers forgot to pack it he wanted to carry it on the plane but I wouldn't let him. With two kids, two strollers, all of the carry-ons and a cat, a hockey stick was not an option. He tried to buy one the other day at the local sporting goods store, but when he asked if they had hockey sticks, they looked at him like he was crazy.

They play from ten to midnight (I know, it sounds suspiciously like "old man" ice to me too.) But he left here at 8:30 because he was so excited. (And he had to find a hockey stick.)

Thursday, April 3, 2008
Luke is Done.

First, an important update to the last entry: John had a successful tryout with the Jayhawks. He was able to purchase a stick for a "few" euros from their shop before he skated. His tryout consisted of an hour of drills followed by a half-hour scrimmage. I don't think John has done drills since high school. They invited him back, so I guess it went well.

We've spent the week dragging the kids around to look at appliances and electronics, not a pleasant task with two busy little boys. Today, we stopped to grab lunch at a local fry stand. We learned that if you ask for pickles on your burger, really, you just get pickle sauce that looks like green goo.

This afternoon, I heard Luke on our steps, banging something around. He had dragged his suitcase out of the closet, and bumped it all the way down the steps.

When I asked him what he was doing, he explained: "I'm taking my suitcase to the airport to get on a plane. I'm going home to Grandma and Grandpa."

"So, you are done with Belgium then?" I asked. "Yep," he said.

The other day, the cat fell out the window. She was upstairs, lounging on the windowsill, but the windows here don't have screens. She rolled over, and promptly fell into the flower pot down below. She was fine, but if a cat could look embarrassed, she did.

Tuesday, April 8, 2008
First Day of School.

Tomorrow, the boys have their first day of school. We found a great little neighborhood school, Saint-Joseph in Ohain. We met with the teachers and principal yesterday and it seemed like it would be a really good fit. Avery thought so too since his class has a bunny that lives in the classroom.

Children in Belgium start preschool when they turn two and a half. We were a little nervous about starting Luke right away, but yesterday at our meeting he talked to anyone and everyone. I also think he would be really lonely at home if his brother was in school all day every day.

Today, I had to go buy lunch boxes! But they won't need them until

Thursday, because on Wednesdays in Belgium, kids get a half-day. But that makes it a perfect day for them to start, and then they only have two days until the weekend.

Friday, April 11, 2008
Happy Friday.

Yesterday, was the first full day of school and the longest day of my life. The boys were sobbing and crying when I left, which means that by the time I got back to the car, I was sobbing and crying too. Although, I'm proud of myself that I managed to wait until I got back to the car.

I went early to pick them up so they could see me right away. The boys did great and talked nonstop the whole way home, and talked a lot about lunchtime. Avery's lunch box has a picture of a monkey and a lion, and the lion is looking down at a banana and the monkey is looking down at a drumstick, and they both look upset. Avery told me about how he showed his whole lunch table this and had everyone laughing at the joke. Not bad, considering he doesn't speak the same language as the other kids. Luke told me about how he took a nap after lunch. "There was a little room, with little beds, but no pillows. And I took my shoes off, set them next to my bed and went right to sleep with my monkey and my nukky." I am so proud of both of them.

Today, they were more nervous about leaving the house, but drop off went a little better. A few tears, but thankfully, none of them were mine.

Monday, April 21, 2008
Whew. What a Week.

Our movers came last week and we are now semi-settled in our new house. I feel like we've been moving for months. Oh wait. We have. But the end is finally in sight.

They unloaded the truck on Wednesday, and two "unpackers," came back to help on Thursday. This was our first "professional" move. I felt spoiled watching the guys move the boxes and furniture into the house for us. We've always had to bribe helpers with beer and pizza.

But I don't think I liked the unpackers very much. Basically, they took everything we own out of the boxes and put it in piles all over the house. On Thursday night, we could barely walk from our bedroom to the boys' room. I wished we had a snow shovel to clear a path. It was stressful and unsettling.

By Friday, things were better. With the boys at school, I had time to get the house organized. It was also nice not to have to deal with all of the papers and boxes, since we don't know anything about the recycling rules. And having piles everywhere certainly motivated me to get everything put away!

Things are better now. We can at least walk from one room to the other.

Monday, April 21, 2008
We Have Our Doggie Back!

Jasmine, our big yellow dog, arrived on Friday. It took a lot of coordinating and planning. Grandma and Grandpa Fowler ran all over the Twin Cities on our behalf to get Jasmine to the vet and her paperwork to the USDA's office, and then of course, the dog to the airport.

John drove to Amsterdam on Friday morning and found the animal retrieval desk. Our dog was so confused to see him. But now we have one tired lab that's been reunited with her family.

Can you believe she has jet lag? She's been waking me up in the middle of the night to go outside, and she's confused when I don't feed her.

The cat was a little disappointed to see the dog. Athena obviously thought we'd left Jasmine behind.

Monday, April 21, 2008
Why Are We Doing This Again?

Avery really misses going to school in English. Luke is having a hard time adjusting to all-day school. I got a note in Avery's backpack and I can't understand what it says. I am overwhelmed that our house here is such a mess and there is still so much to do to put it back together, and keep a daily schedule on top of that. Our dishwasher didn't work when we moved in and it was just one more thing Johnny had to call about in French. Jasmine won't eat because she broke her tooth before she left Minnesota and so she is scheduled for surgery on Wednesday.

Avery and Luke had a party at their school on Saturday, and they both got to be in a little dance with their teachers and classmates. They were so excited to be part of something and Avery smiled the whole time. There is one really great older girl from the primary school who seems to love all of the little kids and her face lights up whenever she sees Avery and Luke coming. She kisses them and hugs them and takes them by the hand. She even asked me if she could take them around to all of the games and activities at the party on Saturday. She spent about an hour with the kids, checking in with me the whole time. While she was playing with the boys, Johnny and I had a chance to have a glass of wine with some of the other parents. And one of the moms really wants to practice her English, so she invited me over for coffee tomorrow so that I could speak French to her and she could speak English to me.

Today, the caretaker came to our house to "fix" our dishwasher by plugging it in. And I bought a vacuum. All by myself. In French. (Ok, so it was only a little bit of French and a whole lot of hand gestures.) But I did it by myself. And I even found a really fun baby gift for Ryan and Jenny, my brother and his wife who are expecting. I also found a shortcut on the way home. And we found a really nice, English-speaking vet that is going to fix Jasmine's tooth on Wednesday. And while I was taking Luke to the potty there, we got to see some baby kittens being born.

Oh yeah. We're doing this because life is too short not to have adventures. And because the harder the struggle, the sweeter the victory.

***

Author's Note:

This was also the weekend that I learned I was pregnant. I couldn't bring myself to blog about it, we'd had several miscarriages and have always held our pregnancy news close and quiet until we knew it was safe to share.

But I will never forget finding out I was pregnant with our third child. When we were in the middle of the unpacking mess, I found a single pregnancy test. We'd had a miscarriage right before Christmas, and it was an extra from that.

And I realized, it had been awhile. In fact, the only reason I knew that I was overdue was because along with everything else, I'd had to deal with that on the plane coming over. But it was still too early to test. Trying to figure out how and where to buy a pregnancy test was not something I wanted to figure out. I tucked the single test away in a safe place, and saved it, just in case.

At the kids' school party, everyone was drinking wine. After my second glass, I realized that I should probably figure out if I was pregnant or not.

The next morning, John was down in the kitchen making breakfast for the boys, and I snuck upstairs to take it. When it came back positive, I sat in shock for a few minutes. Then I left it on the counter. I remember telling John that whenever he had a minute, there was something he needed to see in the bathroom. He of course, went to check right away. Neither of us could even talk about it for a week. While we were of course thrilled, we weren't expecting to get pregnant so quickly after our arrival in Belgium.

***

Sunday, April 27, 2008
A Belgium Birthday Party.

Avery and Luke were invited to a birthday party. When they brought the invitation home from school, I was so overwhelmed by the kindness of the family who thought to include them (and us) that I cried.

The day of the party arrived and it was a beautiful Saturday afternoon. We wrapped our present and made a special card. We found the house with almost no trouble, even though the online map directions led us along a dirt road that went through a field, but that actually turned out to be the right way.

We walked through the house to a beautiful backyard, complete with a swing set and trampoline. Most of Avery's classmates were there along with some of the parents.

But the first and only thing that the boys saw, was the huge table filled with more candy than you could possibly imagine. There were bowls of licorice, gummy bears, cookies and chocolate. It was like walking into Willy Wonka's house. John and I shrugged our shoulders and let them have at it. (When in Rome, and all that, right?)

We talked and visited with the parents. John and I learned how great a glass of French rosé wine tastes on a hot day. The boys had a wonderful time playing with new friends from school. It was a lovely day.

Monday, May 5, 2008
School Update…

At the birthday party last weekend, I mentioned to one of the mothers that Luke was having a hard time adjusting to going to school all day. And she said, "Well, why don't you just pick him up at lunch?" I didn't even know you could do that!

Apparently, children in Belgium start going to school early, but attendance isn't mandatory until age six. I sort of knew that, but didn't really know I could apply that to our circumstances. Anyway, I talked to the teachers last Monday. Ok, I made John come with me to drop the kids off so that he could talk to the teachers (which turned out not to be necessary because there are enough parents that speak English who are happy to help translate if we need it). And since Luke was coming home after lunch, Avery wanted to come home after lunch too. And since my goal is to make sure they both like going to school, that's what we decided to do for a while. (Not to mention that it saves me from driving back and forth to school all day long.)

The teachers were happy to accommodate, and explained that the best time to pick them up would be right after lunch. And the difference last week was amazing. No one cried in the morning. No one complained at breakfast about going to school. And most important, no one fought with his brother all afternoon and all night after school. They came home after lunch smiling and excited about their day and then played NICELY together until dinner. Every day. The difference was amazing.

Wednesday, May 21, 2008
A Day in Amsterdam.

My friend Sally was here for a visit last week. She flew into the airport in Amsterdam, and took the train to Brussels.

To fly home, I was going to take the train back with her. We would stay one night in Amsterdam and then she would catch her flight the next morning. A quick girls' overnight. Sounds simple, right? It wasn't.

Last week, we learned that the Belgian trains were going on strike. I'm not sure how effective a strike is if everyone knows about it ahead of time and it's only for one day, but that's what they did. Of course, it was the day we needed to travel. Fortunately, we did know about it and were able to rent a car which was not easy, especially since I'm "the American" who doesn't know how to drive a stick. I was not all that excited about my first road trip and having to find my way through two countries, but Sally and I travel well together. We were looking forward to the adventure even with a drive.

We made it through Belgium and into the Netherlands, and that's where it got dicey. We had really, really bad directions to our hotel in Amsterdam. Our directions took us to a neighborhood on the edge of the city. And now, Sally and I know that little corner of Amsterdam really, really well. And we know for absolute certain, that there is not a Crown Plaza at the intersection that the printed directions say there is a Crown Plaza.

We asked for directions a lot, so now we also know a lot of people from this neighborhood too. We met an old lady, a police officer, mothers with children, fathers with children, a lady at a hair salon—you name it, we probably talked to them yesterday. It just so happened, that yesterday, my cell phone got restricted to emergency calls only—something about the bill not getting forwarded to the right address. Apparently, getting lost for several hours in Amsterdam didn't count as an emergency.

In any event, we eventually found a hotel (not the right one, but one that was incredibly helpful). The clerk called our hotel, confirmed our reservation for us, and then gave us the right directions. Ok, so the directions were in Dutch, but they were better than the ones we'd found on the internet.

We learned a lot of lessons yesterday. The most important was that Sally and I still travel really well together. And if I'm going to be lost for several hours in a small corner of the world, I'm glad it was with her.

Wednesday, May 21, 2008
Saying Goodbye.

There is a song that the kids have been singing a lot lately. It's from the

Muppets Take Manhattan. (The Muppets are big at our house these days.)

It's a song about why it's not sad to say goodbye, because when we have to say goodbye, it makes us remember the good times.

That song went through my head like a soundtrack when I said goodbye to Sally this morning. But it is very, very true. It was absolutely wonderful to see her, and it was so appropriate that she was our first official visitor in Belgium.

As I was saying goodbye to her today, I realized how very lucky I am. Not just to have a friend like her, but I had just spent ten days with her. The last time we got to spend ten days in a row together was when we backpacked through Europe after college. When in my adult lifetime, would I ever expect to spend that much time with a good friend?

So, thank you Sally. For being such a good friend, and for being our first official visitor.

Wednesday, May 21, 2008
Luke Has the Chicken Pox.

Yep. The chicken pox. About two weeks ago, I noticed a little boy at school (from the older kids' class) that I hadn't seen in a while, and he had red spots/scars all over his face. And last week, there were a few girls missing from the older kids' classroom and they returned with the same spots.

When I realized these kids had recovered from the chicken pox, it never even occurred to me that my kids would get, or should I say *could* get it. They were both vaccinated.

When I was driving back from Amsterdam, John called to tell me that when he got to school with the kids, he noticed Luke had spots on his face. By the time he picked the kids up after lunch, everyone at school decided that yes, Luke had the chicken pox. Everyone was very helpful, and no one seemed too concerned about hustling Luke out of there or anything.

Luke is covered in little red blistered spots. I get itchy just looking at him. We're on day two, and he's keeping his good nature through it all. So far, the hardest part for him is having to stay home from school without his big brother to keep him entertained. And Avery told us that without Luke at school today, he was lonely at recess.

Wednesday, May 28, 2008
Appliances.

I blew up our toaster.

I don't know what I was thinking, but it was something along the lines of, "If my hairdryer works on a trip to Europe with an adapter, then why wouldn't a toaster work with an adapter?" Well, it didn't. I plugged it in with an adapter and it sparked, and popped and I pulled the plug as quickly as I could, but it still smoked for quite a while. I think I completely killed it, which is too bad since it was a good toaster.

It went into the brown box in the basement labeled: Junk from the US that won't work here. Some of the other things in the box are night lights, radios, and a few other random odds and ends that I'm not ready to throw away. Just in case.

Fortunately for us, this is a good time of year to catch the expat moving sales. We've been able to find lamps, fans and yes, even a new toaster.

Monday, June 2, 2008
U.S.A…

The other day, I overheard Luke chanting "E.S.A. E.S.A." And then I heard Avery say, "No Luke. It's U.S.A. U.S.A." Whew. I'm glad we got that figured out.

Johnny took Luke running the other day (in the jogging stroller). They ran past the tennis court, where some sort of tournament was going on. John said he noticed a sign that said "Welcome Belgian Junior National Team." (Although it probably said that in French.)

As they ran by (about three feet from the court and the players) Luke started chanting "U.S.A. U.S.A. GOOOO WILD!" And Luke doesn't say anything quietly these days. Johnny said he ran a little faster, but he thinks the player might have missed his shot.

Wednesday, June 4, 2008
Number 3…

It's official! We are excited to share that we are expecting Baby Number 3 just in time for Christmas.

I've been feeling good—tired, but not sick. Finding a doctor was hard. But I joined the American Women's Club and asked around for a recommendation.

It just so happens that my parents will be here! The week we moved, they booked their tickets for Christmas, arriving a couple weeks before and staying just through Christmas. Not a bad coincidence, even though it's not exactly what they were expecting when they booked their first trip to Belgium!

Friday, June 13, 2008
Cleaning Products

Warning: Type-A personality in full-force and effect.

As everything here, when it came to buying cleaning products and supplies, it was a lot of guessing as I tried to figure out what to buy and how to use it.

Imagine my delight when I recognized "Mr. Clean" smiling down at me from the shelf. Bonus: Most of the back of the bottles show little pictures of where to use the product. I found the picture of the stove for the kitchen, the bathtub for the bathroom and so on. Easy, right? No. Mr. Clean actually ended up smelling like Mr. Pansy.

Maybe this is just my "pregnancy nose" but everything here smells overly perfumed and excessively floral to me: Soaps, lotions, shampoos, everything, and cleaning products in particular.

In the eight months before we moved, I turned into a neat freak out of necessity. With the house on the market, barely any notice before most showings, and two kids and two pets, I didn't have time to mess around. My house was clean out of necessity. Eight months is plenty of time to turn that level of cleanliness into a habit.

Every time I've cleaned here, it ends up smelling like all I did was spray air freshener all over the countertops and toilet. (And no, I didn't. I verified the French on the Mr. Clean bottles.) Give me some bleach Belgium! I miss the tell-tale smell of bleach and disinfectant. Clorox! Lysol! I miss you!

My solution: Earlier this week, I went to the grocery store. I spent an extra twenty minutes in the cleaning supplies aisle. I'm not kidding, I sprayed every bottle until I smelled anything that slightly resembled the smell of bleach and narrowed it down from there. A lot of people stared at me like I was insane, but I didn't care. And I sincerely hope all those fumes didn't hurt the baby. But I found Bref. And it smells better and cleaner than Mr. Pansy.

Friday, June 13, 2008
Last Day of T-Ball

Last Saturday was Avery's last day of T-Ball.

I thought it was funny that the weather last Saturday, was pretty much exactly the same as the first day of T-ball: cold and rainy. Not that I'm complaining, we're not getting floods here like they are at home in the Midwest.

Everyone's favorite day of T-Ball was the last day. It was at the army base. That meant a concession stand with real burgers and hot dogs, orange soda and root beer.

Tuesday, June 17, 2008
A Fun Weekend

Some good friends of ours from St. Paul (they were our old neighbors) made a stop through Brussels on their way to Denmark from Germany. We went to meet them at their hotel and go out to dinner. It was our first attempt at driving downtown, but thanks to our fancy-shmancy GPS we made it just fine.

On Sunday, all John wanted to do was watch Tiger play in the U.S. Open. But the closest he could come to watching it on television, was to hit the refresh button online and get the play-by-play commentator reporting each and every move. I loved when the guy typed, "This is so exciting I can barely even type," to which John yelled, "Just tell me if he made the putt!" Riveting stuff, let me tell you.

I think we're going to have to break down and get the fancy (and questionably legal) satellite cable. He'll never make it through football season.

Wednesday, June 25, 2008
Random Updates.

I had an interesting conference with Luke's teacher the other day. She mentioned that he understands a lot of French, but whenever she says something that he doesn't want to do, he pretends that he doesn't understand. I love two-year-olds.

John is settling into work here and trying to get stuff accomplished before everyone in Europe goes on "holiday." But his traveling has gone well, and he is working hard to find that perfect balance between work and home—not an easy task when you work from home. It's also one that becomes even more challenging with a seven-hour time difference, meaning everyone from the States hits the middle of their morning right as we are sitting down to dinner. But we're figuring it out and adapting quickly.

I have officially given up at trying to keep the cat in the house. Our doors and windows here don't have screens so if the patio door is open, she is now free to move about the backyard. She can't really go much further than this anyway, we have thick hedges and fences. And she seems perfectly happy to sit in the sun and not venture out too far away. I'm hoping that she catches the mouse/shrew that lives in the bushes. Wait, let me also add, "When Johnny is home to dispose of the carcass."

Wednesday, June 25, 2008
It's Hockey Night. In Belgium.

Last Saturday night, we all attended Johnny's hockey game in Leuven.

John's team played the Grizzlies. The Grizzlies are actually the Belgian National Women's Team. I have to say, I was a little scared when we arrived at the rink. These are some tough looking girls. And they all met early so they could go for a run BEFORE the game. I got even more nervous when I saw the guys on the ice when we arrived. Have you ever been to an NHL game? You know how they let the little kids play in between periods for a few minutes? And half of them just fall over for no apparent reason? This was the skill level of the guys playing before Johnny's game. I suppose it didn't help that they had pitchers of beer with them on the bench.

But I didn't have to worry. John's team is actually very good, and it was so fun to watch him play. The last time I watched him at a real hockey game (with refs and a score board) was almost (large, audible gasp) twenty years ago when we were in high school.

The girls were good, but the guys were bigger and faster. Everyone in the rink was really excited when the girls' team finally scored. My little boys did great and actually watched most of the game—when they weren't asking to "play" the car video game in the bar upstairs. And if they didn't want to sit still, they didn't have to because we were the only ones there. They could climb up and down the stands all they wanted without bothering anyone.

All in all, it was a really fun family night in Belgium. And I can't even tell you how awesome it was to sit and watch a live hockey game.

Sunday, June 29, 2008
The Last Day of School…Finally.

The last day of school was a long time coming. My whole life, the last day of school has always been in late May or early June. To have school go until the end of June was excruciating. (In two weeks when the boys are bored and fighting with each other, remind me that I said that.) But now, summer is officially here and we're all excited.

However, Avery woke up on Saturday morning and wanted to know why it was cold and rainy. "It's not summer," he protested when he looked out the window. It's easy to forget how literal four-year-olds take everything, isn't it? I reminded him that this is Belgium. Some days are cold and rainy, even in the summertime. It's why the outdoor swimming pool has a retractable roof and why we really appreciate the warm sunny days when we get them.

Thursday, July 3, 2008
Counting Crows in Belgium.

John and I had our first concert experience in Belgium last night.

When we first arrived in Belgium, John discovered that the Counting Crows would be playing here in Brussels in July.

Last night, we went out. We even made a dinner reservation for before the concert. The tickets said 8pm and we figured we had plenty of time. There's always an opening band, right? Apparently not here.

To our surprise, the concert was held in a small club venue. (The last time we saw the Counting Crows, they played in a field.) We walked in at 8:35 and missed the first song. After accidentally and unintentionally annoying everyone around us as we tried to move through the crowd to the front near the stage, we finally found our way up to the first balcony. There, we found a spot near the rail, about 10 yards away from front man Adam Duritz, slightly above the crowd surrounding the stage.

I was so confused about the way the crowd behaved when we tried to move through it. From our bird's eye view, I took a few minutes to watch the audience. I learned a lot about concert-goers in Belgium in those first few songs. For example, a rather large woman moved through the crowd and left through a side door. No one in the crowd filled the empty space she left behind. It seemed like everyone around her was going to save her spot while she went to get a beer. It didn't make any sense to me.

But it was a great concert. We watched the Counting Crows play about 20 songs in the most intimate settings we will ever see them play.

Saturday, July 5, 2008
Homesick.

I was really homesick yesterday. You're probably saying, "Well, it's about time." Yes, I know. It was a combination of triggers. The change from schedules and school routines to empty days and two little boys to entertain...and if not entertain, at the very least, keep from clobbering each other.

Also, there is no better holiday than the Fourth of July in Minnesota. A day with family on the lake. Fireworks. Food. It's a day on the calendar that (obviously) goes completely unrecognized here. Also, we are all still sick with coughs and colds and I am really tired of not feeling good. Oh, and then there's the rain. Have I mentioned that it rains a lot in Belgium?

But yesterday came with sunshine and Johnny motivated us to get up and out the door. We drove to the coast and spent the day at the beach in the sunshine. And it wasn't a "bank holiday" here, so we had plenty of parking spots to choose from. And if I have to have yet another cough and cold, at least I was at the beach in the sun.

It wasn't a bad Fourth of July after all. It turned out to be a good family day at the beach.

Oh! And my mom is coming next week for a short visit. And at the end of next week, we leave for our first trip home. And after that, John's parents come for a long visit in August. We have lots to look forward to, including our own little taste of summer in Minnesota.

Monday, July 14, 2008
A Visit from Grandma…

Grandma arrived last Wednesday. Unfortunately, we didn't show Grandma as much of Belgium as we would have liked. Instead, Grandma got to go to doctors' offices and pharmacies.

By Friday afternoon, Avery had a diagnosis of pneumonia and Luke, bronchitis. I was sick too. The three of us were on antibiotics and my kitchen could have been mistaken for a French pharmacy. There were antibiotics, cough medicines for day, cough medicines for night and nose drops for the boys. None of it tasted very good. I miss the sugary, flavored syrups from the United States. I've resorted to hiding the boys' bedtime cough medicine (the worst of the bunch) in a chocolate milkshake after dinner. It's just a matter of days before Avery catches on to my trickery.

Saturday, everyone was feeling a little better so we ventured out. There is a medieval castle not that far away that we wanted to find. We were only there for about 45 minutes, and it was cold and rainy. Exploring a cold, damp castle on a cold, rainy day within 24 hours of Avery being diagnosed with pneumonia was not the best parenting choice.

Yesterday arrived with high hopes that everyone would finally be feeling better. These were dashed about ten minutes after breakfast when Avery threw up all over the living room.

This morning, everyone was finally feeling better. We've even seen the sun all day, I think it's the first time in a week. Of course, my mom had to leave for the airport right after breakfast so she missed both the sunshine and two boys who are finally back on their way to feeling normal.

I'm sorry Mom, but at least we'll see you soon. We're going to have a quiet week and get ready for our own flight home on Friday. Here's hoping the next few weeks are free of fevers, coughs and vomiting!

Thursday, July 17, 2008
Summer "Sales" in Belgium.

Everyone here is in an excited buzz about the big sales in July. Apparently, merchants, by law, can only offer substantial discounts during July and January. They have "promos" throughout the year, but the good discounts and best time to shop is during the big sales.

Earlier this month, our town of La Hulpe even closed its main street and made the first weekend of the "sales" into a big party. There was a band and everything. There were activities for kids and the merchants all moved their goods out to the sidewalks.

But shhh…I have a secret. The "sales" weren't actually all that great. Or maybe I am just totally and completely spoiled by American stores. After all, American stores have sales and clearance racks every single day.

Saturday, July 19, 2008
Jet Lag.

After a really long day of travel, we made it back to Minnesota. Our day started with a taxi pick-up at 8:45 am, Belgian time. Our flight was late, and the airports were crowded, but we made it through the check points and security to catch our 1:15 pm flight in Amsterdam with just enough time to spare. My favorite part of the process, was proving to the security officers in Amsterdam that my double-wide umbrella stroller really did fold up small enough to fit through the x-ray machine.

Our flight from Amsterdam to Minneapolis was long. It was a daytime flight and we had more than eight hours to fill for two busy little boys. I chose to look at it as "lots" of quality one-on-one time with Luke. I think Avery watched television until he turned cross-eyed from exhaustion. I knew I was in trouble when I checked the "are we there yet" map projected on the cabin wall only to learn we still had five hours left.

We finally arrived in Minneapolis at our anticipated 3:15 pm, local time. For us that meant 10:15 pm. But I won't complain. Already, in only two trips back and forth across the ocean, we've met expat families with young children traveling from further away than us, heading on to other destinations after Minneapolis.

We stayed with my parents. They had cheeseburgers ready (per Avery's request) and we had an early dinner on the deck overlooking the lake. It was nice to be somewhere familiar.

I woke up at midnight and couldn't get back to sleep. I was just about to, when I heard Luke wandering around in the hallway. I was just dozing off (again) when I heard Avery crying because he was all alone in the basement. I went downstairs to sleep in Luke's bed—and every twenty minutes a little hand patted me to "make sure I was still there" which also made it impossible to sleep. Finally, at about 4:45am, we gave up and went out to watch the sun come up. We later learned that while Avery and I were watching from the basement patio, Johnny and Luke were watching from the deck above us.

Wednesday, July 30, 2008
Observations.

I thought it might be fun to share some of the things that surprised me about being back in Minnesota.

The first one came when we managed to get ourselves into our rental car and out of the airport just in time for Friday afternoon rush hour. There we were, sitting in traffic, and I totally and completely relaxed. It was as if we had just stepped off the plane for a Florida vacation at the beach. I didn't even realize how tense I'd been for the last several months. But just knowing where we were and where we were going was incredibly calming. We turned on familiar radio stations. The billboards were in English. We even knew when to expect the traffic to slow down and pick back up again. We didn't need a GPS system to get us to where we were going.

Seeing white eggs surprised me. I guess I'd never really thought much about the colors of eggs before. In Belgium, eggs are always brown. I was so busy getting used to everything else in Belgium, I'd gotten used to brown eggs without realizing it.

Also, everything felt really big. The cars seemed bigger and the roads seemed so wide. In Belgium, I flinch when I pass a car too closely on a two-lane road.

Another surprise came from how quickly we settled back into an American lifestyle. There were a few days of shock that came along with the jet lag, but we quickly and easily fell back into some familiar habits, like daily lattes.

In all of the years I'd lived in Minnesota I never realized what a great state it is for a vacation destination. We had sunny and gorgeous weather every single day in Minnesota. We could go to the pool, or the lake, or a park whenever we wanted without worrying about rain.

I realized how lucky we are to be Americans. The entrepreneurial nature of Americans in general ensures a constant flow of new ideas and products. It was crazy to watch commercials for things like "cereal straws" who would have thought? Market competition ensures fair prices and trade. A solid work ethic means successful (and completed) projects. Recently, I read an article about road construction in Belgium. Apparently, there's a race to start road construction projects in early July, because school gets out and traffic is minimal. But then, the entire construction industry goes on holiday for the month of August. And everyone wonders why things aren't completed in time for school to start again in September.

I guess what they say is true. "You don't know what you've got until it's gone." But, now we've also had a chance to be away from Belgium for a while too. I'm looking forward to getting home and finding out what we've missed from there while we were back in Minnesota.

Sunday, August 3, 2008
Back Home in Belgium.

We've spent the week readjusting and getting over "the jet leg," yet again. The boys have been waking up in the middle of the night and having a hard time going back to sleep. The good news, though, is that instead of getting up before dawn, I have to drag them out of bed at 9am. But we're close to being back on track.

We came back to summer weather in Belgium. The day we came home it was sunny, hot and humid, but now it's cloudy and rainy again. We all have our "holiday suntans" which somehow makes it easier.

Grandma and Grandpa Fowler arrive on Tuesday, and we are very excited to get to see them again so soon. It made goodbyes in Minnesota much easier.

Oh, and the boys have a new baby cousin! My brother, Ryan, and his wife, Jenny, were heading to the hospital at the same time we were heading to the airport to fly home. I missed holding my newest nephew by a matter of hours.

I am sorry to all of the friends and family we didn't get to see while we were home. It felt like such a short visit. But now that our first trip home is over and done, it helps us feel as though we are not so far away. And now we also know to plan for a longer, even better trip home next summer.

Monday, August 4, 2008
Happy Monday.

The boys woke up smiling at 8:30 which is definitely progress with the jet lag. My day started with a twist when I had to answer the door in my pajamas not long after that. It was Leon, our elderly caretaker who was here to fix the main floor toilet. Leon has a charming smile, but doesn't speak a word of English, and by that I mean, not even a "hello." I couldn't exactly explain why I was standing there in my pajamas. "Recovering from jet lag," is beyond my basic French skills.

After breakfast, we assessed Luke—who has been running yet another fever for the past two days—and decided we needed to call the doctor. The doctor diagnosed an ear infection. While we were waiting for the prescription at the pharmacy, Luke gave me a look and then proceeded to vomit his strawberry yogurt all over everything. Well, mostly himself, me and the floor. At least he didn't throw up in the car?

We got ourselves home and cleaned up. When I took the pukey clothes downstairs to the basement, I discovered HUGE puddles of water all over. Fortunately, Leon was still there.

We discovered a three-foot-long crack between the foundation and the sidewalk outside, and water runs down into the basement. It rained a lot last night. A lot.

Leon happened to have some extra silicon to fill it in. Hopefully, that does the trick. I'm also happy to report that we are getting a brand-new toilet on Friday morning at 8am. I will NOT be answering the door in my pajamas.

Thursday, August 14, 2008
English as a Second Language.

Before we moved to Belgium, and even while we were home in Minnesota for our vacation, people would say to me, "Well, everyone speaks English there anyway, right?"

I can now answer, "No." At least not in La Hulpe. I am absolutely not complaining about this. I am living in a foreign country and I do not expect to walk into a shop or speak to a vendor in English. It has been interesting, though, to observe how different people from different places respond to my inability to speak their language.

For example, in French-speaking Belgium, I always get a better reception if I fumble my way through an explanation in French that I don't speak French very well. Sometimes, the person I'm speaking with will switch to English. More often than not, they won't, but at the very least, they will be patient with me and politely try to help me out. I'm also getting really good at charades and acting out what I need. Never mind that I look like a fool. Maybe the French-speaking Belgians are too busy trying to learn Dutch as their second language to have much time for English?

For the first time since we moved here, I actually came across a clerk at the grocery store who spoke English, and seemed excited to practice. Of course, I was with my mother-in-law, and I had just finished explaining to her that no one at the grocery store ever spoke English. But when it was our turn in line, the clerk heard us speaking English to each other and got excited to practice her own. The biggest challenge has been the pharmacy. Getting prenatal vitamins, or any of the kids' prescriptions when they are sick is a lot of work. Buying the vacuum cleaner I told you about in the first week was probably the most comical.

In Dutch-speaking Belgium, my experience is that it's not well received to speak French first. There are some tensions between the Flemish (Dutch-speaking Belgians) and Wallonians (French-speaking Belgians). In the Flemish region, it's always better to just assume that everyone speaks English and ask in English if they speak English. However, in the Netherlands, I found that people were actually insulted if I asked if they speak English (because everyone in the Netherlands speaks English very well).

We haven't been here long enough for me to really know. There seems to be a lot of tension in Belgium between the Flemish and the Francophones. Specifically, the government is trying to work something out and both sides seem frustrated. A lot of the problem seems to focus on language and who should speak what where. It will be interesting to see how this plays out over the next few years.

In any event, it's complicated. But a smile goes a long, long way, no matter who I'm trying to talk to.

Thursday, August 14, 2008
A Ten-Year Anniversary…in Paris.

We celebrated our ten-year anniversary last weekend in Paris. I feel so "la-de-dah" saying that. "Oh, we went away to Paris for the weekend." Who does that? Movie stars? Millionaires? And apparently, us.

Nothing about the past year has been easy. We have worked so hard to get here, get settled, and just figure out how to live with a young family in a foreign country. Everything takes longer, nothing is easy.

John's parents arrived last week for a long visit, and very kindly offered to stay with the kids for the weekend so we could sneak away. I've never been to Paris and it's only an hour by train from where we live. It was the perfect choice for an anniversary weekend. It was so easy!

And when we got there we just wandered....by ourselves without kids! We went out to dinner...by ourselves without kids! There were a million tourists. In fact, I don't think there were any Parisians in the city at all, they were all on holiday. But we could skip the long lines for museums and churches, because we know we could go back again in the off-season. We felt very lucky to wander, enjoy being together and relax, knowing we didn't have to rush to see it all.

Ten years of marriage is something to celebrate. We've worked hard together to make it this far. We make a good team and are good for each other, but it's still a lot of work.

I appreciate that we had the chance to celebrate it. And it was so great that for once, something was easy. And I'm glad it was Paris.

Wednesday, August 20, 2008
The Olympics.

It has been really interesting watching the Olympics here. In the United States, there are so many top athletes. There are lots of individual stories for the media to cover, just among our own athletes.

But watching the games from over here, really provides a sense of how international the Olympics truly are. We've been able to watch some of the coverage from a television channel in France, some of the coverage from a Belgian television channel, and of course, the BBC. One thing does not change: a country's pride in its own athletes.

One of the BBC channels has provided the most inclusive sports coverage as they have dedicated one of their channels to round-the-clock coverage. Not to mention, it's in English. However. I realized, Great Britain must not be good at the same sports as the Americans. But they are plenty good at other sports I didn't even know about! Who knew that "trampolining" was an Olympic sport? And we discovered the most interesting bicycle race with an indoor track and lots of hills. Apparently, the Brits are good at this, because it warranted an entire afternoon of uninterrupted coverage.

Unfortunately, we saw next to nothing of gymnastics. And coverage of the swimming events was sporadic at best. But Michael Phelps was amazing! At least from what we could see on the internet.

September 2, 2008
First Day of School!

The first day of school in Belgium is like a national holiday. The police were everywhere directing traffic. Drop-off was a family affair. There were cars filled with entire families everywhere. There were lots of parents filming video and snapping photos. It was fun to be a part of it.

The boys did great, they were excited too. It wasn't as scary for them because they know the teachers from last year. It helped that it was Avery's birthday, and he chose to bring chocolate cupcakes for his classmates. Showing up at school on the first day with chocolate cupcakes for everyone is never a bad thing.

The school supply lists were interesting, but I somehow managed to get the shopping done. And I can tell you that I probably feel a deeper sense of satisfaction at being done with the school supply lists than any of the other parents because they were so hard to figure out.

I keep asking Avery about what the other kids brought and if his stuff is the same or different (trying to gauge if I've completely missed the boat on one thing or another). So far, it seems like I've done pretty well. Although, yesterday he said "Mommy, I was the only one in gym class without a special t-shirt!" Fortunately, he seems to think that's funny and he laughed about it for a while.

It will be a good year.

Tuesday, September 16, 2008
School Update.

Luke: Luke is doing well at school. He barely kisses me goodbye before running off to play with his buddies.

But last week, I got an interesting report from his teacher. She was having problems with Luke because he was refusing to listen to her when she spoke in French (even though she knew he was understanding). I told Luke she was his teacher and he had to listen, no matter what language she spoke. He said, "Ok Mommy. I will listen to her in French." And the next day he did and she said he did great. If only all of our school problems that arise over the next fifteen-plus years could be that easy!

Avery: Avery is enjoying school too. There are two new children in his class that both speak English at home. I think it has helped him to not be the only kid who's different, and he's also not the "new kid" anymore. His class has started their swimming lessons. They go with the first and second primary classes once a week on the bus to a nearby town with a pool. This caused a lot of anxiety at first—riding the bus, changing into his swimsuit, not knowing what the pool would be like. Now that he's done it once or twice he thinks it's a really cool thing to do for school, and I agree. But it is very strange for me to think that my five-year old has been to a part of Belgium all by himself that John and I have never been.

The weather here has been beautiful. Sunshine during the day and crisp, fresh air during the evenings, through the night and morning. There is a party coming up at school where the kids get dressed-up. It's not for Halloween, but it is in the middle of October so we will make it work. Now, we just need to find an apple orchard!

Tuesday, September 23, 2008
The Girl with the Red Boots.

Tonight, at dinner, the boys were talking about their friends at school. Luke was talking about the "girl with the red boots." (He refers to kids at school by their shoes.) The "girl with the red boots" is blond and British. She's in Avery's class and she's new this year.

She speaks English at home, but she also speaks French. I think she has become the playground ambassador for Avery and Luke. I asked Avery about her, I was curious what language they spoke at recess. He explained, "She speaks French." And then he got a big grin and emphasized by waving his finger, "But not to me. I get the English."

Wednesday, October 1, 2008
Las Vegas. For Children.

Well. We did it. We took our very first family weekend away and went to Disneyland Paris.

We took the train from Brussels. The stop for Disneyland was underground, and when we walked up the stairs, we really felt like we had arrived in the land of Disney.

There were a lot of British visitors and it was strange to hear "British" all around us for an entire weekend. We'd become so accustomed to hearing French, it was overwhelming to suddenly be able to understand every conversation.

We had one especially bizarre moment, one night at dinner. A British woman, whom I had noticed staring at us, came over to our table. Without any intro she asked, "Why aren't you in Florida?" John and I looked at each other, confused.

She continued. "Why would you come all the way to Paris to go to Disneyland when you could have gone to Disneyland in Florida instead? The food is better in Florida."

We explained that we lived in Belgium. She simply said, "Oh," and walked away.

Sometimes, it feels strange to live in Europe. This was one of those days.

Monday, October 13, 2008
Roadways and Roundabouts.

In Belgium, it seems as if roads have been turned into obstacles as a method of controlling traffic, our town especially.

Here are some of the obstacles erected in our part of the world in an effort to make drivers slow down:

Roundabouts: A roundabout is a giant circle instead of an intersection, where cars have to wait for a break in traffic to enter, and they have to exit at the right spot or you get stuck going around and around. Drivers drive through these really fast, so you have to be ready.

Speed bumps: Speed bumps are self-explanatory, but some of the speedbumps here are REALLY big and in a little car, you can hit your head on the ceiling if you go too fast.

Plateaus: Plateaus are giant speed bumps where you drive up, drive for a few feet, then drive down the other side. If you go too fast, the bottom of your car scrapes against the pavement. It was a good thing I figured this out while we still had a rental.

The Random Squares: I have no idea what these are supposed to be called, but they are two giant squares (with an incline/decline similar to the plateau) positioned next to each other so that each lane of traffic has their own. I have yet to figure out the best way to go around these.

Sometimes, I see cars line themselves up to drive directly over the middle, causing the least interference as you mostly avoid the incline/decline that way, but then I worry about the muffler scraping off of the car. I usually use the half-the-car method where I drive so that one side of the car hits the incline/decline while the other side gets to go in between and remains level.

The One-Way Buffers: (I made up that name too.) These are big wooden boxes, erected across half of the street, turning an otherwise two-lane road, into a one-way section of road. (Usually it's about 25 yards long.) The idea is that if the buffer has been erected on your side, you are supposed to wait until the traffic clears before you can take your turn to go down the road. An observant driver will discover that there is an elaborate signaling system that goes along with this obstacle. If you are the driver waiting, you turn on your left blinker. If you would like to be generous and let the opposing driver proceed first, you flash your brights. Don't ask how long this took to figure out. And also don't ask what happens if you use the wrong signals.

Just to give you an idea of how popular these traffic control tools are, especially in our little town, we are about eight blocks away from the train station. And between our house and the train station, there are: three plateaus; two sets of random squares; approximately five one-way buffers; and one roundabout.

There is one more critical Belgian/European driving rule that is tough for us foreigners to grasp. It is the "yield to the right" rule. No one has been able to explain its origin with certainty, although I think it's something that dates back to the time of horses and buggies. At an intersection where the roads are of equal value (meaning one isn't busier than the other) the driver approaching from the right has the right-of-way. In practice, this means that the drivers from streets on the right break into the flow of traffic by turning out in front of you without even slowing down. Sometimes they don't even watch. I had to learn quickly to watch out for the traffic from the right.

Driving here is fun. And a little dangerous.

Monday, October 13, 2008
Mommy, My Tummy Hurts.

About a week and a half ago, Luke was getting over a cold. He wasn't quite himself, but he wasn't acting sick and he was excited to go to school. On the way to school, however, he announced that his tummy hurt. This was a few moments after Avery and I were talking about how *his* tummy hurt because he was nervous about going to school. I assumed that Luke was just trying to get in on the conversation.

We arrived to the playground, and I sat down on the bench. Luke turned around and looked at me with this really strange face, gave a little cry and a cough, and proceeded to vomit all over me. In that moment, I realized he wasn't kidding about his tummy hurting. There I was, standing next to all the uber-chic European moms, covered in puke.

Thankfully, I was wearing sweatpants because my maternity wardrobe is rather sparse. We cleaned up as best we could, kissed Avery goodbye and I took Luke home to watch movies on the couch.

However, he chattered and acted like his normal self, all the way home. The rest of the day, he was absolutely fine. He ate, talked and played all day, and generally had a pleasant day at home with mommy.

But as I was driving back to school to collect Avery that afternoon, I realized that the exact moment he had told me that his "tummy hurt," was immediately after three quick roundabouts, a sharp left turn that goes down a hill to a winding road, followed by a speed bump, a plateau and then another speed bump. And then I remembered that he had told me on more than one occasion that "his tummy hurt" in exactly the same spot.

Hmmm. Maybe the kid was carsick? Three roundabouts, followed by consecutive speed bumps and plateaus is enough to make anyone queasy and rethink their breakfast.

Last Monday, we took a different route to school. Successfully. No puke. Tuesday, we were not so successful. This time, thankfully, I was spared but our car was not so lucky. He threw up as soon as we parked. If I had only gotten his seat belt unbuckled fast enough! If I had just opened his door for him instead of yelling, "No, you're not sick, you can't be sick!"

Well, he was and he showed me.

We have permanently banned yogurt for breakfast. I now drive around with a bucket in the front seat, an arm's reach away, just in case. We avoid as many roundabouts as we can in the morning, even if it means driving the long way to school. So far so good. His teacher recommended a homeopathic motion sickness chewable tablet for kids that we haven't had to use yet, but I have it on hand, just in case. And you can bet, that if

Luke ever tells me that "his tummy hurts" again while we're driving in the car, I will pull over faster than you can say "roundabout."

Monday, October 20, 2008
McDonald's.

On my limited, overseas travel prior to residing in Belgium, I used to laugh and roll my eyes at the idea of visiting McDonald's in a foreign country. Actually, I did more than that. I issued a strongly worded declaration that essentially swore I would never, ever set foot in such an American establishment as McDonald's, anywhere outside the United States.

That was before I found myself living in a foreign country with two children. I was very, very wrong to make fun of the American enterprise that had duplicated itself on foreign soil.

When we first arrived in Belgium, everything we encountered was new and strange. There was nothing to remind us of our former life in Minnesota. The weather was different, the language was foreign, the culture was new. But, in Waterloo (an area I have heard described here as "the American ghetto" as it contains the highest concentration of Americans in all of Belgium) there is a McDonald's.

From our temporary housing, we had the chance to drive by the McDonald's on the way home from school every day. The boys looked for those golden arches every time as if they were some symbolic representation that all is not lost.

And when we walk through those doors and they can shout their familiar orders of Happy Meals with chicken nuggets and get exactly what they are expecting, it's like magic.

On Saturday morning, we took Johnny to the airport for his second trip back to the U.S. within the last six-weeks. It's hard for me and the boys not to feel homesick when we know Daddy is home (for work) but gets to stay with and visit grandmas and grandpas and aunts and uncles and cousins.

That day, I had an epiphany. We went to Saturday night mass, and I promised dinner at McDonald's as a reward for good behavior. After repeatedly reminding them over and over again what was at stake, I called it good. At approximately 6:35 p.m. we walked through the familiar glass doors of the iconic institution.

After a good twenty minutes of nonstop laps up and down the giant, brightly colored plastic play-land structure with a dozen other children, they were hungry. They happily ate every bit of their Happy Meals.

I love McDonald's.

Now, if only Starbucks could find a location somewhere in Waterloo....

Saturday, November 1, 2008
Untitled.

This baby must be getting close. I barely have a shred of motivation to do anything.

The boys have had the week off of school for autumn break. How cool is that? I think I like the European school schedules. (Remind me I said that when the boys are still in school through June.) It's been a busy but fun week, trying to keep two little boys entertained. Yesterday, we even found the Natural Science Museum and saw the dinosaurs.

Here are a few highlights from the week:

Avery announced (unsolicited) that when he grows up, he wants to be "a Daddy first, and then an English teacher," which he later clarified was a "teacher that speaks English." (His teachers only speak French, I can understand his addendum.)

Luke announced (unsolicited) that he would like to be a construction worker. And when he was all done with that, he'd like to be a super hero. With a cape.

Yesterday, Avery was playing in the attic. The play area is on one side, and John's office is on the other. John was at his desk making a few phone calls. One of these calls was to the phone company, to clarify our phone bill from the last few months. Most of this conversation was in French. Johnny said that a few minutes into the call, he heard a little voice whisper from across the room, "Daddy, it's 'oct-obre' not 'october'." After John was finished with the call, his five-year old said, "Daddy, your French was pretty good, but you need to practice a little more."

Saturday, November 1, 2008
Happy Halloween!

I've been told that in France, Halloween is discouraged by the government because it goes against religious views. (It's so easy to take the separation of church and state for granted in the U.S., isn't it?)

Anyway, here in Belgium, Halloween is a small, but growing holiday. Mostly, it is celebrated by singletons at the bars and clubs. And there is definitely a strong focus on the "horror" aspect. We've steered clear of the Halloween displays at the stores because they feature lots of fake blood, axes in body parts—the sort of thing that gives a grown-up nightmares, not to mention a five-year old.

We missed all of the expat-organized Halloween activities, because they took place before the children went on their school break.

Last night, John helped the kids dress up in their pirate outfits. He took the pirates to the bakery to get bread for dinner, and the fry stand to get fries for dinner (and a few other stores in between). Most stores here give candy to kids anyway when they come in with their parents. Last night, dressed as pirates, my little American boys brought a lot of smiles to the inhabitants and shopkeepers of La Hulpe, and came home with a few pieces of chocolate and candy. Not bad, for missing every other organized Halloween activity. The credit, of course, goes to a daddy that made sure his kids got to experience a little bit of the American holiday they were missing at home.

Wednesday, November 5, 2008
American Politics: A View from Abroad.

I've been asked (by my American friends) what people here in Belgium think about American politics. Our Belgian friends here are really curious about our political opinions. In fact, here, even mere acquaintances ask us which candidate we prefer.

That surprised me. I realized that Americans seem more guarded about their political opinions. (*Author's note: Keep in mind, I wrote this post before Facebook.*) Of course, there are political discussions among friends and within families. But, I would never just walk up to a new mom I met through Avery's preschool, and start a conversation by asking her which political candidate she supported. Those sorts of discussions are eased into much more gradually where I come from.

People seemed more fascinated with the race between the democratic candidates than the presidential election itself. A few months ago, the question was, "Who do you support, Hillary or Obama?" It was interesting that people naturally assumed that we were for one or the other. In fact, interest in the actual election seems to have faded in recent weeks, as if the winner has already been chosen.

Within these discussions, I also came to realize that people seem envious for a chance to vote in the U.S. election. Our foreign friends have strong political opinions, but as Americans, we're the ones with the vote that counts. Voting has always felt important, but from here, I realized for the first time that voting is a coveted right and privilege that only comes with our precious U.S. citizenship status.

Obviously, the best part about American politics from abroad is that we were mercifully spared the barrage of media. No endless political ads on television. No telemarketer phone calls during dinner time. Our mailbox escaped the burden of being stuffed with glossy ads. No door-to-door solicitors. No yard signs. It was interesting to have to seek out information about the candidates on our own instead of having it jammed down our throats.

I sort of miss the yard signs, though. Especially in our St. Paul neighborhood. It was such a sign of Fall to drive down a street and see signs of every color staked among the piles of leaves on the square city lots.

Sunday, November 9, 2008
Luke's Favorite New Word

Luke's new favorite word is responsibility. He uses it completely out of context every time. For example, we recently had a conversation about how they should be nice to all of the kids at school, even if it was someone they didn't particularly like, namely, a really bossy girl in Avery's class. Luke replied, "But it's my responsibility to be mean to her." The other night, John asked Luke for a hug and he replied, "But that's not my responsibility right now."

French Progress Report: When Johnny asks Luke to say something in French, he replies, "Anglais, s'il vous plait." In other words, when John asks him to say something in French, he replies, in French, that he wants to speak English.

Friday, November 14, 2008
Avery's Declaration.

Avery has always been a creature of habit. He loves routines that he can count on and knowing what's going to happen when. Avery is also an extremely observant kid. He will notice things that would easily go unnoticed by a lot of people.

One week when John was traveling, we stopped and got fries from the fry stand to go with our dinner. Avery pointed out how funny it was that we were having "fries" on a Friday. Then he declared that "Fridays" are now "fry days" and we have to have fries for dinner from the "fry guy" on Fridays.

I guess that works for me!

Friday, November 14, 2008
A Guy Walks into a Bar with a Big Yellow Lab…

A week or so ago, Johnny really needed to get out of the house and take a break. As you can imagine, it can be isolating to work from home. Being seven hours ahead of the States, often, some sort of crisis will happen just when he's ready to stop working for the day. And in today's world of technology and Blackberries, having the discipline to "turn it off" is a constant challenge.

All of this is usually balanced pretty well by John's travel. If he's traveling somewhere every other week or a few days here and there, the isolation isn't as noticeable. And spending a couple nights at a hotel every once in a while, gives him a chance to keep working during the business hours of the States, thus appeasing his coworkers.

But with the holidays approaching and the baby coming soon, he's home now for a while. And even though we've met good people here, it's not like we have friends that we could just call up at the last minute and say, "Let's go get a beer." (Brock, and the Nativity Guys, Johnny really misses you.)

The other night after the boys were in bed, John came downstairs from his office and declared he was taking the dog for a walk, and that they were going to go get a beer at the neighborhood pub. He and Jasmine walked down to the bar. Belgians not only love their beer, they love their dogs. Jasmine was invited in, and the two of them sat at the bar and had a pint or two of Belgian beer. Jasmine did a few tricks and earned a few cookies.

Last night, late, Jasmine perked up when Johnny came downstairs and wagged her tail and barked expectantly. I think she wanted to go out for another pub night.

Friday, November 14, 2008
Sunday Night Football.

Aside from not having a good circle of buddies to hang out with, Johnny has also had to re-think Sunday afternoon football. We don't have the expensive satellite television here yet, we're trying to survive without it as long as we can.

But Johnny did invest in an online viewing package through ESPN.com, meaning he can watch football games live on the internet. With the time difference, most of the games start just as the kids go to bed. It's perfect!

Except for one thing: He has to watch on our computer. Sunday nights, he turns the couch around in the living room so he can watch football.

Oh, and one other thing: The "full screen" option doesn't work for some reason. He gets to watch on a tiny window.

Oh, and one more thing: Every thirty seconds or so, our computer goes into "sleep mode." John has become good at kicking the mouse with his foot to turn it back on.

And he doesn't even complain about it—we just laugh! I guess it's just a good example of how thankful we are when we find a little piece of our former, familiar life. It doesn't matter if the football game is on a six-inch screen and turns off by itself every thirty seconds, it's live American football—Budweiser commercials and all.

Wednesday, December 3, 2008
Lists.

A few weeks ago, I was cleaning out the closet in the baby's room. We haven't been here long enough for it to have become too cluttered, which was nice. It was an easy job. But, I came across something in the process that actually made me a little sick to my stomach.

I found my lists; the ones I made when we were getting ready to move here to Belgium. There was a list for things that went to storage. A list for things we weren't sure if we were going to move to Belgium with us or not. A list for things we were air shipping, to arrive early. A list of things to pack in our suitcases. A list of things to bring in our carry-ons. A list of what we were giving away and who we were giving it to. And the list of lists goes on and on. There were at least a dozen—for a variety of different things.

I'm not normally a big list person. But there was no way we could have made this move without all of those lists.

And guess what I did with the lists? I joyfully threw them in the garbage and didn't think twice about it. I'm hoping that I will never again need that many lists to accomplish anything ever again.

Wednesday, December 3, 2008
Thanksgiving. In Belgium.

Holidays here, especially ones that are only celebrated in the United States, are big homesick days for us. I learned after the Fourth of July, to be ready for it at Thanksgiving. The boys have been talking a lot about Minnesota lately. They really miss their friends and family we left behind. I knew Thanksgiving would probably just make this worse.

A few weeks ago, we invited two families from school over to our house for an American Thanksgiving dinner. One family is an expat family from France, and the other is Belgian. Knowing I was going to be very pregnant and knowing I would need any extra time I could find to get ready for Christmas, we invited them over for the Saturday before the actual holiday. (I guess that's an advantage to celebrating an American holiday abroad—you can pick your own day.) Besides, on the actual Thanksgiving holiday, the kids had school, I had a doctor's appointment and we knew our week would just be a regular week.

A week before our planned party, John and I went to the butcher in town and ordered a turkey. In French. I was nervous all week, because I wasn't 100% sure if we had actually accomplished that task. I was also nervous because I wasn't sure if the turkey would fit in our oven.

Actually, I was just plain nervous. It was the first time we've entertained here. At least I've cooked a turkey before. But here, it's not like I can go find a box of Stovetop Stuffing or have a can of turkey gravy on hand just in case I mess it up. I also had to figure out how to bake a pecan pie without corn syrup, because I can't find that here. I was nervous about doing all of it by myself. At home, there's always a grandma, sister, aunt or mom around to help or offer a second opinion.

We kept things pretty basic. Turkey, mashed potatoes, stuffing, gravy, veggies and pie. And of course, Belgian bread. For the most part, the food turned out pretty well.

And one bonus: When you cook for people who have never experienced

Thanksgiving dinner before—they have no idea what to expect. My friend from France told me that when she was a student, she was in New York one year at Thanksgiving time. She and her friend wandered the streets on Thanksgiving Day wishing they could be inside somewhere learning about the American holiday.

She thought our Thanksgiving meal was perfect. And we did too. After all, the original holiday was about stopping for a minute to give thanks after settling in a new country, and sharing a meal with new friends made in a new land. This year, I am thankful that we had a chance to appreciate the true meaning of the holiday, in a way we never have.

Monday, December 8, 2008
It's the Final Countdown.

We've reached the final countdown. In about a week, Baby Fowler will be here, just in time for Christmas. I haven't blogged much about being pregnant. It's been such an easy and mellow pregnancy (and for that I am incredibly thankful) but it often takes a back seat to everything else going on in our crazy-busy life.

I figured something out. We arrived in Belgium on March 17th, St. Patrick's Day. And my C-section is scheduled for December 16th. For anyone who is half-way decent at math, yes, this is almost exactly nine months—to the day—after we arrived. In an absolutely amazing coincidence, the week we moved, my parents booked their trip to visit us at Christmas—before we even knew we were expecting. They arrive in Brussels on December 15th. (Which is just a little *too* perfect, so I'm expecting my water to break at any moment—just to make life more interesting.)

I have my "reservation" for next week, which sort of makes me feel like I'm going to the spa instead of the hospital. I have a whole suitcase packed, just for the baby. Here, they don't supply any clothes or linens or toiletries for the baby (or me for that matter) so I have a lot to bring. I will also be staying for at least four days, if not five. (A five-day stay is normal no matter the type of delivery here.) Will I enjoy the extra time or will I go crazy at the hospital knowing my parents and boys are home without me? I have no idea.

Mostly, I'm excited to find out if this is a boy or a girl. I guess we'll know soon enough.

Monday, December 8, 2008
My First Haircut in Belgium.

This actually happened a couple of weeks ago, and I wasn't quite sure if I would be brave enough to blog about it. But maybe you can enjoy a laugh at my expense.

I finally got up the nerve to go in for my first haircut here. I pride myself in being low-maintenance when it comes to my hair. I'm very easy-going and I go back and forth between long and short (a bob every now and then) without much fuss. Keeping it long is a lot easier, I can get it out of my face and I don't need to dry it. (When it's shorter, I have crazy waves that have a mind of their own.)

Obviously, since it's been awhile since our trip back to the States, my hair was getting pretty long and in need of a healthy trim. I figured that it was a pretty safe length for me to try the local hair salon. My French is a lot better over the last few months, as has my confidence in speaking it. I studied the page on "going to the hair salon" in my *Idiot's Guide to Learning French* and went off to my appointment without fear. I was actually looking forward to it, planning to add it to the "accomplished" column in my mental check list that I've kept in my head since we arrived here several months ago.

I think I need to work on my French. Either that, or the "Idiot's Guide" wasn't exactly the best source to rely on for something as personal as a haircut. In any event, whatever I said must have been something like, "Please make me look like I'm trying to join an 80's rock band."

We made it through the initial consultation (all in French). The small talk that usually happens with a stylist was minimal, as you might imagine. We talked about the baby—which was an obvious topic given my big belly. But after that it was a quiet appointment. I relaxed a lot after the initial snips, she was cutting a little more than I thought I'd said, but it was still going to be a good, low-maintenance length. Whew. Or so I thought.

Panic set in when she combed up a huge section behind my few whispy bangs...and then cut about six inches before I could blink. I tried not to gasp out loud. I was in shock for a moment or two, but then realized I couldn't really say anything anyway. First of all, in my state of panic, the few French words I had been so confident about earlier were nowhere to be found. Second, I realized that if I tried to say anything, she'd probably get flustered and nervous and it would all end up a lot worse.

I held my breath for the next forty-five minutes and watched, helpless, as she cut layer after layer after layer. I'm not kidding—it is not unlike Bon Jovi or David Lee Roth circa 1987. Maybe a little longer. It's the kind of style that requires (especially for my out-of-control waves) no less than a hairdryer, curling iron and lots of product to look half-way decent. I don't even have a hairdryer and curling iron with the right plugs.

Oh, and let's not forget time. I don't have time to "do" my hair. And that's not going to get any easier with a new baby. At least my hair grows fast. Right now, I can just barely pull the "front line" of the layers back out of my face. In a few weeks, that should improve, I hope. In a few months, it will probably look really good. In six months, maybe I'll have enough nerve to get it cut again. Perfect! That's just about what we're planning for our summer vacation home to Minnesota...

Monday, December 29, 2008
It's a...

GIRL?!?! What are we supposed to do with a girl?! I thought for sure it would be another boy!

John and I spent the whole first day with Isabelle, completely in awe of the fact that we were saying the words "she" and "her." More than once, I caught myself saying "sweet boy" and having to change at the last minute to "sweet baby." It's a change we are all welcoming with open arms—of course.

Isabelle is the first granddaughter on both sides of our family. And Grandma Tritz thought for sure it would be grandson number six. But she adjusted quickly and even snuck a "pretty princess" doll with a matching tiara into the Christmas present pile. Avery was pretty fascinated by the fact that his baby already has her own tiara. And thanks, Aunt Jenny, for the quick response and getting us a pink blanket here as fast as you can say, "baby girl."

Thursday, January 1, 2009
Christmas in Belgium.

Saint Nicolas Day (December 6) is a big deal here. At the end of November, all of the chocolate shops and grocery stores have big elaborate displays featuring Saint Nicolas. (The bishop, not the jolly elf.) Avery and Luke brought home numerous art projects featuring the saint, his donkey and his sidekick. And here, Saint Nicolas is responsible for bringing the big presents to the children (not Santa). This required a little explaining to the boys. Somehow, we managed to find a plausible explanation for the coexistence of Saint Nicolas and Santa Claus.

One day, in my French class, we translated a handout about the tradition of Saint Nicolas. I learned more about his sidekick—Père Fouttard. Saint Nicolas was a bishop who lived a long time ago and looked out especially for children. However, as the legend grew, his sidekick came along to "take care" of the children who were bad. Apparently, "fouttard" is French for "whip."

As soon as I had the chance, I asked Avery what he had learned in school about the guy who "helped" Saint Nicolas. He explained, "Oh, that's the joker that goes along with Saint Nicolas to help make the children laugh." Whew. Glad to know that the school had re-interpreted the legend so I didn't have to try to explain corporal punishment as a part of Christmas.

Saint Nicolas Day came and went, and at school, the children left out carrots for the donkey and a beer for Saint Nicolas. (Yes, I said beer—at school. We are in Belgium, after all.) Incidentally, we decided to leave a beer and chocolate for Santa this year instead of cookies and milk. We figured, after all the milk, he might want something a little different. And we are in Belgium, after all.

Thursday, January 1, 2009
Having a Baby. In Belgium.

I'm glad that this was not my first baby. It was comforting to have been through the whole experience—twice—before going to another country to have a baby. As is everything, some things were different, some the same; some better and some not.

One of the biggest differences was the prenatal care. I had monthly, and then more frequent prenatal appointments as my due date approached. But it was a much more personal experience than the U.S. In this entire time, I never once saw a nurse. I would always meet with the doctor first in her office, followed by the exam. Over the course of nine months, this allowed me to really get to know my doctor.

The hospital stay was also different. For a Cesarean, I had to "check-in" at noon the day before my scheduled surgery. I was told by my doctor that I would go in for my paperwork and blood work and then get to go home for a while, but would have to return for bedtime. It was strange to check-in to the hospital, only to go home for dinner, but I was grateful because my parents had just arrived. It was also really bizarre to sleep in the maternity ward that night—still pregnant—and listen to all of the crying babies in the rooms next door.

The food was definitely different. In the maternity wards in Minnesota, there was a "patient" kitchen, stocked with graham crackers and peanut butter for the new nursing moms. I think at Abbott, I even got to order a variety of extras to go along with my meal if I wanted. Here, dinner was usually a salad with a piece of cheese. Lunch was the main meal, and with my special "san gluten" (gluten-free) diet, it was guaranteed to be "sans flavor" as well. Three out of the five lunches were a piece of white fish—probably cod (no sauce) with mashed potatoes (no gravy). Yum.

My actual stay felt calmer and quieter here. The focus was on rest and recovery. In Minnesota, people were constantly coming in and out of my room. Nurses would be in several times a day to check vitals for me and the baby. Blood technicians would come and go at all hours. Here, the doctors did rounds in the morning. Other than that, no one really came in. But my physical therapist came once a day. The first two days after surgery the nurses checked on me frequently, but once I was up walking around they left me alone unless I needed something. It might be my imagination, but it seemed to me the first two days, the nurses spoke a lot of English to me. But after I was up and walking around, they spoke French. In fact, the same nurses that I thought spoke English in the first two days, didn't seem to even understand English the rest of the time. Hmmm. Maybe I had some really good pain meds those first two days.

The nurses were surprised that I wanted to leave early. Believe me. Six days in the hospital was plenty. I was ready to get home with my new baby. All in all, it was a good experience, but one I'm really glad to be done with.

Wednesday, January 7, 2009
A Belgian Blizzard.

We've been having a week of Minnesota weather here. On Monday morning, the first day of school after vacation, we woke up to two inches of snow on the ground. And it was still snowing. It was really pretty, coming down in big, thick flakes.

We managed to get out the door at a decent time, even though it was our first day back from vacation. We slid our way out to the main roads and joined a long line of crawling cars. Driving the Volvo is a little different than driving our old Trailblazer—no antilock breaks or four-wheel drive. Traffic stopped. It took us 25 minutes to go a mile. And once you were in traffic—you couldn't change your mind and turn around to go home because it was the same story in every direction. There were no obvious accidents, everything was just slow. It turned out that cars were getting stuck going up the hills. The sand trucks and plows (or, as Avery pointed out, they weren't really snowplows, just tractors with shovels strapped to the front) were just getting out onto the roads at the same time as everyone else—and were stuck in the traffic jams.

To my surprise, the driver of one of these plows tapped on my window. He rattled off something in French, and I explained that I don't speak French very well. He repeated the exact same thing over again, but louder. He left and I rolled up my window. I commented to the boys that I still had no idea what he was talking about.

Avery replied, "Mommy, 'passe' means pass, he wants you to pull over to the side so he can get his truck around you." Oh. Ok then. Good thing my five-year-old can speak French and good thing he was in the car with me. We scooted over to the side as best we could and the truck drove around us.

It took me an hour and a half to take the kids to school and return home. (School is only five miles away.) It's cold this week (-10C—whatever that converts to). We still have about four inches of snow, and a lot of the roads are still a mess. John also pointed out that they must not have shovels in Belgium. No one cleared their walks, and we haven't even seen anyone out shoveling. I did see a lady out with a broom though.

We are enjoying our week of Minnesota winter weather. But mostly, I'm glad that in a week or two, the snow will probably be gone and it will have warmed up again.

Wednesday, January 14, 2009
Facebook.

Facebook is pretty amazing.

Within a week of joining, John and I connected with a lot of people from all aspects of our life. His hockey team, our friends from St. Paul, my writing group from Minneapolis, cousins, classmates from high school and college. And then he started getting "friend requests" from people he grew up with and hadn't seen or heard from in a long time. It was pretty exciting. And pretty amazing when you think about it, to be connecting with all kinds of people from our past while we're sitting over here in Belgium.

My family moved to the Twin Cities just before I started my freshman year of high school. Before that, I lived in Des Moines, Iowa. I went to a catholic grade school, Sacred Heart, for eight years. Unfortunately, after we moved, I completely lost track of all of those kids. I've always wondered what happened to everyone I grew up with.

A few weeks ago, I got a note through Facebook from one of my best friends at Sacred Heart. She is living in Chicago and has three kids (one of them, a brand-new baby). Last week, I got a note from another friend who lived around the corner from me. We rode the bus together every day for eight years. She is living in Phoenix and has three beautiful kids. A few days ago, I was "tagged" in a class picture from second grade and a few pictures from junior high. Suddenly, my email inbox was filled with names and notes from my classmates at Sacred Heart. In the blink of an eye, I'm back in touch with people I thought were lost forever.

Amazing. And overwhelming.

This all happened while we are living on the other side of the ocean. John and I have both reconnected with all kinds of people that we used to know from various times in our life, at a time in our life when we feel very much removed and far away from people who know and love us. Isn't it fascinating when the universe finds a way to balance things out, all on its own?

Wednesday, January 14, 2009
Updates.

Last week, we survived our first few days with John back in his travel routine. He went to Ireland and was gone for two nights. When he's working at home, I am lucky enough to be able to leave the baby with him while I drop/pick-up the boys from school. I was nervous about this first trip where we'd have to all go. We managed to make it to school in the morning (late, but we made it). Everyone at school was thrilled to finally meet the new baby. Now we're really back into the routine—he left today for a trip back to the U.S. But never fear, Grandma will be here! Grandma Fowler will arrive on Tuesday.

Last weekend, we thoroughly enjoyed our winter weather. John took the boys sledding at the Chateau de La Hulpe—with no less than 700 other people. Belgium hasn't had snow that stayed like that since 1996 (or so we've been told). As we've learned, when there is a chance to enjoy seasonal weather (snow in winter or sunny days in the summer) Belgians don't mess around and they get outside to enjoy it as quickly as they can. Even though energy levels were low on Sunday, John took the boys out sledding again and they were out for about three hours. A good thing too, because on Monday night, it warmed up. We woke up in the morning and all of the snow was gone and it rained all day Tuesday. But with 20 below temperatures in Minnesota, I will never complain about the weather here.

Monday, January 26, 2009
The Politie.

Politie is Dutch for "police." We know this because it's written in large blue letters on the envelopes for the speeding tickets that come in the mail. Yes, in Belgium we get speeding tickets in the mail. And guess what? The tickets are all in Dutch. The only thing we could comprehend with certainty were the numbers: the date, the time and the price.

We've since figured out—a little late—that there is a hidden camera somewhere along the route we used to drive from our house to the language center where we took our French class. We were late to our respective French classes—a lot.

And did you know that it's illegal to talk on your cell phone while you're driving here? Yep. And did you know that the penalty for talking on your cell phone while driving is 100 euros? We know this because of the ticket that came in the mail from the police in La Hulpe last week. At least we can sort of read French—enough to know that the citation was for talking on a mobile phone while driving.

In Minnesota last year, the City of Minneapolis installed several cameras at intersections that triggered a photo when a driver ran a red light. I think it was called "Operation PhotoCop" or something similar. The City then mailed a citation to the owner of the car for running a red light. It didn't take long for someone to challenge this practice as a violation of our protections under the Constitution. And not long after, the "PhotoCop" was indeed declared unconstitutional. The City of Minneapolis ended up with a giant mess involving refunds and expunging traffic records.

But here, we paid our tickets by wire transfer—and reflected on some basic principles that we took for granted when we were living in the United States. Namely, the right to due process under the law and the presumption of innocence until proven guilty beyond a reasonable doubt.

Oh. And we got another notice in the mail yesterday from the Politie. It seems as if they don't believe they received the wire transfer of funds. John has to provide them with copies of our bank records showing that he did, in fact, pay the fine.

I've found myself holding my breath when I go to get the mail lately. As with every household these days, budgets are tight. It's hard to think that an unexpected bill for 100 euro could appear in our mailbox at any moment...especially when I think of all those times I was running late to French class, or making a quick phone call to John without knowing it was wrong to do so.

Friday, February 6, 2009
Planes, Trains and Automobiles.

Johnny loves this movie, but I can't watch it anymore because around here, it just hits too close to the life we live with a daddy who is an international salesman.

Take, for example, last Wednesday. Johnny had a routine sales visit scheduled to France. It was supposed to be an overnight trip. I got up at five to take him to the La Hulpe train station (it was a rare occasion where Grandma was still here to stay with the kids, otherwise, Johnny would have walked).

He took the train from La Hulpe to the main train station in Brussels, where he connected to Paris. From Paris, he caught another connection to Southern France for his afternoon meetings. His plan was to stay overnight and make the return trip the following day.

He was just wrapping up his day, when an architect interrupted his meeting. He wanted John to know that the trains in France were about to go on a nationwide strike that was going to last until Saturday. He rushed John to the train station and John jumped on the last train out of the area, without a ticket. He made it by five minutes.

While he was on the train to Paris, I looked up the train schedule at home so he would know exactly where to go and what train to catch back to Brussels. (Again, he'd be trying to get on the train without a ticket.) He was scheduled to arrive in Paris at just after eight o'clock, and the last train from Paris to Brussels was leaving at 8:55. Here's the catch. His train was coming into a train station on one end of Paris, and he knew he would have at least a 20-minute ride on the metro to get to the other train station.

His train arrived into Paris at 8:25. He jumped off, sprinted to the metro, jumped on and made it across town. He ran to the track for the Brussels train and it was empty except for the conductors which meant that the train had finished boarding. He had three minutes to spare.

The conductor, seemingly amused by John's situation, made a big point of telling John he needed to switch his ticket at the counter before he could board. John tried to talk him into letting him on anyway (in French) but the conductor wouldn't budge. John raced back to the ticket booth—where the agent put an "ok" sticker on his ticket, and then back out onto the track. He made it out of France on the last train. If he hadn't made that train, he would have been stuck in France until Saturday. Oh, and I forgot to mention, he just returned from a busy week in the States and was still recovering from jet lag.

He arrived back in Brussels after the trains stopped running to La Hulpe. He took a taxi from the train station to our house. Well, almost to our house. The end of our road, which is the turnoff from the main highway, was recently closed completely due to major road construction. There isn't an easy way around it, the detour goes all the way into town and around, easily adding an extra fifteen minutes to the drive. To avoid the detour, the taxi driver dropped John off at the end of our road and he walked the last half mile home from Paris at 1:30 in the morning.

At least he didn't get stuck somewhere until Saturday. And at five in the morning when he was holding a huge, heavy window sample, I'm so glad he decided not to take it with him to his appointment.

Saturday, February 7, 2009
A Baby Born Abroad.

Our goal last week was to register Isabelle at the U.S. Embassy and get her passport. Mission accomplished...we think.

Even though Isabelle was born in Belgium, she does not qualify for citizenship. We (her non-citizen parents) would have had to live here for several years before she was born for that to happen. But we still had to register her in the commune where she was born within 15 days after her birth, which we did. Then, we had to register her in La Hulpe—her commune of residence. We did that too.

With her Belgian birth certificate and French paperwork, the next step was to register her with the U.S. Embassy and apply for her social security number and passport. It was no small task. We made an appointment and started on the paperwork. We had her picture taken and put everything in order, including proof that we had previously lived in the U.S. for five consecutive years, and a list of the "specific instances" in which we left the United States for international travel. For myself, that was relatively easy, I could list on one hand the times I'd traveled outside the United States before we moved here. But for Johnny and his several years in international sales....

We arrived at the U.S. Embassy for our "appointment." I don't know what I was expecting, but it didn't come close. I think I had a vision in my head of a cushy office - which was unrealistically based entirely on what I've seen in the movies—movies from pre-9/11 days.

In our post-9/11 days—and the real world—things are different. We went through three police checkpoints, just to get to the front security gate. A man with a clipboard came out and confirmed our "appointment" before we could go inside. John's mom (who is visiting) was not allowed to come with us so she had to leave and wait for us at a nearby café. I had to stand outside in the rain by myself while John and Isabelle cleared security, as only one person is allowed through the security process at a time. Oh! And I almost forgot about the part where we had to wipe our hands on the white pads to prove that we had not touched explosives in the recent past.

I was asked to leave my diaper bag behind, so I took out a diaper and a spit rag to bring along. We then stepped through a door to the service area. There was a long counter with windows (like bank tellers) and a huge waiting area with really uncomfortable wooden chairs. The only thing that was missing was the little tag box where you could "take a number." A very humorless, serious woman showed up at window number six to take all of our paperwork. (John can usually get anyone to smile, but not this time.) We were asked to wait while she sorted through everything.

We almost passed. We had failed to provide a "translation" for Isabelle's French birth certificate. It's a good thing that we know the French words for "born on" and could translate it ourselves.

She took our paperwork and asked us to wait. At this point, Isabelle was insisting "very loudly" that she was hungry, so she got to eat. And I'm sure whoever was watching on the other side of the hidden cameras got an eyeful. When I was burping the baby, she made this really loud, really long, tooting sound. Which was followed by a really strong smell. John and I just looked at each other and laughed. I had to go back out to the security guard and ask him if I could look through the diaper bag for the wipes. (I brought the baby with me for evidence.) He was not happy about this at all, but there was nothing he could do about it and he knew it. I got what I needed and laid her in the middle of the service area to change her. (We okayed this with the one other guy who was waiting.)

Eventually, a guy called us back up to the window so we could take our oath and swear to what we needed to swear to, and sign where we needed to sign. He explained that our application was "almost" complete. First, we would have to go to the post office and get new stamps for our self-addressed stamped envelope because what we originally provided wasn't sufficient. Then, we would have to go to another photo place to get new pictures for Isabelle because the pictures we provided were just a little too small. He gave us a map and sent us on our way.

For the next hour, we ran around figuring all this out, like we were on a "passport-themed" scavenger hunt or something. I felt like I was on the Amazing Race, except that instead of giant backpacks on our backs, we had Isabelle in her Graco car seat. We accomplished our tasks and turned everything back in to the lady. And then we went out to lunch to celebrate. We ordered an extra glass of wine, or maybe even two.

So yes, it was stressful and a lot of work. I'm really glad it's over. But it also made me think. The things in life that are worth having, are never easy. A U.S. passport is a document that is coveted worldwide by a lot of people. It should be hard to get. There should be a lot of hoops to jump through and evidence to provide. And it should be even more difficult when you're trying to obtain it from outside the country. I am thankful for my U.S. citizenship and I am grateful that my children have U.S. citizenship. Yet again, my eyes were opened to something I used to take for granted.

Saturday, February 14, 2009
Lukee Update: French.

On Friday, Luke's teacher told me that she only spoke in French to Luke, and he answered in French all day. This was a major milestone. He was absolutely committed to never speaking French in Belgium. He would chatter all day long in English to everyone at school as a matter of principal. I'd even begun to wonder if the kids in his class would start to speak English before he started speaking French. He told me once that was his plan, to teach them English instead. But Friday, it was only French, all day.

I talked to him about it on the way out of school. I made a big deal about how great it was and how exciting it was to hear his teacher say that he'd spoken French to her all day. He looked at me with a blank stare.

I said, "You didn't even know that you were speaking French all day, did you?" He answered with a frown, and crossed his arms over his chest.

**Thursday, February 19, 2009
Ugh.**

Oftentimes, police patrol the neighborhoods in these big blue and white square vans. With images of swat teams in my head (another assumption thanks to Hollywood) I always wondered what was really inside the swat-team vans. Guess what? The vans have a table and a bench on the inside. I know this because today, I got to sit at the nifty little table inside the blue and white swat-team van.

This morning, I was late to school with the kids, but I felt relaxed about it. I figured, they are three and five and we have a new baby. If there is ever a time to employ the attitude that "we'll get there when we get there," it's now. We parked in one of our usual spots, up on the sidewalk—and yes, I was actually up, on the cobblestone sidewalk. It was just before a turn in the road on a narrow street near the school. As long as your car is out of the way of traffic, pretty much anything goes.

I had just gotten the boys out of the car when a big white delivery truck came barreling down the street. I heard a really loud grating noise—like metal and plastic on metal and plastic. And I thought to myself, "Ohhhh...it would be awful to be the owner of that car." And then I realized. It was my car that was involved in the awful scraping noise.

Ugh.

Avery and Luke stood on the sidewalk waiting patiently, but nervous, while the delivery guy came running back rambling off a bunch of French. I got the baby out of the car and set her next to Avery. The man kept talking in rapid French, even after I explained I didn't speak much of it and asked him to slow down.

I understood that he was telling me to take the children into school and he would meet me back at the car in five minutes. And the my sweet little five-year-old said, "Mommy, he's going to go park his car and come back. He wants to know if you have a pen and paper."

Did I ever mention how wonderful my five-year-old is? That was the part I wasn't understanding. I grabbed the pen and paper, and he wrote down his license plate number and went off to his car. A friend of mine (who doesn't speak English very well) saw the incident. It just so happens that the police were up the street directing school traffic for the morning, so she went and asked them to help us with the accident.

As we were walking into school, I happened to see one of the mothers who grew up in Great Britain. She graciously agreed to help me through the whole situation. She helped me fill out the accident report, talk to the police and find the correct documentation (insurance papers and vehicle cards). At this point, the truck driver was insisting that he couldn't even be sure that he actually hit my car and what if the huge white gash in the side of my car was there before? Grrr. Thankfully, she was there to tell the police that I had heard the awful noise, and we all looked in the street to see that there was white paint that had peeled off his truck on impact.

Then I came home and cried. I cried because it is so frustrating not to be able to communicate in the way I'd like to communicate in a situation like that. I had a lot of words I wanted to say (I'm a trained attorney, after all.) I couldn't say any of them. I cried because just when we feel like we are settled and doing well here, something always happens. Now, I have to call our insurance company. And figure out where, when and how to fix our one and only car. And that all sounds easy enough, but things like that are never easy here and always cost more money that we think.

But then I was done crying. What can you do but pick yourself up and keep going? I am thankful no one was hurt. I am thankful for the wonderful mom who took an hour out of her morning to help me. But I will never, ever park in that spot again.

And now Isabelle and I can say that we know what the inside of a police van looks like.

Saturday, February 21, 2009
Carnival Week!

The boys have the whole week off from school next week for Carnival Week. A lot of people around here escape our cold, rainy, gray weather and head to Switzerland or France to ski. Not us though. I'm just excited to have a whole week where we don't have to get up and out of the house every morning.

Yesterday, the kids had a Carnival parade at school. (Think Mardi Gras without the exposed flesh.) Everyone brought a costume. Luke was a knight and Avery was a pirate. And Isabelle was a bear, thanks to a hand-me-down snowsuit from big brother Luke. The big kids went on a walk through town with their costumes (which was really just a loop down the street by the church). Almost all of the boys in Avery's class were pirates, and almost all of the girls were princesses. Luke's class was too little to go on the walk, so they just stayed in their classroom and had a dance party.

This morning, Luke and Avery woke up with horrible fevers. That's really not a surprise—since they've started every single school vacation sick. We've spent the day on the couch watching Belgium television and movies.

Tuesday, February 24, 2009
A Really Fun Vacation Week. (Not Really.)

Help! We're trapped in our house in Belgium. We are being held hostage by this horrible, rotten virus that has hit our household hard. It's day number four of vacation, and our sickness. Luke and Avery didn't move from the couch on Saturday and Sunday.

Sunday night was rough, Luke whined all night and had terrible dreams. He fell out of his bed around 6:30 and I made the executive decision to just end our horrible night and get up for breakfast. But yesterday, the boys finally ventured off the couch to play a little bit. However, now John and I have it. Aches, fever, runny nose, cough...yuck. (So far so good with Isabelle.)

Last night, mercifully, everyone slept. But Luke woke up with a fever again today...we'll be off to the doctor tomorrow if he still has it. It goes without saying that boredom is high. Out of desperation, I turned on the BBC kids channel this morning and just left it on.

We suffered through (read this next part with a British accent) a horrible children's show about numbers. But our persistence paid off. Imagine our sheer delight when we heard the first few notes of the Bob the Builder theme song. Hooray! A show we miss from Minnesota! And it's not even dubbed over in French! But wait. As soon as Bob started talking, I noticed that something was off. Bob has a British accent when he's on the BBC. Why would they go through the trouble of dubbing over an English-speaking show, into British?

John loves to talk with a British accent. Anyone who's heard him, knows that he's "quite good, actually." I've teased him in the past that he needs to add it to his resume under his list of foreign languages. Of course, I was joking. But now that I've seen Bob the Builder in British, maybe British really is a language of its own...

Saturday, February 28, 2009
One Year Ago, This Week...

A year ago this week, Johnny and I were here in Belgium looking for a house and school. Every time I've been out of the house this last week (which wasn't often, given that the plague was here for a visit) I think about how unfamiliar the streets were when our relocation agent drove us around.

For the next few weeks, I know I will constantly think to myself, "Last year at this time, we were doing this, that, or the other thing." I'm a little surprised by how much residual emotion is tied up into that, crashing around inside of me. On the one hand, it makes it easy for me to see how far we've come and how well we're doing. I am so thankful that we are in this space and time and not just arriving here—fresh off the plane. But it also feels like delayed trauma. Things were so chaotic, that we didn't even realize how traumatized we were by the move. But because I'm looking back and remembering, it's almost like I'm experiencing the trauma now. It's hard to explain.

Not to completely change topics, but I recently discovered a side effect of Facebook. While it's amazing to be so connected to what the world back in Minnesota is doing, if I'm the tiniest bit homesick, it's sort of terrible. And Johnny is back in the U.S. this week for business. We are always a little more prone to homesickness when he is there and we're here.

So here's what I will do: I will control what I can control. If you are looking for me on Facebook this week, I'm not there. I'm taking a break. I am going to look forward to my Target bag—the big duffle bag that John takes with him and stuffs full of goodies to bring back to us from Minnesota. And I'm going to plan a party—even if it's just for our little family—to celebrate our one-year anniversary in Belgium. We deserve to celebrate our year.

Saturday, February 28, 2009
Here Comes the Sun.

In case anyone is interested, that's my all-time favorite song. If you haven't figured it out by now, I'm an optimist and that song speaks to my glass-half-full personality.

In all of the years they've been keeping such records in Belgium, this February was the darkest month in the history of Belgium.

BUT, we've had three days IN A ROW of sunshine. Anyone who knows anything about the weather in Belgium will tell you that's a big deal, especially in February. I have learned to appreciate the sunshine here in a way I never have before.

There is a park near our house where the kids like to ride their bikes on the basketball court. Saturday, I managed to walk up there with all three kids and the dog, by myself.

We were quite the sight. The baby was strapped to my front and we held onto the dog. Avery rode his scooter and Luke rode his tricycle. It's a good thing the park is only about three blocks away, and the end of our road is under construction so there's hardly any traffic right now. Whenever I had to help Luke with his trike (like over the grass to get to the court) I made him get off and hold the dog leash. Inevitably, within three minutes he would get bored and let go. It's a good thing the dog is getting old and likes to stay by us.

On our way out of the park, we found a whole big patch of little flowers that were growing on the side of a hill. Mostly, they were purple. Some were white and there were a few random yellow ones. I can't tell you what kind of flower. They looked like baby tulips, but they were clustered together in a way that isn't typical of tulips. Anyway, we almost missed them completely because they were growing up through the old, leftover leaves from last year. In fact, Avery and I found one that had sprouted right through the middle of a big dead leaf. Can you imagine? A beautiful little flower growing right through a big rotten leaf.

How's that for symbolism?

Thursday, March 5, 2009
Dinner Without Daddy, Part One.

Our refrigerator and freezer are miniscule. I usually keep enough food on hand for two or three meals, which means I typically make a trip to the grocery store twice a week. I actually like living like this. It feels more efficient. I find myself cooking with fresher ingredients, because I buy to use, I don't buy to "stock up." Grocery stores here are not open at all on Sunday, but there are several "express grocery stores" that do stay open on holidays and the weekend. I shop at these a lot because often, we just need a few things, and one thing we always need is milk.

John left last Saturday, and over the weekend, I realized that our cupboards were pretty bare. I had to make lunches for Monday, we were out of milk and we needed something for dinner on Sunday night. To date, I have avoided having to take all three kids into the grocery store. Just the thought makes me quiver with fear. The grocery store was closed on Sunday anyway, but I knew there was an express store next to the indoor gym I was planning to go to with the kids on Sunday. Perfect! I would only need to get everyone in and out of the car once during our outing.

Sunday came, and the four of us made our way into the very crowded express store. I always feel like the obnoxious lady with a whole gaggle of kids when we're out in public, with the baby strapped to the front of me and I'm hollering at the other two.

Here, it is not uncommon for stores to just "run out" of products. They just don't have it, and they don't put anything else out until they get it. On this day, this store was out of a lot. There wasn't any ham for lunches—not a single package. In fact, the whole "lunch meat" section was almost completely bare. I snatched up a lonely package of turkey before the guy next to me could grab it and figured I could sell the boys on turkey sandwiches. Which is sort of funny in itself because I have NEVER seen turkey on the shelves here.

Meanwhile, Luke was attempting to load my basket with chocolate, so when the turkey went in, I had to put back all of the stuff he'd added.

Next, milk. There wasn't any. Not a single bottle. (A lot of people here buy canned milk, and there was plenty of that, but my kids refuse to drink it.) I did a quick mental calculation and figured if I made oatmeal for breakfast the next morning, we could make it without buying milk. (I was trying to avoid another stop at a different store at all costs.)

Next up, something for dinner. I don't usually buy fresh meat from the express stores because it never looks very fresh. We opted for chicken nuggets from the freezer by the checkout. Guess what? Third strike. They were out of the kind I usually buy. Next to the empty space, there was another box of something that looked like chicken fingers and the box said "poulet" (French for chicken). At this point, Luke had found a box of chocolates that looked really expensive and he was trying to open them. I grabbed the poulet, wrestled the chocolate away from Luke and we got in line to check out.

Later, as I tried to throw dinner together, I realized the poulet I purchased was supposed to be cooked in a deep fryer. We don't have a deep fryer. Shuddering at the amount of cholesterol I was planning to feed my kids for dinner, I dumped a bunch of oil in a pan and figured I'd fry them up the best I could.

Before anyone would eat it, the boys made me cut one open to see what was inside. Well, it turned out to be a bunch of goo. It was some cheese concoction with chicken bits. Gross. No one would eat it so into the garbage it went. Peanut butter sandwich anyone?

Thursday, March 5, 2009
Dinner Without Daddy, Part Two.

I like to cook, because I love to eat, but when John is gone, we have kid friendly-fare, like chicken nuggets, fish sticks or the occasional hot dog. We also eat in the kitchen instead of in the dining room. It's just easier.

We also eat dinner earlier—between 5:30 and 6. (I am all about early bedtime when John is out of town.) Yet eating at this time also happens to be the same time all of our neighbors usually get home from work. We don't have drapes in the kitchen. Our kitchen therefore turns into a fishbowl and all of our neighbors get to glimpse "an American family at dinner."

The boys insist on waving at everyone as they walk by, thus calling attention to our dinner in the window, but also forcing our poor neighbors to acknowledge that they are peeking at us. Here's a replay of the conversation from last night, I can only imagine what it all looked like to our neighbors.

Avery: "Mommy, I don't have to wash my hands before dinner because I had gloves on when I went outside."

Me: "That's a creative argument, Avery."

Avery (about to melt down into a fit): "So does that mean I have to wash my hands?"

Me: "Did you pick your nose or put your hands down your pants?"

Avery (Laughing): "No." (Whew. Meltdown averted.)

Me: "Then sit down." He got points for creativity, and I was picking my battles.

Avery: "Mom, we're not having goo again for dinner, are we?"

Me: "No, Avery, they're fish sticks."

Avery: "Good. Let's never have goo again for dinner."

Me: "I agree."

Meanwhile, the baby was happily watching the whole time with coos and smiles from her bouncy seat. Jump ahead about ten minutes.

Me: "Luke, are you done eating?"

Luke: "Nope, nope, nope."

Me: "Then please get your fork out of your hair."

Luke: "Milk!!"

Me: "Is there a manner word in there somewhere?"

Luke: "Please!!"

Avery: "Is it a dessert night?"

Me: "What did you have in mind?"

Avery and Luke together: "Biscuit bucket!" (That's what we call our cookie jar.)

Me: "Ok, one Prince cookie for boys who eat their fish sticks."

Avery: "Mommy, the baby smells."

I picked up the baby and sure enough, she smelled. And my whole hand got wet. And I realized that it was covered in poo. Upon peeling all of Isabelle's clothes off, it became obvious right away that there was poo everywhere. In her belly button, behind her knees, she was covered in it.

I guess there was a little goo with our dinner after all.

March 26, 2009
How Do You Know You've Lived in Belgium for A Year?

As I mentioned a few weeks ago, our one-year anniversary has put me in a reflective mood. I find myself thinking things like, "Now I know what the weather is like for every season here." (Which is funny because it's pretty much the same all year; a combination of cold, rain, and sometimes a sunny day thrown in just for kicks.) I've also noticed the little things in my daily life that prove how far I've come.

Here are a few:

I always remember my coin for the grocery cart and my bags for my groceries when I go to the store.

I have figured out the complicated recycling scheme and no longer have to watch to see what the neighbors put out on the street on what day. After the first of the year, I even went into the maison communale and asked for the new recycling schedule. In French.

When I take the shortcut to school (a really narrow road, think alley-width in St. Paul) I've stopped flinching, squeezing my eyes shut and jerking the car to the right when I pass an oncoming vehicle. Ok, occasionally, I still flinch. And I still jerk the car to the right if the oncoming vehicle happens to be a bus or a truck.

I instinctively look to my right when driving through neighborhoods to watch out for cars flying out of streets on my right.

The five and three-year old know how to operate Skype on the family computer by themselves. Every now and then, I hear a Grandma or Grandpa's voice coming from the living room and it's because they've called us and the boys answered on their own.

It no longer irritates me that grocery stores are closed on Sunday or that certain shops are closed on Monday. Or that some businesses, like pharmacies and the post office, close for two hours over lunch.

When I go out to eat, I order a "Coca Light" instead of a "Diet Coke" without thinking about it.

I remember to specify if I want "still" or fizzy water.

I have finally memorized my home phone number. And my cell number! The cell phone numbers here have one extra number, and that really messed me up.

In the car on the way to school, I can now understand one out of every three words on the radio, instead of one out of every twenty or thirty.

I keep a rain hat in my purse.

We buy a fresh baguette almost daily. (And I'm allergic to bread!)

We've become absolutely and totally addicted to the frites from the frite stand in La Hulpe—with cocktail sauce. (Cocktail sauce here is different. It's ketchup and mayo with a little Scotch whiskey thrown in for flavor.) We've become so programmed that if Johnny and I even see the jar of cocktail sauce in the refrigerator we get hungry for frites. (I figure there are worse things.)

I no longer miss Starbucks or giant lattes-to-go on a daily basis. I am perfectly content with my home brew. (Tradeoffs, see the previous two statements.)

This morning at breakfast, Avery and Luke were talking about how they loved living in Belgium. We certainly have come a long way in one short year.

March 26, 2009
An Earthquake!

Did you know that they have earthquakes in Belgium? If you did, how come you didn't tell me?!

We just had an earthquake! I don't even know what you are supposed to do in an earthquake. Go to the basement? Hide in the tub? No, that's for a tornado. I'm a Midwest girl, we have tornados, not earthquakes.

I was sitting on our bed about an hour ago, working on my laptop. There was this really loud noise. It sounded like a large truck was driving behind our house and in front of our house at the same time (even though that is impossible). The dog and cat (who are never more than three feet away from me in the evening) both looked up.

It lasted a few seconds and I never really even thought about it in the moment. I guess I just assumed something along the lines of a truck theory. BUT THEN, I went online to check my Facebook page. Two friends from here were talking back and forth about the earthquake that happened and the time stamp was 55 minutes ago.

And I realized I'd been in an earthquake. It took a minute for that to sink in, and even now, I'm still a little in awe of the whole thing.

Tomorrow morning, I'll tell Avery and Luke that they were in an earthquake. After I figure out how to explain to them what an earthquake is without giving them nightmares, I'm sure they will think it's cool too. For now, I'm just going to try to come to terms with this new natural disaster that I get to worry about.

Saturday, April 4, 2009
The Wrong Way.

Do you ever leave the house in the morning and no matter what, you feel like you're going the wrong way? I do.

I think I've mentioned in the past that the roads in La Hulpe, or pretty much anywhere here for that matter, aren't exactly efficient. Coming from a land of city blocks and organized municipal planning, this was difficult for me to comprehend for a long time. Often, there is only one way to get somewhere. For example, if a road is blocked by a garbage truck going about its route, the choice is to wait behind the garbage truck until the road is wide enough to pass. Or, like when we were in the snowstorm, we couldn't turn around and we couldn't turn off the street we were on. There is simply no other choice but to sit tight and wait.

At first this was mind boggling and beyond frustrating. But with acceptance comes peace. Now, I don't bother wasting emotion on getting upset. If we get stuck behind a garbage truck, we breathe through it and wait until we can pass. It's simply not worth getting mad about.

But I digress. Last year, La Hulpe started a construction project on our road. The end of our road connects to the main road that leads to "the Ring" (the freeway that loops around the center of Brussels). During rush hour, cars used to fly back and forth in front of our house, slowed down a little bit by the one-way road obstacle that forces cars to go by our row of houses one at a time.

Depending on what is happening with the construction, sometimes our road becomes a one-way street and we never know which way that's going to be. This is even more complicated by the fact that we live in the middle of the road.

At some point, the city of La Hulpe put up a "no entry" sign about 500 yards down the road. Not needing to drive that direction for a while, it was a week or so before we even realized there was a new sign. Which meant that every time we left the house we were going the wrong way and didn't even know it. No wonder people were looking cross and wagging their finger at me!

Then, one day the end of our road was completely closed, so they covered up the "no entry" sign and put up a "local traffic only" sign. Again, this was not only confusing, but also annoying because the detour took us quite a bit out of our way and through town. Finally, after almost a year, the construction work is finished. They built a nice new roundabout that helps a lot with the traffic flow. Thinking that things were back to normal, we came and went again with ease.

But one day last week, I got a really angry look and a finger wave from an oncoming car. She was really mad. But I was sure it was my turn to go through the one-way part so I couldn't figure out what I'd done wrong. Then it happened again. This time, I got flashed with the high beam/brights. What the heck? And sure enough, the traffic is now officially one way and every time we left for school, we were driving the wrong way without even realizing it.

It's a good thing I realized it when I did. The other day, when I was coming home from taking the children to school and thus, driving the correct direction down our street, I noticed a police car sitting off to the side. Most likely because someone complained that a lady with three kids squashed together in the back seat was repeatedly driving the wrong way down Avenue Solvay.

Saturday, April 4, 2009
Holiday in Spain.

I have learned not to set expectations for things like holidays. It's a healthy lesson, learned relatively early in life, and it keeps me sane as we travel with three little ones.

We had been talking for months about what we could manage for a vacation. We talked about a road trip to France. But the thought of staying in tiny expensive hotels with three little kids had us dragging our feet. John had to plan a trip to Spain for work and he realized that the prices of airline tickets had dropped significantly. Within ten minutes he found a vacation-rental-by-owner and within an hour, we had our first vacation as a family of five all planned out—leaving in less than ten days.

Last week, two days after planning the trip, Luke got sick. He's on antibiotics for "brown kitus." But the first day of our vacation, he started running a new fever. He's the only kid who would get a new virus while he's on antibiotics for something else. But then again, I did catch him licking the counter at McDonald's the other day when we were ordering our dinner. If you're going to lick counters in ultra-public forums, you will get sick. Even if you are already on antibiotics.

The boys were really excited to swim every day, but the pool (unheated) is really, really cold. Avery insisted that he could handle it so he and John went down the other day "for a dip." Avery jumped in, turned blue and screamed, "Daddy get me out of here." But they laid in the sun for a while, warmed up and even jumped in a few more times just to say they did it.

I studied Spanish all through college and I was excited to finally get a chance to visit a country where I could use my Spanish. Upon turning on the television, I found that I could understand almost everything. It was a refreshing change from the Belgian programs in French. However, when I open my mouth to say anything when we are out and about, the only thing that comes out is French. Sigh. I'm not kidding. I've said "Oui," "Sil vous plait" and "Merci" to everyone in town. And at dinner the other night, I was completely tongue tied. Good for my French, I guess, but not so good for the Spanish Minor.

It's really good to be on vacation, but it will be really good to be back home. And it's fun that our "home" now is Brussels.

Sunday, April 12, 2009
Happy Easter from Belgium!

Happy Easter!

Today, is the first time we've celebrated a holiday in Belgium without being homesick.

One factor is definitely exhaustion. But another contributing factor is that we've made some new friends. We met them at the park near our house, they are from Canada (Quebec City) and they've lived in France for the last six years. They moved to La Hulpe in the fall and live just a few blocks away. They have a little boy exactly Luke's age, and a six-month old. I feel like we just got a bridge between the cultures. For example, they came across an invitation for an egg hunt at the Chateau de La Hulpe that I think we might have otherwise missed.

They invited us for Easter dinner and an egg hunt for the boys. It was a lovely afternoon, and so much fun to go to someone else's house to celebrate a holiday.

Saturday, April 18, 2009
A Duck.

This morning we woke up and it was raining—a drizzle that makes for a cozy Saturday morning. I was alone in the kitchen finishing my coffee and taking a minute to read the news from the weekly English-Belgian newsmagazine. Two mallard ducks (a male and female) flew in for a landing right in front of our house. I called the boys to the window and we watched the mommy and daddy duck waddle around for a few minutes.

I went upstairs, set Isabelle in her crib and went into my bedroom. I peeked out the window to check on the ducks and in that short amount of time, a car had come along. Daddy Duck was dead in the middle of the road.

In tears, I explained to John what had just happened. My amazing husband went out in the rain with a shovel and scooped the duck out of the street and put it in the woods.

The rain washed away most of the blood in the street. By noon, the sun came out. All day long I watched cars whizzing by and I was so thankful that the duck didn't continue to get hit by every single one of them.

I've been thinking about that duck all day. It made me stop and think about how precious and fragile life is and how everything can change in an instant. It made me remember that life is a wonderful gift and we need to take advantage of each minute. Any time I am given a reminder like that in life, no matter the tragedy, I try to be thankful. It's the something good that can come out of something bad.

We went for a walk this evening before dinner. The boys (Avery) made a comment about the feathers everywhere. And I realized, we managed to spare our children from a tragedy, so I'm thankful for that too. Because the Lord knows that we won't be able to spare them from very many.

Friday, April 24, 2009
Oh, What a Week.

Monday morning, John left for Spain. By Monday afternoon (after only his second day of school in a month) Luke was sick again. By Monday evening, Luke was having difficulty breathing with symptoms of asthma. It's a good thing I know a lot about asthma.

After a mostly sleepless night, on Tuesday morning, I took Luke to the doctor after we dropped Avery off at school. Thirty euros later, we left with a handful of prescriptions, including one for a rent-a-nebulizer. For now, Luke's asthma symptoms are part of his virus. But I wouldn't be surprised if an asthma diagnosis follows in the near future.

We then raced to our local pharmacy to try to get there before they close for their daily two-hour lunch break. About a hundred euros later we left with our rent-a-nebulizer and a bunch of medications.

It took a few days for Luke to get his breathing back to normal, which meant consecutive sleepless nights for me. What's that expression about having time to sleep when you're dead?

We've decided to make some changes in Luke's school schedule until his health improves. We cut his school schedule in half, and he will only go to school for two-and-a-half days a week, effective immediately. As such, Luke stayed home from school on Friday, and I can't believe the difference it has already made in his attitude about everything, but especially school. I'm looking forward to some extra time with my three-year-old.

We were all happy to have Johnny back (on Thursday). And we were all ready for a Friday Night Family Frite Night. Beer and frites in front of a family movie was the perfect way to end a long week.

Monday, April 27, 2009
What the...?!

Excuse my French, but what the [insert your favorite four letter swear word here]?

Do you remember that bad day with the truck scrape along the side of the car?

The damage is a scratch along the passenger side wheel well. It's not that bad, you have to know what happened and look for it. But if you know where to look, it's pretty obvious.

John has made no less than eight attempts to call the insurance adjustor, during normal business hours. The adjustor answered once. The adjustor also only spoke French so it wasn't a very effective phone call anyway. I hereby vow to never complain about customer service in the United States, ever again.

Trying another approach, Johnny called the Volvo dealership where we purchased the car. Our sales agent was much more helpful, especially when John mentioned that our car was a little too small for three car seats and we were *thinking* about a new, bigger, one. (When we win the lottery.)

The sales agent is going to arrange for "the expert" to meet us at the dealership to assess the damage. Then, they give us a temporary car while ours is getting fixed. Easy enough, right? Nope. Of course not. This is Belgium.

(Here's where it gets fun. Hysterical even.) John said to me, "We should schedule this for after your Mom comes to visit." And I said, "Why? She's not coming for another three weeks, they should be able to get it back to us sooner than that, right?"

And with a straight face, he said, "Well actually, they send it in." "What you mean they send it in?" I asked. "They have to ship the car to the Netherlands to have it serviced. It will probably take about three or four weeks," he answered.

Are you kidding me?

They send it in?! It's a car. Not a mail-order-do-hicky thing. IT'S A CAR! To fix a scratch, they put the car on a semi-truck, ship it to a different country, fix the scratch and then ship it back? ARE YOU KIDDING ME? How is that cost-effective? Where, when and how did anyone ever decide that that was a good idea?!

We don't really need to fix a scratch, do we?

Thursday, May 7, 2009
It's the Little Things.

On Tuesday, I had a day.

Over the last year, I've posted a lot of entries about some of the difficult moments. The difficult little things can easily add up, become a really big deal and drag you down. But this week, I realized that the converse is also true. Yes, the difficult little things can drag you down. But the small victories can pull you right back up. I have found extraordinary triumph in some of the most ordinary every-day tasks.

So back to Tuesday. Tuesday and Friday are now "stay at home days" for Luke. It's going well and the little breaks in his week have made a huge difference for him. I am enjoying having him around more too. On my "Luke days" I schedule errands, which can be enormously fun when there is a three-year-old with you chattering away. I also jump at the chance to take him to a coffee date or to the Women's Club Library—the same sorts of things I would get to do with him regularly if we were still living in Minnesota and he was in a half-day preschool program. It's been great to take a step back.

On this particular Tuesday, Johnny was in England. (The fact that he was traveling should tip you off that something bad is about to happen because bad things always happen when he's out of town.) We were on our way to one of the above-mentioned coffee dates. Out of nowhere, I heard a gagging noise and within seconds, there was vomit all over the car.

By the time I dug the bucket out of the trunk he was covered. The car reeked. We were twenty minutes away from home with leftover rush hour traffic in both directions.

But we made it and we got lucky enough to get a parking spot in front of our row house.

Most of the mess was on him so I got him out of the car, stripped him down on our front step and took his clothes and rain jacket right down to the wash.

Sidenote: A rain jacket is a great thing for a kid to be wearing in a round of carsickness. I hosed off his car seat and wiped everything down with bleach. I got Luke re-dressed and reassessed. Not bad, if we left right away and I held off on feeding the baby, we could actually make it back to our coffee date and salvage our morning.

I got Luke back in the car. And that's when I noticed the flat front tire. This just about broke me. We noticed last week that the tire had a slow leak, but we both sort of ignored it. Neither of us wanted to deal with figuring out what to do about it, and it wasn't at the critical stage. We (and by that, I mean he) pumped it up at the gas station and we hoped that it would magically go away. Well. It didn't and it reached the critical stage during this particular hour on this particular day.

Ok, so I guess those aren't really little things. They were two really big things that happened within the same hour. Now I will skip over the part where I called John in hysterics. And I won't go into details about my meltdown. Let's just say I'm not very proud of how I handled myself in those twenty minutes.

But I persevered. The tire was only half-flat. Yes, I am fully aware at the obvious comparison to the "glass is half-empty" analogy. One choice was to drive it to the gas station at the end of our road, try to figure out the tire pump thingy and take my chances until John got home and make him deal with it. This was tempting. But had major potential to cause even bigger problems somewhere with the children in the car on the way to school or something. Plus, I seriously doubted my ability to figure out the tire-pump-thingy. My other choice was to drive it the other direction to the garage I had noticed by the train station and try to fumble my way through a "flat-tire conversation" in French—and hope that he didn't charge me thousands of dollars.

I opted for the later. I figured, if a lady showed up in my garage with a baby and a three-year-old and a car that smelled like puke and bleach and had a flat tire, I'd help her out. It was a good choice. The guy at the garage was awesome. After three minutes of me pointing and trying to remember my French despite the recent hysterics, he suggested we speak slowly in English. He checked my tire, switched on my spare and he promised me my tire back within 24 hours.

And then Little Thing Number One happened. Frite Guy came walking down the street and he said hello to Garage Guy and to me. And it made me feel like I belong here and that this is my town. And then the little things kept happening. I returned to the garage at the same time the next day. After a day of driving with the windows open, the car smelled less like pukey-bleach and my tire was fixed and back on my car within minutes.

And it only cost 23 euros.

More little things happened this week. Mostly just little milestones for the kids. But I tried to stop and notice all of them. Because the little things can pull you up, if you let them. And I'm going to try to remember to let them do that more often.

Tuesday, May 19, 2009
Yay! Grandma is Here!

My mom is here right now and we are having a really nice time. The first time she came to Belgium, we were all very sick but also very new to Belgium. We were still trying to figure things out. And it was hard enough to find the doctors' offices, let alone take Grandma anywhere fun.

The second time she came to visit us, we were busy having a baby. At Christmas. That came with its own specialized chaos. But this time, it's just normal. No one is sick. (Except that Luke is fighting yet another cold, but that's nothing new.) We've been able to relax and enjoy Grandma's visit. We've even been able to take her around and show her some fun things. That's major progress.

Last Friday, Grandma got to tag along to Isabelle's five-month check-up. Then, Isabelle and I took Grandma to our favorite coffee shop for a "lait russe" and an omelet. On Saturday, the boys had their "Fête de Printemps" (spring festival) at school, and Grandma got to see their performances live and in person. We stayed for the BBQ and Grandma got to experience a Belgian pot-luck dinner first hand.

Isabelle and I took Grandma to Bruges on Sunday (in a blog entry to follow). The boys had a last-minute day off from school yesterday due to a late notice teacher in-service day. Thursday is a holiday here, so the boys won't have school again. Tomorrow, John is taking Avery and Grandma on a special overnight train trip to London.

In other words, we've been able to spend lots of time with Grandma doing normal, everyday things (and a few special activities) and for that, we are very thankful.

Tuesday, May 19, 2009
In Bruges.

As you know by now, we don't do a whole lot of touristy stuff with the kids. For so long, we were just focusing on settling into our life here. Then, the baby brought new mobilization challenges and the economy brought new budget challenges. When we do go somewhere, we try to make sure it is something the kids will enjoy and remember. John and I have both done the backpacking-around-Europe thing as students. Plus, we've had a few trips over here before we had children. And while we have a list of places we want to see with the kids, neither of us feel that it's necessary to head off every weekend to tour museums, cathedrals and castles. However, it is nice to get a visitor, as it encourages us to get out and explore something that we might not have otherwise done.

Back in the U.S., on more than one occasion, when I mentioned "Belgium" the response was a ten-minute monologue about the city of Bruges and how wonderful and beautiful it is. It is also a favorite of the expat community. Only an hour's drive from Brussels and easily accessible by train, it is an easy destination to take (or send) out-of-town visitors. I've been anxious to see it for myself.

John has been to Bruges when he was in Europe for one of his backpacking adventures. He's told me on more than one occasion that he has no desire to go back. This intrigued me. Why wouldn't he want to go back to one of the "most beautiful cities" in Europe? I've been waiting to get a visitor so that I could take a day trip to Bruges.

On Sunday, Isabelle and I took Grandma to Bruges. It was easy enough to get there, thanks to my faithful GPS. We didn't have a whole list of places to see or anything, but we decided it would be cool to go to mass at the Church of the Holy Grail. (Ok, so it's not really called that—John started calling it that.) It's really called the Basilica of the Holy Blood, and it has a relic from Christ that sits in a golden box during mass.

After church, we took a leisurely walk and found a market and a lace shop. We found a really fancy outdoor cafe for lunch. We ordered and I left to go refresh our parking time.

Did you know that all of the streets in Bruges look exactly the same? Cobblestones and row houses. I ran at least a half-mile down two wrong streets before I found the right one. The car was really lost for what felt like a really long time.

I was gone for about a half-hour. When I was about a block away from the cafe, I could hear my baby screaming inconsolably. Still stressed from losing the car, I pulled myself together and settled her. But I vowed then and there that I will never, ever have aspirations to try out for the Amazing Race. I would be really bad at it.

Bruges is a pretty city. The canals make it interesting and add to the beauty. It is old and you can feel the history as you walk down the street—with thousands of other tourists. There are some cool churches. The markets are fun. But did I mention that you are there with thousands of other tourists? I think I'm with John on this one. I'd rather find the cool places that the rest of the world doesn't already know about.

Tuesday, May 26, 2009
Memorial Day: A Perspective from Abroad

Yesterday, was not a holiday in Belgium. But I have come to realize, that some holidays—especially the ones not celebrated by people here—mean more to us now that we are living on foreign ground. This is especially true about Memorial Day. Back in the States, Memorial Day always meant a three-day weekend for us. The start of summer where we could retreat away to John's parents' lake home up north.

Celebrating Memorial Day here is a little daunting. We are in the middle of Europe. We are living very near the towns and villages where thousands of American soldiers lost their lives fighting for freedom on foreign soil.

There are several Memorial Day services held in Belgium, at the three main American cemeteries. These services are usually held on the Saturday before the American holiday, and all three are only about an hour's drive from where we live (in different directions). We weren't able to attend a service this year.

Last year, on one of the last days of summer, we went fishing in a sheep field in a small town not far from one of these cemeteries. We walked through the quiet field along the river. All I could think about, was what it must have felt like for those American boys. They carried supplies and weapons instead of fishing poles, and never knew if and when they were going to get shot at.

In a couple of weeks, we are going on a road trip to Strasburg, France with some friends of ours from school who are from Strasburg. It is in the Alsace Region (the border of France and Germany) and it just so happens that it is where my grandfather's family came from. I'm excited to see this little corner of Europe.

But on the way, we will drive through the town of Metz, France. This is the town where Johnny's grandfather died as a soldier in WWII. He was crossing a river when he was shot. We will stop in Metz to find the river.

A few weeks ago, we were at a school dinner with some of the parents from Luke's class. At one point, the conversation shifted to what European ancestors we (Johnny and I) could trace ourselves back to. And then the conversation shifted to World War II and John mentioned that his grandfather died fighting in France. A dad looked Johnny in the eye and said, "Thank you." With these two words, the meaning of Memorial Day forever changed for me.

Tuesday, June 2, 2009
A Temper Tantrum.

Whenever the sun comes out after there have been a few consequtive days of clouds and rain, there is a mass exodus of people down our street as they flock to the Chateau at the end of our road.

On Friday, the sun came out. I decided to join the collective pilgrimage to the park for an outing with Luke and Isabelle. We had bread to feed the ducks. I was even ambitious enough to think I might jog for part of it, just like the old days.

I loaded the kids into the jogger stroller, packed it up and leashed up the dog. When I got the stroller out of the garage, I noticed it had a flat. No problem. I dug the tire pump out to fix the flat. Luke got out to "help."

Then I realized. We recently took the wheel of the jogger stroller to the bike shop because it had a hole. They fixed it, and this was the first it needed air since it came back from the shop. I noticed it now had a different air nozzle and our tire pump from the U.S. no longer fit to pump air into it.

Huh. Unfazed, I found the new ball pump we'd purchased, the one that came with three different sized attachments. Surely one of those would work.

Nope. That's when I had my temper tantrum. (When you read the title of this entry, I bet you weren't expecting that the temper tantrum was going to be mine.) But it was. I carried on for a while as I tried to get one of the four attachment-thingies to fit even the slightest bit to pump some sort of air into the tire. I hollered as I tried everything short of putting my mouth on the dirty nozzle and blowing. When none of that worked, I called John (who was in Ireland) to "tell" him what was going on. He let me carry on for a while. Luke watched the whole show, his big brown eyes wide.

It was just so infuriating. I came outside with a plan for the morning. The baby and the three-year-old were all packed up. I had fixed that tire a million times before. Only now, it was impossible to fix it because we'd replaced it here in Belgium and now it was different.

After I ranted and raved over the phone for a few minutes, Johnny said, "Why don't you take the other stroller?" Hmm. The other stroller. Good idea. I wouldn't get to run, but who was I kidding? I wouldn't have really run much anyway.

We went on our walk. Luke fed the ducks. Isabelle fell asleep. Morning salvaged.

Do I wish I'd handled myself a little better? Of course—especially in front of my three-year-old. But I also found a lot of value in a good-old-fashioned temper tantrum. It was like this huge release. I didn't know I'd been carrying around all that tension, and after my fit, it was gone and this huge weight had been lifted. (Though I'm sure there are probably better ways to get rid of that, maybe I need to start running again.)

The next time one of my kids throws a fit, though, I'm going to let them. I will step aside and let them go at it for a few minutes. I'm not going to get mad or let it upset me. And when they are done, I'm going to give them a big hug and say, "I know just how you feel."

Tuesday, June 2, 2009
The Chateau de La Hulpe

We live about 800 meters from the entrance to the Chateau de La Hulpe. The Chateau de La Hulpe was once owned by our landlord's ancestors (our landlord is a baron). The estate was given to the town of La Hulpe some time ago (the previous generation, I think) and now its massive gardens and hiking trails are open to the public. People come from all over Brussels to spend time there.

When we found our house, we knew that we lived near "The Chateau." But we didn't realize how cool that would turn out to be. The Chateau is different things on different days. This winter, when we had 48 hours of snow, people came from all over to snow shoe, cross-country ski and go sledding. At Easter, the city of La Hulpe had an egg hunt in the back garden. There is an art exhibit going on there right now—with huge, painted pieces of plywood strategically placed throughout the estate. They are beautiful.

I've seen children taking horseback riding lessons (there is a stable and pastures somewhere on the premises). The Chateau (house) itself is usually closed to the public, but it is rented out for big parties and weddings. It is not uncommon to see and hear fireworks on a warm summer night coming from the Chateau because of a wedding. Supposedly, there is a cafe somewhere on the grounds, but we have yet to discover it. We usually just get an ice cream cone from the truck parked at the entrance. Unless it is winter; then he serves "gaufres chaud" (warm waffles) instead.

I've gone there with Jasmine to run in the morning when no one else is there. We've hiked there with visitors. When my friend Sally was here last Spring, every time we turned a corner in the trail, there were new blooms of all colors. We take the boys there with their swords and shields and they hike through the woods, pretending to be knights or Robin Hood. Sometimes, John takes the boys there with their baseball gloves and the bases and they play a game of baseball. (They even get a few spectators.) We also flew a kite there one windy day last month.

But so far, my favorite visit to the Chateau was yesterday. Jasmine and I started our day with a run (see my previous blog entry as to why). And it was one of those days when we were the only ones in the park. I saw one other person—a photographer taking pictures of the mist on the lake and the vast, rolling green lawn in front of the Chateau. It is a sacred moment to find yourself in a place like that, alone.

Yesterday was a holiday here in Belgium and we had a three-day weekend. The weather was beautiful each and every day of it. We felt like we should do something to get out and enjoy the weather, but energy levels were low and we didn't know what to do. We decided to "just go over to the Chateau."

We got ourselves together mid-afternoon. I packed a "snack-picnic." This consisted of cookies and fruit for the boys and wine and cheese for me and John. (When in Europe...act European, right?) We hiked over to the Chateau. Avery rode his scooter. We can always tell how busy it is by how far down our road the cars park. There were hundreds of visitors. Everywhere we looked, there were families sitting on blankets, couples making out on park benches, kids riding bikes, scooters or rollerblades, lines of people waiting for ice cream.

We found a spot near some trees in the shade and sat on a blanket of our own. The boys kicked around their soccer ball. We enjoyed our snacks. It was so crazy to think that just a few hours before, I'd been all by myself in the park. And I felt so lucky. (Beautiful family and amazing life-opportunity aside) I felt lucky to look around and know that most everyone else had driven into La Hulpe just for this, just for the day. And we get to go anytime we want. Twice in one day even.

The next time you visit, we'll take you over and show you our Chateau.

Wednesday, June 10, 2009
Belgium, 1555.

Every now and then, it's fun to let myself get sucked into the history of my surroundings. When John's parents were visiting last summer, we were at the train station in La Hulpe. John's dad pointed out the corner stone on the building and said, "This building was built the same year Minnesota became a state." (1858 to be exact.)

A few weeks ago, the boys brought home a flyer from school advertising a special day of worship and celebration at the Church of Saint-Joseph in Ohain. The parish is celebrating its 450th anniversary. Wow. That's old. Two weeks ago, we went to the 10am service in La Hulpe at Saint-Nicolas, in French. The bulletin announced that preparations were underway for the celebration of their 450th anniversary. Last weekend, we went to our church on the other side of the forest, at Saint-Anne's in Rhode-St. Genese. A big banner hanging near the altar announced Saint-Anne's 450th anniversary year.

It got me thinking. What happened in Belgium with the Catholic Church 450 years ago? Something must have. Or these three churches would not all be celebrating their 450th-centennial-whatever-you-call-it-when-it's-450-years-of-something (I wouldn't know, because the U.S. has never celebrated anything that old.)

I started with my history book. Does the *Idiot's Guide to European History* count as a legitimate research tool? Probably not, but that's what I started with anyway. It's actually a good read and provides a solid "big picture" perspective.

I read about the problems with religion in Europe in 1555. (Wait, what do you mean there were problems with religion in Europe? Just kidding, I at least remembered that much from my European History class.)

But what about Belgium? I found a history of Belgium on the internet. As you might have guessed and I already knew, Belgium has had some practice at being in the middle of things. It was no different during the battles between the Catholics and the Protestants.

Ultimately, I never really answered my own question to the satisfaction of my inner research geek. If you find a better answer, let me know. But in any event, it was fun to stop and think about it for a minute.

Thursday, June 18, 2009
I'm Tired.

I'm tired because there have been a lot of nights in a row with little boys wetting beds or having nightmares and a baby that thinks she needs to eat all night long. But I'm also really tired of living overseas. This week, anyway. I know it will pass. It has before.

We got another ticket in the mail from the friendly neighborhood police department. This time, for going the wrong way on my own street (150 euros.) John took Avery to the police station to ask about it. He was told that if we try to contest it in court, the judge usually just doubles the fine. Nice. I guess that's one way to keep the court calendars clear. I miss the legal system in the United States.

Friday, June 26, 2009
Homesick. With a Capital "H"

I am more homesick than I've ever been. We all are. I don't know why. I am hoping that blogging about it will make it go away.

Maybe, it's because we've been waiting and planning our summer trip back to Minnesota for so long and it still isn't here yet. Maybe, it's because it is the last day of school and there's that transition period from schedule to no schedule and that's always tough. Maybe, it's because Avery has "graduated" from maternelle and will start his first year of primary next fall at the "big kid" school. Maybe, it's because this is the longest John has ever gone without a trip back to the U.S.

Probably, it's because my nephew turns one next month and I haven't even met him yet. Probably, it's because Isabelle hasn't met her Grandpa Fowler yet. Or her aunties, her uncles and lots of other important people in our lives.

I'm sure it's a combination of all of these things.

Nope. Blogging about it didn't make it go away. But I've started packing for our trip. I've filled our calendar with "things to do before we leave." I hope the next two weeks pass quickly.

Tuesday, July 7, 2009
Our Ducks.

One day last month, there was a pair of ducks wandering around in front of our house. We found a piece of bread to encourage them to wander on out of the middle of the street. We didn't want to deal with another dead duck in the road.

A few nights later, John and I were watching a movie. The kids were in bed. John paused the movie and asked, "Do you hear that?" We went to the kitchen, and there, standing on the walk in front of our house, two ducks were quacking rather loudly. Apparently, they were looking for another handout. We obliged. We were impressed that they had remembered which door and window were ours, considering we live in the middle of a row of ten houses that all look the same.

They don't come regularly, every couple of days or so and at different times of the day. Until yesterday, they were low maintenance friends.

We had a Fourth of July party at our house on Sunday for some friends. Ten minutes after we started the grill, rain dumped down and it was a soggy afternoon. But the ducks made a guest appearance, quacking for a handout when everyone was in the kitchen. The children were all very excited and the ducks ate very well that day.

Last night, I was feeding the kids in the kitchen because John is off to London for a few days. Isabelle was squawking and impatient. The boys were hungry and arguing about everything. The dog would come lay two inches from my feet wherever I was because I hadn't fed her yet. The cat was meowing because her bowl was empty. It was chaos and I was just trying to make everyone happy as fast as I could. When Avery announced that the Momma duck was here, I told him to tell her to "get in line." I explained that the ducks would have to wait until after our own family was fed and the boys had eaten, so we went about our business and I think Momma Duck sat down to wait.

About 20 minutes later, the boys were gone from the table, the baby was quiet, the dog and cat had been fed and I was cleaning up dishes. The duck flew up to the windowsill and probably would have pecked her beak at the window if I hadn't screamed.

Thank goodness the window wasn't wide open (no screens in Belgian windows) or we would have had a duck in our kitchen and Jasmine would have had duck for dessert. And even though it was completely the wrong thing to do, we threw bread out the window to make her get down. (Positive reinforcement for negative behavior is a definite "No" from any Parenting or Puppy Training 101.)

She kept quacking, but I held my ground. She got her one piece and that was plenty. She engaged in surveillance, by flying straight up and down—I think to try to see what was going on in the kitchen. She flew up to the windowsill one more time.

For tonight, I think I'll let the kids eat dinner in the living room and watch a movie. A fun summer vacation activity, right? And by next week at this time, she'll have to find another food source anyway, as we will be on our way to the good ol' U.S. of A. Although it would have been pretty funny to look out one morning and see her with all of her babies quacking at our door. Maybe she'll bring them by to meet us when we get back to Belgium in August.

Friday, July 24, 2009
Home and Home.

Getting ready for our vacation caused a little confusion. Our home, obviously, is Belgium. It feels like home, our life is there. However, when we were preparing for our trip, we often said, "When we go home..." or something similar. It made me think.

For a long time, I was conscious and careful not to call Minnesota "home." I thought it might be confusing to the boys, especially for Luke who really only knows Belgium as "home." When we would talk about our trip I was constantly correcting myself by saying "When we go home, I mean, when we go back to Minnesota...."

But then I thought about it. I was always catching myself because Minnesota was still home to me and probably always will be. We left pieces of our hearts behind in Minnesota. No matter how long we are away, whenever we get off that plane and walk out of the Minneapolis/St. Paul airport, it will always feel like coming "home," even if it's just for a vacation.

I guess the old saying, "home is where your heart is," is true. And I guess that means we have two homes. Because our hearts belong in Belgium now too. We are working too hard to integrate our family into life for it not to feel like home. We have good friends, a good school and we love our life in Belgium, even if it does wear us out sometimes.

Part of me worries about this. We will never be living in both places at once. Will we always feel like we are "missing" something from here on out? But then I guess there's that other old saying. "It is better to have loved and lost, than never to have loved at all."

I suppose if our hearts are going to be forever in two places at once, it's better to feel like we are missing something, than to have never had it at all.

Sunday, July 26, 2009
Exhausted.

We are about a week and a half into our vacation. And we are totally and completely exhausted.

Yes, there is the jet lag, not to mention dragging three little kids half-way around the world. But I didn't realize how totally and completely exhausted we are just from living in a foreign country. There have been some culture shock moments, but those deserve their own blog entry altogether.

We arrived in Minnesota on Wednesday, July 15. Thursday, I repacked our four suitcases so we would be ready for our trip up north and the wedding on Friday night. Friday morning at 8:30am, we began the four-hour road trip to Bemidji.

A four-hour road trip took us all day and was quite a production. We passed 13 McDonald's throughout the morning (yes, we counted). But of course, when we were ready for lunch, we were off the main highway and we couldn't find one. The boys were bound and determined to hold out for those golden arches. Eventually, the screaming baby and Luke's green, carsick face required that we would stop at whatever was in the next town. Luke started throwing up right as we spotted those elusive golden arches. I gave him a plastic ziplock bag, but didn't realize was that it was a plastic bag for fruit and it had tiny holes in it. I'll spare you the description.

Johnny helped Luke finish up in the grass next to the parking lot. Luke used the back of his sleeve to wipe off his mouth and said, "Wow. I feel sooo much better. Let's go eat some nuggets!!" And we did.

We made it to Bemidji just in time for the five o'clock wedding ceremony. The next day, we drove to John's parents' house, an hour away. We've spent a good week catching up with family and trying to relax and ease ourselves back into American culture. Although Luke had to go the doctor for a cough that he's had for more than ten days, and I've been sick as well. Last summer, I actually had time to sit and read a book or two while we were up here. Not this year. But that's to be expected with a baby who needs to be fed and put down for naps, and two little boys who are far away from their home. Next week, we head off to try to catch my brothers for a quick visit and then back to the Twin Cities.

Looking ahead, I'm anticipating the next leg of our journey to be exhausting. More packing, unpacking and getting the kids used to a whole new venue. We have doctor and dentist appointments to sneak in, lots of shopping to do and lots of friends to try to catch up with, no matter how brief the visits might be. But how can we not look forward to this? Isabelle will get to meet her Godparents for the first time. Avery will get to see some of his preschool friends. We are very lucky to still have all of these people in our lives, and I can't wait to give them a hug and tell them so in person.

Monday, August 3, 2009
Culture Shock.

I am a little surprised by the culture shock. It's easy enough for me and John to step back into life here. We remember the choices and conveniences. But to live them again is a little overwhelming compared to what we are used to now.

What do you mean the stores are open on Sunday? I forgot about that. You mean you can pick up milk on your way home, even if it's 8 o'clock at night? And the store you choose will actually have the item you want to buy? That spot on the shelf won't just be empty for no apparent reason?

What do you mean there is a McDonald's at practically EVERY exit on highway 94 heading North to St. Cloud? Do you mean we can actually let our kids sleep in the car and not have to wake them up because we know there will be lots of food choices and gas stations to choose from further down the road?

It's pretty easy for us to pick-up again with the American lifestyle. Except for the fact that I eat way too much when I'm on American soil, it's all good.

But our kids are over-stimulated. As I write this, they are watching "Diego" and shouting Spanish back to the television whenever prompted. And they are amazed at the commercials on television here. (We are used to watching DVDs from the U.S.)

They re-experienced Kraft macaroni and cheese and loved it. They

LOVE frozen American waffles which are for breakfast and not dessert. I brought a big box of chocolate waffles with us from Belgium. When I told my aunt I was bringing waffles to the BBQ, she was confused. It was after I hung up the phone that I realized she probably didn't know that waffles in Belgium are for dessert.

Overall, I feel lucky that we can travel back to the U.S. for so long while we live overseas. I think it's a good thing that the boys get to experience American culture like this as they get older. It has been fun to see Avery watching baseball. It helps me remember how my own brothers would rattle off batting averages and statistics without hesitation and I'm glad Avery gets to enjoy a little piece of that too. It's fun that the boys will get to go to a baseball game while we are here. I'm glad that when Avery sees a Target, he shouts, "There's Target!" at the top of his lungs from the back seat. I'm glad that Luke hasn't stopped sampling any kind of new breakfast cereal he sees.

All of this makes the idea of reintegrating to life back in the U.S. a lot easier, whenever that may be.

Sunday, August 16, 2009
Peanut Butter. Check.

Well. We're packing up. At this point, I need to borrow a suitcase from my parents, and I'm leaving a few things here for John to bring back to Belgium in October. It's been a fun-filled, busy month.

We have mixed feelings about heading home. We certainly fell right back into American life and I hope we fall right back into life in Belgium the same way.

I thought you might find it interesting to learn about some of the items that are already packed up in our suitcases and awaiting departure:

Peanut butter. Check.

Plain Cheerios. Check.

Maple syrup. Check.

Reece's Peanut Butter Cups. Check, Check, and Check.

Baby Rice Cereal (plain, not chocolate, like they have in Belgium). Check.

Ortega Taco Seasoning. Check.

Lipton Onion Soup Mix. Check.

Hidden Valley Ranch Packets. Check.

Buffalo Wing Season Packets. Check.

Are you noticing a theme, yet? I have discovered that season packets are very efficient. Minimal suitcase space, and maximum potential for satisfying an American craving.

Life Cereal. Check.

Kraft Macaroni and Cheese. Check.

Aveeno Baby Eczema Lotion. Check.

A giant bag of white rawhide chew bones for Jasmine. Check.

Lots and lots of new DVD's including the vintage Justice League Super Heroes and Transformer cartoons. Check.

Wii. Check. (Just what I always wanted for an anniversary present.)

Back-to-school clothes. Check.

Back-to-school shoes. Check.

The 1/2 price pair of shoes mommy got to pick out each time she went back-to-school shoe shopping. (Thank you, Famous Footwear BOGO Sale.)

Levi's jeans for a good friend from France. Check.

A whole suitcase full of new girl clothes for Isabelle. Check. (Thank you, Target, Baby Gap and Herberger's.)

Birthday trimmings for the boys. Check. (Transformer invites, party bags and napkins for Avery, Batman for Lukee.)

Birthday cards for each kid—in English. Check.

New books—in English. Check.

And finally, here are a few things that I remember packing in our suitcases last year, that didn't make the cut this year:

Starbucks coffee. (Yes, we finally figured out that Europeans make excellent coffee.) Oh, and there's now a Starbucks at the Brussels Airport just in case we ever need it.

Gluten-free pasta. (I've found a new organic store that has lots of gluten-free options.)

Candy. (Aside from the Reece's, we don't need a whole bunch of junk candy like we did last year.)

US Weekly. Can you even believe that I broke my weekly tabloid habit?

Hot Wheels Cars. There are new and improved fads this year - like Transformers and Bakugan (which I'm still trying to comprehend.)

Maternity clothes.

Friday, August 21, 2009
Fowler Vacation Stats.

We are home, safe and sound in Belgium. It has been a busy week of unpacking and dealing with jet lag. We are very glad it's Friday!

You might find it amusing to see some of our vacation stats.

Suitcases we checked to the United States: 4 (plus a car seat)

Boxes of chocolate we brought to the United States: Somewhere between 15 and 20

Bottles of wine: 4 (The max allowed by customs—two per adult)

Boxes of waffles: 4 (We accidentally-on-purpose forgot to mention these to customs because we weren't sure what they would say about it.)

Suitcases we brought back to Belgium: 8 (Plus a car seat.) We had to carry one on with us.

Suitcases we had to borrow from my Mom and Dad: 2

Days it took me to pack it all up: A lot. I started at least a week before we left.

We shop a lot on vacation. Prices here are insane. We try not to buy anything we don't have to in Belgium. For example, everyone got new shoes and back-to-school clothes. Between Old Navy, Gap and Herberger's, I bought a new winter/spring wardrobe for Isabelle and spent what would have bought three outfits here. I should have done some Christmas shopping, but I wasn't that organized. Besides, John returns to the U.S. in October, and there's online shopping for that.

Number of fish that the boys caught: Too many to count. But they each reeled in a memorable "big one" at some point.

Number of trips to Dairy Queen: 2? (I think.)

Number of trips to McDonald's: 6 or 7 (We were in the car a lot, and once was a bribe for good behavior at the Mall of America.)

Number of visits to Starbucks or other similar coffee establishment: About 7? (I can't count for Johnny.) But considering we were in the U.S. for a month, I did an excellent job at keeping this old habit from recurring.

Number of US Weekly's purchased: 2 (I held off as long as I could. And I'm glad, because this habit would have resurfaced much more easily, I think. Even with just two, I'm suffering a little bit from withdrawal.)

Number of new television shows we have to try to find on YouTube or iTunes: One. As my brothers can attest, we are totally and completely sucked into the show, *Deadliest Catch*. Aren't you glad I didn't say *Jon and Kate, Plus Eight*?!

Number of visits to the MOA: Just one. Thank God.

Number of visits to the St. Paul house: 3 (It hasn't sold yet, and that makes me sad.)

Times we got to see our next door neighbor, Frank: 0 (Sorry we missed you Frank.)

Number of Transformers Avery and Luke brought home to Belgium: 5

Number of Transformers hidden in the suitcase for birthday presents: 2

Bakugan Battle Balls purchased: 4 (Thanks Grandma.) I don't know what this is either, except that it appears to be all the rage with American boys with the average age of seven.

Number of Belgian kids who will even know what a Bakugan ball is: To be determined.

Number of boxes of Mac and Cheese: 7

Number of bottles of Maple Syrup: 2

Number of hugs and amount of love we received from family and friends: Hopefully, a year's supply.

Sunday, August 30, 2009
The Last Week of Summer.

Wow. It was a crazy-busy week. The first day of school is Tuesday, September 1 which is also Avery's 6th birthday. That's a lot to pull together!

Last weekend, I took Saturday morning to tackle the school supply list. Or, as I like to call it, "the scavenger hunt." Last summer, it took me several trips to several different stores. This time, I fared much better. I came home with most everything on both lists, but it still took me three stores. Why is it so difficult? Well! Let me explain.

First of all, the list is in French. Second, some of the French doesn't translate exactly, you just have to know what it is. This year, I knew what a lot of it was. (A major confidence builder.) However, you can't just walk into the Carrefour (the closest thing we have here to Target—and it's a distant second by comparison) and expect to knock off the whole list. Why? Because it's Belgium, and I'm American, that's why.

The list specifies certain sizes and weights of paper, specific sizes of paint brushes, specific brands of glue sticks, colored pencil packs with specified colors in them and a whole bunch of other random odds and ends. The boys needed special shoes in a cloth bag for gym class. Avery's list also had a deck of playing cards and a pair of dice on it. Hmm. I'm going to go out on a limb and say they aren't going to learn to play poker or anything, but who knows what they'll do with those?

Avery's list also requires a shoe box for his painting stuff. This made me laugh as we don't have a single shoe box in the house. We bought all of our shoes in the States and didn't bring any of the boxes back with us. I improvised and found a plastic box with a lid that's the right size.

I am a little nervous about Avery's birthday party. He wants to have a big party and "invite his whole class" the way everyone else does here. Yikes. Twenty kids who only speak French and our tiny house with me and John to entertain and supervise. I don't think so. Instead, we invited all the kids from his class last year (minus the three who moved away or are going to a different school this year) so that brings the total down to about 13. We're having it at a playground. And we invited some other parents along to help. We'll supply the wine and beer and snacks, they can be our interpreters. Oh, and I suppose I have to make a cake.

Speaking of cake. Avery informed me that cupcakes would not suffice for his class birthday treat. Instead, he wants a cake like all the other kids bring. Hmmm. I guess I have, what, about 24 hours to figure that one out. (Because I don't have enough to worry about for the first day of school.)

And I haven't even told you about the dog yet! Jasmine is going in for surgery tomorrow. She has a lump the size of a baseball under her shoulder and the vet will remove it for a biopsy. Probably nothing serious, but it still adds quite a bit to the general Fowler family chaos.

In other news, Isabelle is crawling and pulling herself up on everything. She has a cute little dainty crawl which is very different from the boys who would put their heads down and charge like a bull. But in all fairness, the tile floors slow her down a little. If she has pants on, her knees are slippery and she can't get a good pace going. And now that I know that I put pants on her every day. (I've got three kids! I need every advantage I can find!) The other day we had a race to see who could get to the spilled coffee grounds first and I lost.

Thursday, September 3, 2009
A Heavy Heart.

My heart is heavy today.

On Monday, the day before the kids started school, we found out one of Avery's friends at school lost his mother over the weekend. The circumstances are incredibly tragic. She leaves behind four children, ranging in age from 2 to 12.

The little boy in Avery's class, was one of Avery and Luke's first friends. Just over a year ago, I would stand in the play yard at school with my two little boys clinging to me, sometimes crying but always shy. This little boy would come over, each and every day and try to get them to come play, or even just smile. Eventually, Avery and Luke settled in and adapted, but he was still always one of the first kids to greet them on the playground. And he always, always had a big smile for me.

We've never really talked much, he and I. The kids at school are often shy about talking to me because my French isn't as good (or easy to understand) as Avery and Luke's. But he will always have a special place in my heart for the kindness he showed to my two little boys, and he will always have the distinction of being their first friend at their new school.

This morning, after we took the boys to school, Isabelle and I went to his mother's funeral. We were in one of the back rows, I wasn't sure if Isabelle would cooperate for the whole service. When the family came in behind the casket, it was difficult not to cry. But when Avery and Luke's buddy looked up and saw me, he got this huge grin on his face and he waved—you would have thought we were out on the school's playground just up the hill. I was glad I could be there for him in whatever small way I could.

I suppose there is one good thing about going to a funeral in French. After the initial procession with the family, it was relatively easy for me to hold it together. I couldn't follow along very closely so that made it less emotional. But my heart is still heavy, and very, very sad for Avery and Luke's little friend.

Wednesday, September 9, 2009
We Survived the Big Kid's Birthday Week!

Barely. (No, I'm just kidding.) It really did turn out to be a whole week dedicated to Avery's birthday, as it should be, I suppose, when you're six.

The first day back to school was Tuesday, Avery's birthday, so I made my first of several cakes so he could take one to school for his class. Thankfully, I happened to have a Pillsbury mix. I was a little nervous but the cake was obviously a hit, because he only brought home the Tupperware and a few crumbs. (Yay, me.) While he was at school, I made another cake, so we could have a cake at home for his birthday dinner.

Not that long ago, I made a really wonderful discovery at the grocery store. Here, they have cake mixes that come in a bag and all you have to do is pour it into the cake pan and put it in the oven. It's pretty awesome. So that was the family cake (but I doctored it up a little by adding some coconut—from the U.S. as the coconut here is unsweetened. Blah. Who wants unsweetened coconut for baking?) I frosted it with blue, coconut cream cheese frosting. Yum.

The last cake, was for his birthday party at the park, which I'm happy to say we survived. We didn't lose a single kid, and they all went home in one piece. We were doubtful for a moment when the whole herd of them came up surrounding one little guy who was holding his arm. I repeated, "Please don't be broken, please don't be broken," a few times, but it turned out that it wasn't even his arm he just scraped his knee. Nothing the first aid kit and a kiss on the cheek couldn't fix.

One of my favorite parts of the party was when a group of the boys ran into the woods to have saber fights with the really long, sharp sticks they'd found. Johnny marched into the woods after them and yelled, "Knock it off, give me all the sticks." In English. The kids, who only speak French, immediately handed him all of their sword-sticks and went back to whatever else they'd been doing before they got into trouble with sticks.

But back to the cakes. I made yet another cake for Avery's party, and brought the leftover blue one too. Our friends (the parents we'd invited along to help) had fun taste testing the cakes. Apparently, I make "American" frosting. (Go figure. I'm an American and anything I ever learned how to make or bake, I did so in America.) But I was told that you would never, ever see a blue cake here as they would never, ever think to put food coloring in frosting.

But Avery's favorite color is blue. And food coloring and frosting is so much fun!

Now. On to planning Luke's birthday at the end of the month. I wonder what color I should make the cupcakes for his class?

Sunday, September 27, 2009
Settled.

It feels as if there is not much to blog about these days.

The last few weeks I've had a strong sense of feeling "settled." We're well over a year into this overseas adventure. I feel like I know what I'm doing here and don't get as rattled by the culture shock incidents as I used to.

There are still plenty of "only in Belgium" occurrences, of course. Like last week was Car-Free Sunday, a day where the city of Brussels encourages people to leave their cars at home for a day and use bicycles, public transportation and their own two feet. And by "encourage" I mean, cars are prohibited in certain areas. Except, it seems, on Avenue Ernest Solvay. Our street happened to be one of the routes around the car-free zone. On Car-Free Sunday, every time I looked out the window, there were so many cars whizzing by our kitchen window I couldn't even count them.

But, for the most part, I feel settled. I love living here, I love our life here and I am grateful for this experience. I decided I'm going to enjoy and appreciate every single second of it, and live it with an awareness and consciousness. Some day, we'll be back in the U.S. Whenever that day comes, I want to know that I did the absolute best I could with this amazing opportunity.

Monday, October 5, 2009
Swine Flu Anyone?

Oh, wait. I mean H1N1, that's the politically correct name in the States, right? Here they call it the Mexican Flu. So much for political correctness.

Whatever you call it, I think we had it last week. It's hard to know for sure. I looked up the symptoms, and they are pretty vague. Fever, check. Chills, check. Sore throat, check. Upset stomach, check.

Luke got it first. It hit him like a ton of bricks during his soccer game. One minute, he was running and the next he was stopped in his tracks and looked as white as a sheet. By the time we got home he was shivering with a fever. He was out of commission for the rest of the day but by the next night he was doing a lot better. It hit Avery the same way. We were walking home from a street fair in La Hulpe and all of the sudden, he complained that he was cold. By the time we got home, he was shivering with a fever. By ten o'clock that night, I was shivering with a fever too.

But by Wednesday, we were all on the mend. If it really was H1N1, then it wasn't that bad and I'm glad we're done with it. We scheduled family flu shots for this afternoon—hopefully this will be it for our flu season.

There is one good thing about H1N1. There is a public awareness about general hygiene that didn't exist before. For example, last year, Luke's class didn't have a sink in their bathroom, and the kids never washed their hands. In the big kid bathrooms, they only had cold water and no soap. This year, hand-washing is more important. The big kids got soap in their bathrooms and they replaced the old, icky towel rack thing with paper towels. I've also seen Purel dispensers at the grocery store. Progress.

I still pack hand wipes (imported from the U.S.) in their lunch boxes. We are still probably the only family at school getting our flu shots. Isabelle's pediatrician practically laughed at me when I suggested it for her. But that's ok. The Belgians can think we're crazy if they want. We've been sick enough here already. If getting a shot might possibly spare us from another round, sign me up.

Monday, October 12, 2009
Daily News Updates

We are well into autumn at our house.

Here are some updates:

Soccer is in full swing. Coach Fowler is well-liked by his team and the parents appreciate his "let's have fun" attitude. It is the "under six" league after all, is there any other attitude to have?

The keyboard for our main computer is almost dead. The "a" doesn't work, nor does the space bar. (I'm not an expert but it's probably because of the red wine I spilled on it a few weeks ago.) John went into the Mac store in Waterloo to see about getting/ordering a QWERTY keyboard (as a French keyboard would do us no good). The employee had no idea what John was even talking about. It's a good thing he is going to the United States for sales meetings next week. There will be a Mac QWERTY keyboard in his suitcase upon his arrival home. Meanwhile, if we send an email from that computer....

itwilllooklikethisndwetrynottousewordswiththeletter"a"

In other computer news, we can now listen to our favorite radio stations from the Twin Cities live via webstream. Hooray! These used to be blocked "to users in our area and only available to users in the United States." But now they work. Now, if they could just do this for network television websites and then we wouldn't have to find our favorite television shows on the probably-not-very-legal websites we've been watching them on.

Monday, October 12, 2009
What Were We Thinking?

Yesterday, we had a birthday party for Luke at our house.

We had a little party for Avery for his fourth birthday and I was so organized. It was a pirate theme for six or seven kids. We did a little craft where the kids made their own treasure chest. Moms stayed to help. We went on a scripted treasure hunt around the neighborhood. And we finished everything just as the parents were pulling up to collect their children.

Yesterday, that did not happen. Luke's party was very last minute. We knew we were just going to invite a few kids. As it turns out, his class only has about six boys this year so it worked out perfectly to just invite the boys. He picked out Batman stuff at Target this summer, so it was a "Batman" party. Last week, I went online and did a search for "Batman Birthday Party" to get some ideas. The first website I found was an entry from a mom who did a morning party with waffles and had batman games and all kinds of Martha Stewart-type activities. It completely freaked me out. I stopped looking and instead I adopted the attitude, "We'll just figure something out."

That wasn't such a good idea. The morning of the party came and I managed to bake a cake and stick a plastic Batman on top. We had Batman gift bags with goodies inside. We hung balloons outside and Avery made a sign that said: "Bon Anniversaire Luke." But that was about the extent of our pre-party planning. Oh, and about twenty minutes before party time, John was searching for party games on the internet. We thought the kids could just play in the backyard and we were praying the rain would hold off.

About twenty minutes after the boys arrived, they were in a hog pile in the back yard, which was muddy. They were also swinging the plastic baseball bats at each other. John and I scrambled to bring some order to the chaos.

Did I mention that the kids at the party only speak French? It's a good thing that our six-year-old speaks French. He was the designated interpreter for the day.

John supervised "American sports time" and put some of his coaching skills to use. T-ball, basketball and soccer took up about twenty minutes. When it began to sprinkle hard, we pretended it wasn't. And when the kids started yelling, "C'est pluie!" I pretended not to understand. (Fortunately, it only sprinkled for about five minutes.) I racked my brain and remembered musical chairs. We set that up on the patio and I stretched that for as long as I possibly could. Another twenty minutes gone. We followed up with an "M&M" spoon relay (thanks for the idea Grandma Fowler) and "Hot Potato." Everyone was ready for a juice break after that so we brought out the cake and presents.

During cake-time, John thought it would be funny to skype his parents to show them what we'd gotten ourselves into for the day. They helped us sing "Happy Birthday" (in English). Then they got their coffee and settled on their couch to watch our chaos. For the next 45 minutes, they laughed as John and I ran around like crazy and they helped us count down the final minutes until pick-up time.

So, Luke. Ten years from now when you are reading old blog entries from our time abroad, I am sorry that your parents weren't as organized as they should have been for your fourth birthday party. But I think you had a fun day with your buddies just the same.

I am so glad that the fall birthday season has come to a close for this year. Bring on the baby's first birthday in December! I'll be ready. (Oh, and John's parents will be here live and in person to help us celebrate.) Hooray!!

Monday, October 19, 2009
Rice Krispie Bars.

I am on a mission: A Rice Krispie Treat mission.

Each year, our school celebrates fall and spring with a big party. (In French, fête.) They aren't as elaborate as the Nativity County Fair, but there is plenty of family fun accompanied by great food, Belgian beer and French wine.

At every fête, they ask for helpers, of course. However, not speaking French and with three little ones, volunteering to help at a stand or organize anything is still somewhat beyond our capabilities. But I always sign up to bring desserts. These are either sold during the day or put out after dinner in the evening.

At the first fête, I made Rice Krispie Bars. I thought it would be fun to bring something "American." And what's more American (and easy to make) than marshmallow treats? Let me tell you, they looked very lonely and so obviously different than the rest of the fruit pastries, crêpes and cakes. We were the only ones who ate them. But right then and there, I vowed that I would win Le Ecole Saint-Joseph over to the wonderful world of gooey marshmallow goodness that is a Rice Krispie Treat.

Last fall, just after school started, the boys and I were invited to lunch at a friend's house. It was Wednesday, the half day. I offered to bring dessert, and I was told that offering to bring something was a very "American" thing to do. (It's a good thing I'm American.) All of my friends here are very good at telling me what's considered "American."

Which, of course, is very fun because I'm so American I don't always know.

Anyway, I brought Rice Krispie Bars. And then, I laughed when my friend brought bowls and spoons to the table. I jumped in to cut them up and pass them out. The whole family loved them so much that I left them all at their house (much to John's dismay.)

At the next fête a few weeks later, I happened to notice that the kids who had been at lunch with us that day were buying and eating up all of the Rice Krispie Treats. Score one for the American!

In the spring, I made them again. This time, I bought one of the last two for myself. The woman behind me in line was confused about what it was, so I broke off a piece so she could have a taste. She bought the last one. Touché!

We celebrated our fête d'automne this weekend. Our fête d'automne is filled with family fun and the afternoon consists of the grand jue (which translates to "big game.") The big game is a really long walk through the neighboring fields and forests. There are about ten stations set up with a game to play or family activity and a stamp or sticker to earn at each stop. The goal is to fill all of the empty spots on your card.

Last year's theme was the farm. This year's theme was "space" and all of the children are supposed to dress up according to the theme. Luke was a "Blue Moon" and Avery was a "Starry Night." I'm pretty sure that the names of their costumes were lost in translation, but they looked good just the same.

And guess what I volunteered to bring? Rice Krispie Treats, of course. This year, I never even saw them. Maybe, one of the head volunteers decided they were too strange to put out next to the waffles, crêpes and cakes. (I honestly wouldn't be surprised in the least if that happened.) The French-Belgians are very particular about their food. But maybe, just maybe, they were all purchased and consumed before I even got to see them?

In any event, it doesn't matter. I'll be making them again next time.

Tuesday, October 27, 2009
We're Going to....Disneyland?!?!

Anyone who has followed our adventures in Europe, knows that we don't do a lot of traveling. But that doesn't mean we don't have a wish list of places to go with the kids while we are living here in Belgium.

Number one on the list is Paris. This destination recently earned top priority after we drove by an ugly cement water tower and Luke shouted, "There's the Eiffel Tower! I see the Eiffel Tower!" Avery and I tried to explain that it was a water tower and not the Eiffel Tower but he would have none of it.

Paris is an hour by train and about two and a half hours by car. And yes, if you're thinking to yourself, "Just get in the car and go already!" We know. We need to take the kids to Paris. Here's the problem. It's just far enough, and traffic is just unpredictable enough that it's not a feasible day trip. (Especially with three little kids.) That means, a hotel. Well, the boys have soccer on Saturdays, we have a dog that has to find a place to stay for the night, etc. etc.

And then there's the whole task of finding a family friendly hotel in Paris. John is an expert, seasoned traveler. He is familiar with hotels all over the continent. But when it comes to finding a place for our whole family, he gets a bit...shall we say...picky.

Next week, is a holiday week and the boys have the whole week off from school. We talked about trying to go somewhere on our "list." There were cheap tickets to Ireland. But honestly, we feel like we've just recovered from our summer trip to the U.S. We're not ready to take a plane. (Not unless it involves somewhere with a beach.)

So we went to number one on our list: Paris. We have a whole week. At some point, we can drive for an overnight in Paris, right? Right. On to the task of finding a hotel. Finding the perfect family friendly hotel, close to the sights and within our budget is not an easy task. Last night, John pulled me aside before dinner and said, "I know somewhere with family friendly hotels and it's only twenty miles from Paris." I know that place too. We were trapped in the wonderful world of Disney for two nights and three days with a whole lot of Mickey Mouse shaped pizzas and burgers about a year ago.

Even so, he is absolutely right about it being family friendly. A quick internet search yielded an "ala cart" hotel that doesn't require an extended stay and multiple days of park passes. It has a pool! We can stay for two nights on what we would have spent for one night in Paris. We can drive and park there for free. Which means we can bring a cooler and some of our own food and not get sucked into the "twenty euros a plate" for the buffet restaurants. Also, we've been there, so we know what it's like and what to expect. (A huge bonus for traveling with small children.) AND, it's not even that expensive to get park passes for one day.

Early Sunday morning, we'll drive to the Eiffel Tower in Paris so that Luke knows that it is in fact, bigger than a water tower. We'll probably add a few other kid-friendly sights so the boys have an early appreciation for the amazing city that is Paris. Then, we'll drive to Disneyland. Maybe, we'll even make it there in time to attend the kids costume party Halloween event. (Or maybe we just let the kids wear their costumes around and tell them that's the party.) On Monday, we'll go to the park. And if Isabelle doesn't want to cooperate, I can retreat with her to our hotel room. We can all go swimming! And then, we'll get up on Tuesday morning for a short drive home.

I think this might just work out after all!

Thursday, October 29, 2009
Garbage.

Two weeks ago, our neighborhood had its annual "junk garbage" day. We have an interesting garbage collection scheme in Belgium.

Here's a quick lesson. Once a week (Wednesday), we get a regular garbage pick-up. We have to buy special white "La Hulpe" garbage bags (they are expensive) at the local grocery store and garbage will only be collected if it's in this bag. Sometimes, in the summer, cats and other animals get into the bags which creates a big mess. But mostly, it works. Every other week (Tuesday) we get a cans/bottle pick-up. These also have to be in a special clear blue bag, also purchased at the local grocery store. However, these are much cheaper. If you try to recycle something that is forbidden, they will put a big red "stop" sticker on your bag and the whole bag sits on the curb. The offender is left to wonder which one of the fifty or so aluminum or plastic bottles was the prohibited item. Cardboard and paper pick-up is once a month (on a Tuesday). This is all printed on a flyer that we get from our Commune, complete with a chart of calendar dates, and pictures of the numerous "forbidden" items with big red "x's" through them. Long story short—garbage in Brussels is complicated.

Twice a year, in the fall and spring, we have a "put all your other junk on the curb" day and pretty much anything goes. Our scheduled pick-up day was October 14th. We put a few things out the night before. By the next morning, our stretch of houses looked like it could have been mistaken for a landfill. (I know what landfills look like because I worked at one once.) There were couches, cardboard boxes, a dog bed, wooden crates, construction left-overs. You name it, it was probably sitting on our street on October 14th.

Within the first few hours, scavengers came by. Mostly, these were scruffy looking men driving white, beat-up vans or pick-up trucks. They would drive slowly down the street, and then if they saw something they liked, they would jerk the truck over to the side, jump out and grab what they wanted from the various garbage piles. Yikes. You can have the broken toilet seat. Take it. Really. It's all yours.

But, the real garbage guys never came that day. Or the next day, or the next. For the next ten days, we got to look at garbage, walk around garbage, watch it blow in the wind, get rained on, you get the idea. Finally, last Thursday morning, a garbage truck slowly rolled down our street and picked up every last piece. (The poor cars that had to wait behind the truck. Our roads are narrow, if you get stuck behind a garbage truck—especially on "random junk pickup day," you're stuck for a while!)

They missed a few itty-bitty pieces here and there. But somebody at the Commune must be good at planning and foresight, because the street sweepers/cleaners came by today. Or probably, it was just a lucky coincidence. Whatever the case, it was mostly all good.

However. This week was cardboard and paper pick-up, which is once a month if you were paying attention above. The garbage truck came down our street as I was walking into the kitchen to make coffee. Bummer. Now we'll get to look at a month's worth of paper and cardboard sitting around our house for another month.

Everyone else on our street missed it too. But I think I'm the only one who knows the truck did in fact, drive down our street at the ungodly early hour of seven o'clock. I've come to this conclusion because throughout the day on Tuesday, more and more cardboard showed up in front of our houses. There are paper boxes, stacks of paper and magazines. Cardboard, cardboard, everywhere.

So now, my question is, will we have to look at a month's worth of cardboard and paper in front of our houses, for the next four weeks?

I'm guessing...yes.

Thursday, October 29, 2009
Things That Have Made Me Laugh

I have had a few laughs this week, so I thought I'd share.

Earlier tonight, Isabelle was wearing a diaper and crawling around the upstairs before bath time. I happened to look over, and noticed a spoon (from our flatware set, not even a baby spoon) sticking up out of the back of her diaper. First, how the heck did she get a spoon stuck down the back of her diaper? And second, how on earth did I miss that when I took her clothes off ten minutes before?

Last weekend, John returned from a week of sales meetings in the U.S. He brought three suitcases full of goodies home to Belgium. (Don't ask what he paid to check the extra luggage.) He brought a lot of Halloween related stuff, including candy. My mom sent some goodies along, as did John's parents. Yesterday, we were in the car driving to school, talking about Grandma and Grandpa's upcoming visit. Luke said, "Mommy. We'd better call Grandma and Grandpa." "Why?" I asked. "We need to tell them NOT to bring us any more candy corn because we have enough!" So Grandma and Grandpa Fowler, we're good on candy corn.

Sunday, November 15, 2009
We'll Always Have Paris!

Well, we did it. We took three little kids to Paris. And now Luke knows for certain that the water tower we drive by every day is not the Eiffel Tower.

We left at 10am (very good for us) and programmed "Eiffel Tower" into our GPS. The drive was just under three hours. We even saw a sign for a McDonald's once we crossed the border into France. I love the trains, they are fast and easy—most of the time—but you really get a better idea of where everything is in relation to each other by driving.

We hit the city and were fortunate not to have too much traffic (it still felt like a lot, after three hours in the car with little kids, but it was nothing compared to what it could have been). After three hours of asking "Are we in Paris yet?" every ten minutes, I turned around to tell Luke that we were finally in Paris. He was asleep.

Our trusty GPS took us right to the Eiffel Tower, and even showed us the Arc de Triumph along the way.

We found parking easily, and got situated and on our way with the stroller and rain gear. The exact moment we stepped out of the parking ramp, it started to rain steadily. We only had about three blocks to walk to the Eiffel Tower and the advantage to a rainy day was that there was not a line. We walked right in and started climbing steps.

We made it to the first floor and celebrated with warm, spiced wine and ice cream (I tried to sell them on the hot chocolate, but they insisted on ice cream.) It was cold, rainy and windy, but it was still very cool. We decided to save the second floor for next time.

John and I tried to think what to do next. We decided that the Louvre might be a good idea, as it was indoors and maybe we could spend the rest of the day wandering in a really cool museum. We took a cab and stood, in the pouring rain, looking in amazement at the line of 1,500 or so people that had the same idea we did. So that's why there wasn't a line at the Eiffel Tower, everyone was at the Louvre!

We took a short walk down a street with a lot of cafés (even bypassing the Starbucks for something more "Parisian") to have a glass of wine, coffee, hot chocolate, whatever. We chose one and walked in. The front-door-guy took one look at us with our three soggy kids, shook his head and pointed to the door. Nice. We went back outside, hopped a cab back to our car, and we were soon on our way to where we knew we (and our credit cards) would be welcomed with open arms—our hotel at Euro Disney.

I don't care how many guidebooks there are on having fun in Paris with little kids. It is not a kid-friendly city. Although, maybe it would have helped if I'd read one or two of those books.

We still had fun, even in the wind and rain, and I'm sure if we try again in better weather, it will be a better visit. The rest of our weekend was awesome. The hotel had decent restaurants, a really fun pool with water slides and our day at Disney was very fun. We had a beautiful day (even though it was chilly, it wasn't raining). The kids knew exactly which rides they wanted to go on and didn't mind waiting in line. John and I took turns with rides or staying with the baby. And, they never once asked to go into a shop or asked for us to buy them anything. I was proud.

My favorite part of the Disney experience was when I asked, "What should we do next?" Avery answered, "I think I'm ready to go. But first, we should all go to the Small World Ride so that Isabelle gets to go on a ride too." Isabelle was in complete awe. It was the perfect way to end our day at Disney.

So. If we ever take the kids back to Paris, we will stay at Disney and drive into Paris for the day. Let us know if you'd like to come along, we know our way around!

Wednesday, November 25, 2009
Happy Thanksgiving!

After living here for almost two years it's safe to say that one of the hardest holidays to celebrate is Thanksgiving.

We have to work hard to find the traditional favorites. Turkeys have to be special ordered from the butcher this time of year (they are easier to find closer to Christmas). Cranberries are hard to find. Pumpkin pie filling has to be bought at the British store. This year, though, the Thanksgiving shopping seemed a little easier than last. (Or maybe I'm just a lot more laid-back than I used to be about trying to make it all perfect.)

The biggest challenge is that the American holiday always falls on an ordinary weekday. The boys have school tomorrow and Friday, just like always. We thought about keeping them home, but they missed several days last week because they were sick. Avery is still working on his homework from that. Also, Avery (by Belgian law) only has a few days he can miss "unexcused." Unfortunately, keeping him home for Thanksgiving would probably qualify as "unexcused."

We celebrated our Thanksgiving on Sunday. We kept it simple, but special enough to qualify as a holiday. (Champagne and Kidi-boul—i.e. kid champagne—went a long way to help with this.) I cooked a turkey breast, a box of stove top (imported via John earlier this fall), mashed potatoes, vegetables, and voila! We had a Thanksgiving dinner.

Tomorrow, it will be hard to wake-up to an ordinary day here in Belgium, while everyone we know and love is celebrating a special family day in the U.S. But it was kind of nice to pick our own day and celebrate it early. It also lets us ease into our Christmas celebration a little bit early too.

Since John doesn't have to work tomorrow, we will have a special "date" day. After we take the kids to school, we're going to do some major Christmas shopping!

Thursday, December 3, 2009
An Advent Lesson

Yesterday, there were numerous examples of how preparing for Christmas and the season of Advent can teach us all about patience. This is especially difficult if you are four. And if you are the mother of said four-year-old.

Here are a few excerpts from our day yesterday:

Luke: "Can we decorate the tree?"

Me: "No, Luke. Not until your brother gets home from school. He would be really mad if we decorated it without him."

Luke, *five minutes later:* "Can we decorate the tree NOW?"

Me: "No."

Luke: "Can I have some chocolate?"

Me: "Nope. Not until after lunch."

Luke: Tears and crying and carrying on.

Repeat the first set of dialogue, above.

Me: "Luke, if you open all of your advent calendar windows now, you won't have anything new to open tomorrow, and the next day, and the next day."

Luke: "But Mommy! I don't remember what's behind the door anyway!"

Me: "It doesn't matter, you still need to wait until each new day to open a new door."

Luke: "But Mommy! I only opened two."

Repeat the first set of dialogue, above.

Me: "Luke, would you like to help me put up a few Christmas decorations?"

Luke: "Hooray!"

Me, screaming at Luke: "You may NOT use the colored glass ball wreath as a hula hoop!"

Luke: "But Mommy! It fits me perfect."

Repeat the first set of dialogue, above.

Me: "I have a great idea for these Christmas tree branches."

Luke: "What mommy?"

Me, putting on my shoes: "I'm going to stick them in my flower pots in the back yard."

A few minutes later, standing in the rain, losing my patience, "Luke! Get back in the house! It's raining and you are wearing your brand-new slippers!"

Luke: "But mommy! Here are some more branches for you!"

Repeat the first round of dialogue, above.

Luke: "Can we decorate the tree now?"

Me: "Not yet, Luke, we have to wait for Daddy."

An hour later, just before dinner:

Luke: "Can we decorate the tree now?"

Me: "Yes!"

Luke: "Hooray!"

Me: "If you find an ornament you want, bring it to mommy or daddy to open it for you, and then you can hang it on the tree."

Me: "Luke! What did I just tell you about opening ornaments yourself?! We don't want to break them!"

Luke: "But Mommy!"

Me (last night to Johnny): "We're out of super glue."

This morning:

Luke: "Mommy! Our Christmas tree is so beautiful!"

Yes, Luke, it is. And so are you. I am so blessed and grateful that I get to be your mommy. I will try to do my best to teach you about patience, and I will try to do my best to learn about patience from you.

Monday, January 4, 2010
Christmas Chaos.

With three little kids, I have come to accept and expect that a certain amount of chaos will now accompany Christmas for the next several years.

At a glance, here is a peek at some of our Christmas Chaos from 2009:

Friday, December 11: Luke and Avery had a last-minute scheduled day off from school for teacher training. Daddy had outpatient knee surgery. The boys had a dinner date with some good friends of ours so that Mommy and Isabelle could pick-up Daddy from the hospital at 9pm.

Saturday, December 12: John's parents arrived for their Holiday visit. (By far, this was one of the best parts of our Christmas chaos.)

Sunday, December 13: Our friends from Quebec dropped their dog off at our house while they are in Canada for the holidays. This is a sweet little dog, but she is very nervous and only understands French. It's very funny, but also confusing, to have to speak two different languages to the dogs.

Monday, December 14: Avery had conferences at school. Daddy was walking well enough to come along.

Tuesday, December 15: Luke's class had a Christmas market at school. He was absolutely thrilled that his Grandma and Grandpa could be there.

Wednesday, December 16: Isabelle turned one!

Thursday, December 17: I took Grandma and Isabelle to the American Women's Club for a holiday luncheon. As we were leaving, it started to snow.

Snow in Belgium, even just a little bit, always means very bad driving conditions and major traffic delays. (Seriously, anyone from Minnesota would laugh hysterically at the crippling effect three-to-four inches can have on this city. I did at first, but not anymore!) After almost sliding into a stuck car, I got to school and brought the boys home without further incident. We were supposed to go out to dinner, but we had to cancel, because it was too difficult to drive three miles to the restaurant. We heard from other families that collected their children after 4 o'clock, that it took them hours to drive 5km home.

Friday, December 18: The boys had their last day of school before Christmas break. Avery needed to take all sorts of things for his class party, including a "homemade" gift. It was also Luke's turn to bring "group snack" and I didn't remember until that morning. I didn't have 20 of anything healthy in the house and the grocery stores don't open until 9am. We took our time getting ready, stopped at the store on the way and arrived late to school. It was a wise choice. We missed leftover snowstorm traffic and we were hardly the last ones to school.

Saturday, December 19: Luke had symptoms of the stomach flu (while we were all at our friends' house for dinner). He was sick for a few days but began to feel better by Monday.

Sunday, December 20: I got the same stomach bug. I couldn't even talk about food until Wednesday.

Monday, December 21: John took Grandma, Grandpa, Avery and Luke to the wrong La Roche. There is this great little town in the Ardennes with a WWII museum. John looked up the train schedule and figured it all out. Except he didn't know there is more than one town called La Roche in Belgium. The train that takes you to the middle of a field and drops you off on the side of the highway 5KM from the nearest town, is the wrong one.

Christmas Eve Chaos: We had lots of last minute shopping, grocery store visits, and general business. Even so, Johnny took the kids over to the sledding hill at the Chateau. As the day wore on we tried to relax and slow down as much as possible.

Christmas Day: We shared a blissfully peaceful day filled with presents and excellent food.

Saturday, December 26: We took the train to downtown Brussels to experience the Christmas market.

Monday, December 27: We said our "goodbyes" to Grandma and Grandpa Fowler.

The rest of our holiday break was quiet. The boys went back to school today, and were not excited about it. I reminded them that Carnival Week was just around the corner and I managed to get them out of the house with smiling faces.

Monday, January 4, 2010
Happy New Year!

Our New Year's Eve was relatively uneventful, but at the stroke of midnight, became a bloggable event.

The kids stayed awake as long as they could, but were still tucked into their beds with enough time for John and I to watch a movie before midnight.

When midnight arrived, our neighbors next door (with kids just a little bit older than ours) started their fireworks display.

My dad and brothers would have been proud. Bright lights and big booms filled the next several minutes. Our boys didn't budge. But the baby woke up, and was thrilled to see that the night sky out her back window was filled with color and excitement.

The dogs (yes, plural, we still have the nervous little French dog) were in a tizzy and started barking. We watched the neighbor look up nervously at our kids' windows and John decided to go out and wish them "Happy New Year" to assure them that we were fine with our front row seats to their fireworks.

Well, anyone who knows my husband for more than five minutes, knows that he is a sociable guy. Johnny can make friends in an instant and has a personality that extends across cultures. It's a very special gift and something that has helped us a great deal as expats. It didn't surprise me in the least when he came back inside to tell me that our next-door neighbors had invited us over for a glass of champagne.

As an American living abroad in a country where neighbors are kind but reserved, that's just not the kind of invitation you can ever pass up. We threw on our shoes, wrapped a blanket around the wide-awake baby and went next door.

Our next-door neighbors were clearly in the midst of a fabulous family New Year's Eve. The kids had each invited a friend and the children were running and playing all over the house. The mom was wearing an elegant black backless gown and stilettos. The dad wore a tie and a vest and had a funny little paper hat on his head.

Johnny was wearing sweatpants and a sweater. I had on my flannel Christmas tree pajama pants. And black socks. It will go down as one of the more "unglamorous moments" in my life. Did I mention I was wearing black socks?

But we enjoyed a glass of champagne, laughed at Isabelle who was so clearly discombobulated by the change of scenery at such a late hour, and appreciated our kind neighbors who invited us in as their first guests of 2010.

Monday, January 18, 2010
Coffee, To Go.

One major adjustment we had to make upon moving here was how we think about, drink and enjoy coffee.

In St. Paul, we lived around the corner from a coffee shop. (Who doesn't?) I tried not to go every day, but I went a lot. John tried not to go more than once a day, but he went a lot.

Here, coffee "to go" is non-existent. Here, people "go out" for coffee but they actually go, sit down, drink it, pay for it, and then leave.

About six months after we moved here, Starbucks arrived at the airport. It's right inside the front doors so it's possible to get a coffee, even if you aren't flying. Sometimes, we pick Daddy up at the airport and get a treat at Starbucks. It's fun. And expensive.

We decided, if we added up all the money we've saved getting rid of our Starbucks habit, it's a lot. We bought a fancy espresso maker, and taught ourselves how to use it.

But we still take our coffee "to go" now and again. Honestly, most mornings when I'm trying to get the kids out the door, I don't have a single second to take a sip of coffee before I leave the house.

During break, John took the boys to get their haircut one morning, with his coffee "to go" mug in hand. When he arrived at the shop, a woman asked him if he wanted some coffee. John, being the caffeine addict that he is, accepted. Upon seeing his coffee mug, the staff erupted into a disagreement with one another about whether or not he really wanted a beverage as he already had one. Then they asked John if he was drinking whisky out of his "to go" cup.

The concept of coffee "to go" is not catching on here very quickly. But then again, maybe that's ok.

Monday, January 18, 2010
I Don't Want to Have to Figure Out Stitches.

We've had to figure out a lot. One thing we've been spared is an Emergency Room visit with one of the kids. Our insurance here is messy, requiring lots of cash up front, international claim filing, and eventually, reimbursement. Although lately, it seems there are more denials. Denials require a whole lot of extra hoops to jump through to appeal and appeals require additional proof. Trust me, it's not fun and I don't want to see what an ER visit might do to that process.

Every time John gets on a plane to fly overseas, I pray for two things. Please don't let me get sick with three little kids to take care of by myself. And please don't let one of them get hurt and need to visit the

ER while I'm all alone. Beyond the insurance mess, the logistics of something like that with three kids makes me shudder. I've even been known to yell across the room to two little boys: "STOP RUNNING IN THE HOUSE I DON'T WANT TO HAVE TO TAKE ANYONE TO GET STITCHES WHILE DADDY IS OUT OF TOWN!" (By the way, we have tile floors.)

John left last Friday for a week in the U.S.

Ever since Christmas, the boys have been playing together on a whole new level. They've required very little supervision and hardly any mediation. Avery is diplomatic in guiding his little brother's overactive imagination and Luke happily follows Avery's lead.

The boys played together all weekend, but by Sunday, the fighting began. I heard screaming from the other room and Luke ran in with blood all over his face.

Uh oh. "It's nothing," I said, but it isn't. "It will stop," I said, but it didn't.

I heard something about an elbow (belonging to Avery). To the face (Luke's.) (Obviously.) The cut was on Luke's lip and it wouldn't stop bleeding. He wouldn't stop crying and with the blood and drool and tears, it was nearly impossible to see the extent of the damage. It was four in the afternoon. I didn't know what to do. It's not easy to think straight and problem-solve when there's blood and tears and three little kids looking at me with their big beautiful eyes. A half-hour later, it was still bleeding everywhere. I made the decision to go.

As Avery was helping me gather coats and necessities to get us through the next few hours of the unknown, my brilliant kid asked a question. "Mom, do you think Margaux (the babysitter) is home?" One phone call later, Margaux's mom dropped everything to come over and stay with the kids so I could take Luke to the hospital. I was so grateful, I cried.

When she arrived, there was still blood everywhere, so we left. Luke was quiet on the way. Twenty minutes into our car ride, I asked him how he was doing and he announced that he was "starving." I traded him his dark green bloody-drooly kitchen towel for a rice cake. He gobbled (yes, gobbled, puffy lip and all) it down and asked for another and another and another. Then he guzzled half a bottle of water. Hmmm. Maybe we should pull over before we get to the hospital and see if it's still bleeding?

And guess what? No more blood. The kid was eating and drinking and then he started talking about school. We turned right around and drove home.

We were spared our visit to the ER. For now. Please God. Don't let that be the practice run.

Monday, January 25, 2010
Traveling with a Toddler.

When the hangover of the holidays finally clears, we find ourselves thinking ahead to our spring and summer travel plans. There is something about having that ticket reservation in hand, and travel dates booked that seems to stave off the cold winter days and the encroaching homesickness just a bit.

There are two events that seem to trigger homesickness around here. The first is saying goodbye to visitors, and the second is when John makes a work trip back to the U.S. Both of those events happened in the last few weeks.

However, the thought of traveling back to the U.S. with three kids, one of them a toddler, makes me a little ill. Last year, going with a baby was hard. I've never worked so hard at being a parent. Making the connections, dealing with heightened security, keeping everyone busy in the confined space of an airplane, and then the aftermath of jet lag and culture shock...it was exhausting, to say the least. At least I was naive about the whole thing. I never expected it to be as hard as it was with the baby. After all, babies aren't mobile.

This year, that baby—who at least sat on my lap or slept—is already a toddler. She is a busy little person who likes to walk, run and climb. She is a little girl who has perfected a screech reminiscent of a pterodactyl and she uses it to get what she wants, when she wants it. This year, I'm not naive. I know, without a shadow of a doubt, that this trip will be H-E-Double Hockey Sticks. I've been thinking about not going. Just this once, John can handle the two boys on his own, right? They could have a fun filled week or two with Grandma and Grandpa while John works, right?

But I suppose that would make me a chicken. So, we've been studying the flight schedules like we are preparing for a final exam. What travel options provide the least amount of stress? What connections would be the least stressful on everyone? How do we plan our time in the U.S. so as to balance the stress of travel while maximizing our visits?

Last week, an American friend of mine who has lived abroad longer than I have, described it like labor. It's just something you do and you forget how hard it is so you do it again. I'm not sure. I haven't really forgotten about how hard it was. Maybe I will by June? Another friend of mine suggested bringing chocolate for the flight attendants. Now there's a brilliant idea. I will bring chocolate. Lots and lots of chocolate.

We might be in the U.S. for my birthday this year. Maybe, I should start lobbying now for a spa day....

Thursday, January 28, 2010
It's Been a Tough Week in Belgium: Progress, Part One.

We're having one of those "it's dreadful to live in a foreign country" kind of weeks. On a positive note, I realized that our tough days and weeks are fewer and further between than they used to be. And I guess it never hurts to get a reminder that "what's worth having is worth working for." So here it is.

The biggest problem this week has been with our internet, and more specifically, our wireless internet. Last week, our internet slowed to a screeching halt. What little service we had, trickled in. Websites were slow to load and watching something online was next to impossible. In our house, the internet is vital to our existence. It is our lifeline to our friends and family, our American culture, news from the U.S. and Minnesota and English news and weather reports for Belgium. The slow internet was still internet, so it was a tolerable problem for the moment. Until it became clear that the connection was too slow for John to use his NFL pass to watch the Vikings get smoked in overtime.

Miraculously, John managed to get through to the only person working on a Sunday in Belgium at Belgacom, our internet provider. We were told we'd used up our "gigabytes" for the month. John begged and pleaded and was able to get extra gigabytes for "the important work he had to do in his home office later on in the evening" (i.e. watch the Vikings get smoked in overtime). Did I mention the game was on at 2am our time?

Later phone calls during normal working hours revealed that our internet usage increased significantly a few months ago (suspiciously coinciding with the same time our new neighbors moved in). Huh. Maybe we should secure our wireless network?

My friend's husband works for Google, based in Brussels and he was kind enough to talk John through the process of securing our Wifi network, for the moment. In fact, the network was so secure that John couldn't even access it with the password the next day.

Several attempted phone calls later (filled with frustration including long hold times, language complications and customer service reps who simply hang up if it's a problem they don't want to deal with) finally resulted in a promised visit from a Belgacom techy later in the week, some time during the hours of 10:30 am and 2:30 pm.

No problem. I'll gladly stay home all day on Thursday if you can please, please, please help us figure this out.

The techy visit did not start off well. It probably had to do with the 100-pound lab that tried to eat her way through the front door to get to him when he rang the doorbell. He was not impressed. And for some strange reason, I assumed that the English customer service representative would send an English-speaking tech. I should know better, I've lived here for almost two years. But he probably would have been nicer if I hadn't started rambling in English before the blank stare on his face made me think to ask if he spoke English. Which he did not. I switched to French faster than you can say, "Pardon moi pour mon terrible Francais."

He was completely delighted by the three sets of stairs that he needed to navigate between the modem in the attic and whatever wires he needed to check in the basement and the computer on the main floor. We made the trek up and down and around several times. And he was clearly infatuated with the 100-pound lab. (Not really). While she might have wanted to eat him for breakfast, now she insisted on following him everywhere he went in the house.

After running all his tests, everything was reset and ready to go. Or so he thought, but not really. To make a long story short, we (me and the Frenchy techy) worked together to discover that it is completely impossible to secure our wireless network and expect to access it via a password with both a Mac (our home computers) and a PC (John's work computer).

I guess we'll be purchasing the unlimited gigabyte package from Belgacom. You're welcome new neighbors.

The silver lining from today was that my French, while less than perfect, was good enough to help us fix what needed fixing. I was confident enough to keep Frenchy techy from walking out the door until I had my poorly phrased questions answered. Progress.

Thursday, January 28, 2010
It's Been a Tough Week in Belgium: Progress, Part Two.

Last week, Avery came home several days in a row very upset about school. The big kids have been playing really rough at recess. On Friday, Avery specifically told me how some big kids picked him up and threw him on the backpacks. Understandably, he was upset.

But the behavior surprised me. The schools here are very strict. The children are usually friendly, polite and respectful to each other. Just the same, I sent a note to Madame Directrice (the principal) asking her to look into everything. This note was in French, (thus basic and lacking particulars) but I asked her to talk to Avery so she could get the whole story.

Monday morning, Avery was nervous and I stayed with him before the bell. I was completely shocked to see children running around, completely out of control. Everywhere, there were kids punching and kicking and hitting each other. This was happening right in front of me, standing there with Avery, Luke and Isabelle. Over the course of five minutes, I had to yell, and boy did I yell, at two different groups of kids (boys AND girls) who were kicking and punching. (It's a good thing "stop" is the same in French and English.) After shouting "stop" four or five times the kids finally looked at me and broke themselves up.

What the heck?! This behavior is completely out of character from the same kids I see every day on the playground. Was there something in the water? Over the last several weeks, I had heard parents talking more and more about escalating violence at school, but this was ridiculously out of control. No wonder Avery was nervous about coming to school.

We try to be as involved as we can at school. We try to go to as many of the teacher meetings and planned parent and family activities as possible. Obviously, the language is still a barrier. We are fortunate that a lot of the parents speak English. We are also fortunate that the teachers (and the parents who don't speak English) are patient with our French.

But having to go talk about an issue as important as the one I was faced with this week got me thinking. It's easy enough when the children are little. But as they begin to face problems that get more and more complicated it will be increasingly difficult to accurately communicate. It made me homesick for a time when I could collaborate with teachers and parents in my native language.

But I sucked it up and that afternoon I went to school early so that I could talk to Directrice and tell her personally what I saw for myself that morning on the playground. For the most part, she understood my French. (Along with the game of charades I had to play because I didn't know the French words for "kicking" and "punching" and "stomping.")

I told her what happened, I told her why I thought it was happening (at the beginning of the school year, kids were busy with trading cards and toys but then when the snow came they couldn't do these sorts of things outside anymore. Or maybe they were acting out something they'd seen in a movie? I gave her a suggestion for how to fix it (organize a few parent volunteers to help when needed).

I was proud of myself for handling the situation the way I did. The next day, I noticed an immediate difference in the number of teachers out at recess. They were more attentive in their patrol and they seemed to be breaking up confrontations before they escalated. Avery's teacher made a point to tell me that they'd had a meeting. And during the morning assembly (I stayed to listen) Directrice completely admonished the children. I couldn't understand everything she said, but her tone invoked the fear of God. After winking at me, she pulled Avery aside to talk to him individually.

Huh. Progress.

But I'm still nervous about whatever school challenges still lie ahead.

Monday, February 22, 2010
It Was a Dark and Dreary Day...

Winters in Belgium are mild, as far as the temperatures go. We had a few cold days this winter where the temp dipped below zero Celsius, about 20 degrees Fahrenheit. I know, if you're reading this in Minnesota you're shouting, "That's nothing!" I've been known to shout that myself whenever anyone complains about the weather.

However, the one thing that sneaks up on you during winter here in Belgium, is the dark. Because of our latitude/longitude, our days are shorter than in Minnesota. But that's not really it. It's the endless days of dark, gloomy clouds. Day after day of rain and clouds, can really start to take its toll on a person's psyche.

The last few weeks, we've had a bad case of the winter blah's. I've had a hard time finding motivation. I've been homesick. I'm going to blame it on the weather.

This morning, though, the sun came out. I put on my hiking boots, grabbed the dog leash and tucked Isabelle into the stroller and we were out of the house in fifteen minutes. The air smelled fresh, the birds were chattering like crazy and the sun felt terrific. Two hours later, Isabelle was tucked up snug in her bed for her nap and the clouds came back. The wind began to blow. And now the rain that's been falling for the last several hours is beating directly against the window.

But, we got to see the sun today and we enjoyed it, at least for a little while.

Monday, February 22, 2010
Lukee-Luke.

Luke is especially clever with ultimatums.

My favorite thus far:

One day a few weeks ago, John was working in the attic office adjacent to the playroom. He had conference calls so the boys were temporarily banned from the playroom. Luke said, "Mommy. If you don't let me go play with my Star Wars guys in the attic [insert long pause while he tried to think of something good] I'm not going to let you decorate the house for my birthday party." (His birthday is in September.)

Tuesday, February 23, 2010
Cooking Challenges

I love creative competition reality shows, especially the cooking shows.

I've grown to love cooking in Belgium. I love the challenge of trying to recreate some of our favorites from the U.S. with ingredients I find here in Belgium. And more importantly, without the convenience-focused American products. In the U.S., I used to think I needed certain brands or particular mixes to make our favorite dinners. But now I know that I don't.

Another challenge now is our budget. Life here is really expensive and our tight budget is proof of that. We also have different space constraints here. Basically, it boils down to this: I cannot afford to shop like I used to, nor do I have room to keep lots of groceries around like I used to. My shopping is careful and thoughtful.

And guess what? This means, I buy fresh and we use everything we buy. You would not believe how creative I can get with leftovers these days. I've created dinners using leftovers and no one has any idea that they are eating the same ingredients they ate two nights ago.

I am especially proud of a dinner I made for friends last week. John returned from his last trip to the U.S. with an overabundance of corn tortillas (we can't get those here). We wanted to make enchiladas (it's hard to find decent Mexican food here so I knew it'd be unique). The first hurdle—sauce. First, I was going to try to make green sauce, but a few trips to different grocery stores proved that finding tomatillos might be too ambitious. And even if I could find them, I probably didn't want to know how much they cost. I reassessed and decided on a red sauce. Prior to this, the only enchilada sauce I've ever used comes in a can with the words "Old El Paso" or "Ortega" on the label. A quick search on the internet yielded a new revelation. Enchilada sauce is really, really easy to make from scratch. And guess what? It tasted better than ever. (But that could be because I haven't had it in a really, really long time.)

My next hurdle was salsa. The salsa here that comes in a jar is...well, not good. It's either too sugary, or too salty. There just isn't a balance between the tomatoes and peppers. I have yet to figure out the translations for all of the various chilies and peppers - nor do I have the patience for all that chopping (a blender is on my "must find" garage sale list). So I faked it. I bought a jar of the bad stuff (but it had chilies and peppers in it) and then I added fresh chopped tomatoes, fresh onions and cilantro (here, coriander—I had to open the package at the grocery store and smell it so I could be sure). I made my own guacamole. Our guests, quite accomplished cooks themselves, could not stop raving.

If I could just figure out how to import corn tortillas we can make this more of a regular thing...

My upcoming challenge this week? It's the end of the month. Can I make it through the week without a major grocery store run? I sure as heck am going to try. Do you think anyone will notice if I chop up the meatloaf we had last night and mix it into a spaghetti sauce?

Tuesday, February 23, 2010
Rice Krispie Bar Update

I've made a breakthrough. Remember my entry about Rice Krispie Bars and my personal challenge to make them a staple at the boys' school events? A mom (who I don't know very well) approached me last week and asked for my recipe. That, in and of itself, provided a new culinary challenge. I don't use a recipe to make them, I just mix stuff until it looks right. I had to make them yesterday so I could write down my quantities (and convert them into grams and ounces). I brought her a giant chunk of the batch along with the recipe so she'd know what they were supposed to look like. She couldn't stop smiling and saying thank you.

Huh.

Score one for the American.

Tuesday, February 23, 2010
A Field Trip.

Last week, the kids had the week off from school. The Thursday before break, Avery brought a note home in his backpack. (Don't forget that all the notes that come home from school are in French.) A brief glance told me that it was about a field trip for Avery's class with today's date, February 23. Well, I had two boys who needed costumes for school, a baby to drag along and all the other craziness that is triggered a week before a school vacation.

Needless to say, the note did not end up in the "need to do right now" pile and I never got around to retyping the whole note into my translator website to figure out the exact details.

Yesterday, the first day back at school, Avery's teacher reminded me that he needed a picnic lunch for today (which didn't matter anyway because he always brings a picnic lunch). And Avery reminded me several times throughout the evening that we absolutely, under no circumstances could be late this morning. He didn't want to miss the bus with his class. No worries there, we're never really that "late." Ok so some days we cut it a little close when we can hear the bell ringing as we're still walking up the big hill on the other side of the sheep pasture, but only when we can't find a parking spot. We left ten minutes early today, just to be safe.

I'll pause here for a minute to explain the revelation I had today. The old me, never in a million years would have let my six-year-old get on a bus without knowing exactly where, when and what they were doing in the form of a detailed itinerary. The new me, the one that's lived-in-a-foreign-country-for almost-two-years-and-dealt-with-a-lot-of-crap, shrugged my shoulders, gave him a kiss and told him to have a fun time on his field trip.

Oh, and note that I never had to sign a permission slip.

When I picked him up, this was our conversation:

Avery: "I had the best day today, Mom! It was such a cool field trip."

Me: "So where did you go?" (I was completely in awe of the fact that I had no idea. This was about the time of my previously stated revelation.)

Avery: "I don't know. It was this church that they redid into a museum."

Me: "Was it downtown?"

Avery: "No, but we had to drive past the airport. When we got there, we walked up this hill where there was a bridge over the mud. When we got inside there was a lot of art and we got to watch a bunch of movies about the artist."

Me: "Who was the artist?"

Avery: "I don't know, but he lived in Belgium, then he moved to France but then there was a war, not the war where Grandpa's daddy was killed but the first one, and then he got really sad and he didn't want to go to the dungeons so he went to Spain where there wasn't a war."

Huh.

At dinner:

(Pretty much repeat the entire conversation above, but this time with me and John both asking whatever questions we could think of to figure out where the heck our six-year-old spent his day, with our very limited knowledge of art history.) We concluded that he was in Belgium (good, he didn't leave the country without us knowing at least) and here are some other highlights:

Avery: "He liked to draw stars."

Johnny: "Was it Van Gogh? Was it called 'Starry Starry Night'?" (Major points to John to knowing that Van Gogh painted stars.)

Me: "No, I think Van Gogh was Dutch." (At least, the Van Gogh

Museum is in Amsterdam, so I assumed he was Dutch.) "Was it Picasso? I think he lived in Spain."

Avery: "No, I don't think so. But he drew stars like this…" (He drew an asterisk-type star.

Me: "Let me try one more time to find the paper from school." (Picture me digging through a HUGE stack of paper on my desk.)

Johnny (on the internet searching: art museums Belgium church): "Nothing. I've got nothing."

Me: "I found it. 'L'exposition 'Miro,' Chateau de Waroux a Alleur in Liege'."

Johnny: "You went all the way to Liege today?! That's where my hockey game is this weekend."

Avery: "It was a long bus ride. Juliette even fell asleep on the way back."

We looked the artist Joan Miro up online and studied at his paintings together. Avery likes the ones with the circles.

Then, we found a picture of the chateau and Avery pointed out where they put a wooden bridge to get over the mud.

Maybe our kids are ready to venture out to more art museums while we live here?

Friday, February 26, 2010
The Olympics.

As I type this, the U.S. Men's hockey team is playing in the final playoff game before the gold medal round. I only know this because someone just posted a Facebook update with the score.

My current "live" prime-time coverage on Eurosport is of the ever-suspenseful bob sledding event. Oh, wait. Apparently, there is a "delay of game" because it's snowing so hard they have to shovel and sweep the track. No matter how loudly I shout "CUT TO THE HOCKEY GAME," they don't. Now, I'm looking at a bunch of guys standing around, kicking at the snow. Oh wait. Now they're back, heading down the hill. Good, I was worried.

One thing is for sure, watching the Olympics from overseas is enlightening. It's sports. Plain and simple. In the two weeks we've been watching, we haven't seen a single biography of an athlete. No voiceovers cut into the latest Snow Patrol song with shots of the feature athlete in their hometown intended to stir the heart. Not a single mention of the wondrous Canadian mountain location or a special feature on the local cuisine of Vancouver. In fact, if there wasn't the official "2010 Vancouver" signs hanging in the background every now and then, I wouldn't even know these Games were in Canada. And we realized yesterday that we haven't seen a single medal ceremony. They just don't show it.

And the events that are covered! Did you know that there is a cross-country relay race? Pretty much every time we turn on the live coverage, we're guaranteed to see some sort of cross-country ski race. The biathlon is especially popular. I'm learning that there are a lot of sports in the Olympics that I never knew existed.

And, I don't think Europeans care much about figuring skating. When I was a little girl, that's all the Winter Olympics ever were to me—figure skating. Today, I turned on the television and Eurosport showed a brief recap of a Japanese skater's performance. I realized it was the only time in two weeks I've ever even seen the inside of the figure skating arena. Maybe it's a sport that doesn't have a lot of European competitors at the Olympic level.

Last week, the boys were on a school break and one night, they watched the biathlon. Five minutes before we were going to put them to bed, Eurosport announced they were going to show the first U.S. hockey game (against Switzerland, I think). We whooped and cheered and let the boys stay up late. (Plus, we figured they could help us translate the commentary if we needed it.) Our excitement was short-lived. After the first period (the Americans had just scored), the coverage cut away to show a men's biathlon event. (A French athlete was in the lead. He ended up losing in the last few minutes, though, just in case you were wondering.) Little did we know, that would be about the only hockey we would ever get to watch for the next few weeks.

The other night, John seemed to be in physical pain wandering around the room. He knew the men's hockey team was playing and he couldn't watch it. With the time difference, a lot of these games are even on in the evening. (Usually, when a sporting event is on in the evening in the U.S., it's the middle of the night for us.) It would be so cool if we could just sit on the couch and watch a hockey game! On our own television! At a normal time! Instead, John had to get the updates via the internet—by hitting the "refresh" button on a stats page to find out what was happening.

John yelled a few times in frustration. I pointed out that somewhere in the United States, there was probably a European expat shouting at his television and wondering why on earth the Americans don't show more of the cross-country ski races.

Last night, we watched an intense curling battle between Sweden and China. And then we got to see hockey! Ok, so it was the women's bronze medal match, but still. Hockey!

When I was a little girl, I would twirl around the living room and pretend to be a figure skater. Avery and Luke slide around the dining room table in their socks and every now and then, stop, kneel down, and pretend to shoot at the ceiling. The biathlon is a pretty cool race, actually.

Oh wait! The French announcers just said something about the men's hockey game. If you'll excuse me, I have to go hit the refresh button on my web browser to find out if the Finn's managed to score at all against the Americans.

Wednesday, March 17, 2010
Two Years Ago Today...

Two years ago, the Fowler family arrived in Belgium. We were tired and disoriented. We've come a long way since then. The anniversary isn't as poignant as it was last year, but St. Patrick's Day will always have a special, alternative significance for us.

Aside from the obvious (like an extra child), it's fun to acknowledge some of the other, more subtle changes and reflect on how we've grown.

Here are some that come to mind:

I can parallel park our Volvo station wagon, with two inches to spare front and back, without breaking a sweat and without more than four motions.

I no longer have to announce that I don't speak French. It's not that my French is all that great, but I've learned how to fake it really well. I know enough to get around the stores and my daily errands, it's when the store clerks try to start a conversation that I get tripped up. However, I've picked up some survival techniques. I'm better at reading body language and gestures and paying close attention to what's going on around me. Plus, I do know a few words here and there. And when I nod and smile a lot, I can get through a conversation without having to declare that I have no idea what the sales clerk just confided in me. This strategy often gets me in trouble at school, where I need to know what's going on. So especially at school, I try to make sure I ask questions and practice a lot. Avery is an excellent tutor. And Luke is really good at telling me when I'm saying something wrong.

We've begun to venture out more as a family of five to try to find a new park, or spend the day somewhere exploring. But this isn't as much about a comfort level with our small country of residence, as it is that the baby is easier, the boys are older and it's just not as complicated to go do stuff.

We don't miss products from the U.S. like we used to. There will always be a few things on my "must have" list for John to pick up when he's in the States or that we ask people to bring when they visit. But I definitely don't feel like I will melt away without those things.

Certain situations here don't phase me like they used to. I have a new-found level of patience for traffic jams. I've learned that it's a complete waste of emotion to get upset about sitting in traffic. Mostly because there's not a damn thing you can do about it. The garbage truck or delivery service van will move eventually. The same thing about trying to figure out strange nuances about life here. When a store is closed, even though the posted hours say it should be open, I can shrug it off and say, "Oh well, it's Belgium." Because really, there's nothing I can do about it, so why waste energy being mad?

After two years, I can finally brag that I've memorized not only my cell phone number but also John's cell phone number.

However, we still have no idea how to pick-up messages from our home voice mail. Maybe next year that will be on the list....

I no longer mind when I find an occasional feather or piece of straw stuck to my eggs in the carton. And when I see chicken coops and chickens in backyards, the first thing I think of is "fresh eggs" not "bird flu" (like I used to).

When I listen to the local radio station, it seems totally normal for me to hear Janet Jackson sing "Nasty" followed up by Lady Gaga's Paparazzi song. The random play lists used to make me crazy. Now I just laugh.

Overall, we feel settled in Belgium. Crazy stuff still happens, but those days of feeling overwhelmed and like a "stranger in a strange land" are less likely. I love living here, and I appreciate how far we've come in two short years.

Wednesday, April 7, 2010
Our Historical Journey.

It goes without saying that we're living in the midst of historical places. In our first house, our furnished cottage, we could look out over the battlefields where Napoleon made his final stand. I've had coffee at the restaurant where he ate before his battles (and at the time, I was completely oblivious, I was just there for a coffee date).

As an American, a citizen of a very young country in WWII, this history can sometimes be a little overwhelming. But the history that we've found ourselves caught up in the most, is much more recent than all of that. Living in Belgium, we've embraced the opportunity to learn as much as we can about World War II.

Aside from living in the heart of what was an occupied country and near where battles and eventual liberation took place, there are other reasons we are drawn to this time in history. The most obvious is our grandparents. Our grandfathers served and fought in World War II in various ways. Some were pilots. Some served here in Europe, or the South Pacific. My Grandpa Tritz used to joke that he was the "guy who gave everyone their underwear." Some died serving their country. But our families have personal stories that tie directly to this time in history.

We've asked some of our new friends about their stories from their grandparents during this time. Their answers are eye-opening and sobering.

Not long ago, we worked our way through the Band of Brothers series produced by Tom Hanks and Steven Spielberg for HBO. Usually, I cannot handle a lot of violence, let alone in a war movie, but wow. This series that depicts real events about real people. And we watched it here, where we can walk into any town in any direction and find monuments declaring liberation dates, and names of American companies and soldiers that fought and died; or to take a picture of a building on a street corner in a quiet little town, and then see that same building in a photo taken on the town's liberation day, is nothing less than fascinating.

As a result, we've embarked on our own, self-guided Band of Brothers tour. In blog entries to follow, I'll share some of what we've found.

Tuesday, April 13, 2010
Washing Machines.

It's been awhile since I've had an "expat lesson." But I had one today.

It goes without saying that my washing machine is one of my most important appliances. Three kids, a dog and a cat—I easily average at least two loads a day.

Yesterday, it locked up. Of course, it locked up during the cycle where I was washing the lovies. When I went to switch the load, Luke's monkey and Isabelle's bunny were glaring at me from the inside looking rather soggy. The load was stopped, and I couldn't open the door. Of course, this was about 20 minutes before Isabelle was supposed to go down for a nap and Isabelle needed her bunny.

After several attempts to switch programs and trick it into thinking it was done with the load, I at least got the machine open. Isabelle had a very wet doudou for her nap but she didn't care. And then I did what I do a lot: I pretended it was a fluke and denied that there was a problem. That strategy only worked for about 24 hours until I had to wash more clothes.

This morning it jammed again. I called the store where we bought the washing machine to ask about service. This time, I was smart. I know that no one speaks English at the store where we originally bought the machine, so I called their location in Overijise, in the Flemish region. Usually, people who speak Flemish also speak English very well. In fact, they would much rather speak English than French. The man was very helpful and told me to find my receipt (which, surprisingly, I did) and call the general number and they could help me get in touch with the manufacturer to schedule a maintenance call.

After only 10 minutes on hold (a record time for Belgium) the customer service rep advised me to clean out the filter before I scheduled a service call. Filter? There's a filter I've been supposed to be cleaning out this whole time? Since I stopped worrying about looking stupid ages ago, I asked her, "What filter?" and "How do I clean it out?"

She told me that it was all explained in the manual that I should have read cover to cover when I bought the machine. I pointed out (very politely) that the manual was in Dutch and French and that I couldn't read it. (As soon as I master French and/or Dutch well enough, reading my service manuals is at the top of my to-do list. Really. I swear it is.) Obligingly (although clearly a little irked) she told me where the filter was and how to open it.

I spent the next hour pulling apart pieces from my washing machine and scrubbing out bits of grime and gross stuff. I found the filter. There were two pennies, (U.S. currency which makes me wonder how long they've been stuck in there) three sticks, a piece of plastic and a clump of dog hair. I'm hoping that will do the trick?

And if it does, I saw a really cute sweater today at a shop in La Hulpe. I'm sure the sweater costs less than the cost for a service guy to come clean out the filter and bits of gross globby stuff that I cleaned out? A fair trade, don't you think?

Friday, April 16, 2010
Washing Machine Repairs.

Yep. You guessed it. I was overly optimistic about my ability to fix the washing machine. One long, wet and smelly load of wash after my last blog entry put me in my place pretty quickly.

A phone call to schedule repairs secured me an appointment two days later with a five-hour window of time where I had to be home for the service person who was due to arrive sometime between 8am and 1pm.

No new sweater for me.

No laundry for three days means a serious backlog.

This morning, the service man arrived at 8:45. Hooray!

And while he did not speak English, he was very patient with my French. He even laughed at my joke that I have two little boys and the problem was most likely a toy or rock from somebody's pocket.

After only 25 minutes he was done. The problem was indeed a clog. However, it wasn't because of a little boy, but the dog who had ripped an old towel, a clump of which got stuck in the drainage tube.

When he was explaining the problem, I thought he was telling me that it was after the warranty and that I'd have to pay for it. "C'est la vie," I told him. But when he handed me the invoice, the columns for parts, service and labor all read: 0.00 euros.

Zero Euros?!

I wonder if that sweater I liked is still hanging in the window...

Friday, April 16, 2010
A Volcano in Iceland…

Once upon a time, there was a volcano in Iceland. One day, it began to blow, and blow and blow. It blew so much, that it shot ash and dust straight up into the air. It blew this dust so high into the sky that the airplanes couldn't fly. It made a cloud of gray and white dust that was so big, it blocked the sun.

It caused major problems for anyone trying to get from one side of the ocean, to the other. Unfortunately, our daddy is one of those people.

John was supposed to fly home from Minneapolis to Belgium yesterday. He was supposed to walk through our front door just after breakfast this morning. Tomorrow, we were supposed to take a much-needed mini-vacation for a couple of days to try to sneak something fun in for the kids before the end of their spring break. Did I mention that the hotel for this mini-vacation was pre-paid?

This morning, we woke to a bright and sun-shiney day. At about the time our daddy was supposed to be walking through our door, a big, gray cloud covered the sun. It's still there.

There are people stuck in the airport in Brussels, who can't leave the airport because they don't have a visa to enter the country. At least John is stuck in Minneapolis.

He was able to get on another flight. But the earliest they are rescheduling passengers is for Sunday afternoon. That puts him back in Belgium at the same the boys are supposed to leave for school in the morning on Monday. That means he'll have been gone for 11 days, all of it during their spring break.

But at least he has a ticket home.

The best-case scenario, is that they open the airspace today and don't have to cancel any more flights, and he is able to get on a flight today or tomorrow. The worst-case scenario is that he gets on his flight Sunday. We're going to expect the worst, and hope for the best.

Thursday, April 22, 2010
That Darn Volcano...

Who would have thought a volcano in Iceland would cause so much chaos??

It has been almost a week since my last blog update and John is still in Minnesota. His rescheduled flight on Sunday was cancelled. Upon re-re-scheduling, he got the last seat on a flight that leaves tonight. Although, he's been told that the flight is more than overbooked so we're remaining cautiously optimistic.

John's work travel has always been a part of our life. He and I make a good team and we've learned a lot over the last ten-plus years about how to make it work. I like to think that we're taking this volcano thing in stride. Although I will confess to a moment or two of pouting. I'm also prone to indulging in a little retail therapy every now and then. Especially in extenuating circumstances such as volcanos in Iceland. (Yes, I bought the sweater in the window after the washer incident, and I bought another one today. It's a really cool green one.)

John has always had a lot of control over his travel schedules. While his trips are frequent, none of his trips have ever been this long. This whole experience gives me a new respect and admiration for military families. I've often wondered how they do it. How does a family function with one spouse gone for so long, sometimes without a definitive end in sight? I've had a tiny glimpse at that this week. The answer, from what I've learned this week, is that they just do it. You do what you have to do.

I can't control a volcano in Iceland. I can't control the airline schedules. I can only control how I react and respond, and honestly, I just don't have any extra energy to spend on being mad or frustrated. I am thankful that John was stuck in Minneapolis where he could stay with family and work out of his old office and take some time to do some things he never has time for when he's passing through on business.

The kids have their spring festival on Saturday, the annual "fête du printemps." In any event, think good thoughts that John will get home to Belgium in time for the festivities on Saturday. The little ones are ready to see their daddy! (As am I.)

Wednesday, May 19, 2010
Getting Back in the Groove...

Daddy made it back to Belgium just in time for the kids' school fête. We had a beautiful day and a fun BBQ.

We had about a week to put ourselves back together, and then Daddy was off to Spain and my dear friend Sally arrived for her visit.

Sally and I had a chance to sneak off to Paris for the day. I can't even believe how easy it was (for us, that is, not for Johnny who was left with three little ones for the day). We left the house early, took the train and were standing in front of the Louvre by 11am. We spent the day wandering and took an evening train back. We were home by 9pm. It was a perfect day. Sally and I have traveled a lot together over the years, and I am so grateful we can add a daytrip to Paris to our list of adventures.

Last week, the boys had Thursday and Friday off. We left last Wednesday for a four-day road trip to the Normandy region of France. Words cannot describe it, but words are my specialty so I'll give it a try in an upcoming post.

It was a great weekend, but after which, we had to say "goodbye" to Sally. She left on Monday morning—amid threats of airport closures due to that troublesome volcano again. Her flight made it out fine, even though I was wishing the volcano would cause a little chaos in my favor for a change. But I was lucky to have the time that we had and I think she'll agree that it was probably the best of our travels yet!

Wednesday, May 19, 2010
Arlon, Belgium

We stopped in Arlon, Belgium by accident. Last June, we took a road trip to Strasbourg, France. We were on the highway with stopped traffic. We were all tired and hungry. We took the next exit, found the center of town and parked. By the American tank.

I had always known that Belgium was occupied by the Germans during WWII. I knew enough to know that there was fighting in and around the towns all around us, but I never really knew specifics. Parking in the center of Arlon, Belgium was specific. The authentic tank with the U.S. serial number was real. The attached plaque honored Americans for their service and marked the town's liberation day: September 10, 1944.

Last week we were in Normandy, and we learned that each town has a big party to celebrate their liberation day, and it's possible to trace the path of the resistance forces by going from town to town and following the parties. That sounds fun—but it will have to wait until we win the lottery. For now, we'll see what we can see, one road trip at a time.

Thursday, May 20, 2010
Our Cleaning Lady.

The next-door neighbors (Belgian) have a cleaning lady. She comes on Wednesday morning and for several hours, there is a lot of noise and bumping around. By the afternoon, if the windows are open, there is this nice, lemony smell of cleaning products wafting through the backyard. I once saw her on her hands and knees scrubbing the algae off the back patio. Yesterday, she was sweeping the front walk so hard I thought her arms might fall off. And once, John saw her load up her car with random garbage to drive it to the dump.

We have a cleaning lady at our house too. Me.

Sometimes, I'm a little jealous that the neighbors next door get to come home every Wednesday evening and walk into a sparkly clean house. But even though cleaning services here are affordable and tax deductible, it's just not something I want to spend my money on. Also, I fully admit to having control issues.

My European friends think I'm crazy to clean my own house. Perhaps this is a cultural difference? After all, here there are hundreds of years of social class distinctions going back to before the time of serfs. Hired help has, and still is, very much a symbol of status and wealth. A lot of Americans come from fourth or fifth generation immigrant families and their lives in the New Country required a lot of blood, sweat and tears. My pioneer ancestors did everything for themselves, and they were proud of it.

In any event, yesterday the next-door neighbor's cleaning lady came. (Even though they were on vacation for most of the week.) Yesterday and today, our cleaning lady came too. And from the front sidewalk, you can smell that our kitchen is lemony clean through the open windows.

Sunday, May 30, 2010
La Roche en Ardennes et Bastogne

La Roche en Ardennes:

A little village in the middle of the Ardennes forest was our next stop on our WWII tour. La Roche is just over an hour's drive from our house, and it's a beautiful one. Upon leaving the main highway, the winding roads twist and turn along the river. The road finally opens to a sleepy little town on the river below. An old castle looks down over the town.

At one time, this was nothing but a sleepy resort town offering a quick and easy escape from the hustle and bustle of the city of Brussels. But a military museum in the center of town preserves the memory of how this town was changed forever by the German occupation and the subsequent battles for freedom.

Bastogne:

Not far from the town of La Roche, is the town of Bastogne. The area surrounding Bastogne was famously cut-off from the rest of the allies during the Battle of the Bulge. On the edge of town, another military museum and monument to the fallen soldiers acknowledges those dark days of this area's not-so-distant history. A movie documenting the Battle of the Bulge plays on repeat in the small theater—in English with French, Dutch and German subtitles.

We've been to these museums several times. I have yet to be in one of these museums without seeing a German family, making the same pilgrimage as us, but no doubt with a very different perspective. I usually have to remind Luke over and over again not to talk too loud and I try to discourage him from shouting things like, "those are the BAD GUY guns!"

These museums are poignant, of course. But the most impressive site we've found in the Ardennes is something that's not in the guidebooks. Through a little research, Johnny was able to find where the 101st EZ company dug their foxholes just outside the town of Foy. And those foxholes are still there...

Monday, May 31, 2010
Foxholes in Foy.

In the seventh episode of Band of Brothers, Easy Company holds the line in the woods overlooking the occupied town of Foy, Belgium just outside of Bastogne.

Driving into Foy today, there's not much there; just a church and a few old farm buildings. Given its proximity to Bastogne, it probably wasn't rebuilt after the war.

Driving out of town, towards Bastogne, there is a wide-open pasture. About 500 meters down the road there is a small forest with impressive trees. Parking the car at the side of the road, we ventured into this forest, not knowing if it was private property. It doesn't take long, maybe a minute or so, before you see the foxholes.

These are the holes dug by American soldiers, 65 years ago. Although, some of what we assumed were foxholes, are actually craters from the German shells. The difference being that the foxholes are smaller and a crater from a shell is wider, more jagged and less likely to have big trees around it. It doesn't get much more real than that.

Monday, May 31, 2010
Normandy.

Our road trip to Normandy when Sally came to visit was amazing and emotionally exhausting all wrapped up together. It's a beautiful part of France, and as we drove along the coast to our B&B just outside the town of Carentan, I wondered what this part of France would be like today, if not for the monumentally historic day, June 6, 1944.

We stayed at a country house, managed by a retired British Navy Admiral and his wife. It goes without saying that he knew a lot of facts and figures about D-Day. Our D-Day tour included a lot of stops he marked for us on a map that we probably wouldn't have found on our own.

After breakfast, we drove to the nearby town of Saint-Mere Eglise. There, we toured the Airborne Museum and the famous church featured in the movie *The Longest Day*.

From there, we drove to Utah Beach, Pont du Hoc, Omaha Beach and finally the American Military Museum. At that point, we declared it "our longest day." The kids were troopers, especially Isabelle who was hauled in and out of the car more times than we could count. (And this, after eight hours in the car the previous day to get there in the first place.) But of course, this is not exactly something to complain about in the sacred shadow of all of the sacrifices made in this small corner of the world.

So on this Memorial Day, 2010, my thoughts and prayers and immense gratitude is with all military families. Past and present.

Monday, May 31, 2010
Classes Vertes

Translation: Green Class. At our house, we've been calling it "Green Week."

When we joined Ecole Saint-Joseph two years ago, we were told about Classes Vertes. All first, second and third primary classes at our school go on a one week trip as part of the school curriculum. They go to a camp in the Ardennes forest where they learn about the environment. At the time, I tucked that information away in my brain under the category "things to worry about later."

The subject came up again at the beginning of the school year, at the teacher open house the first week of school. Again, I maintained the attitude that "we'll cross that bridge when we come to it." The departure date was nine months away and it only takes one pregnancy to know that a lot of growing and changing (for both kids and parents) can happen over the course of nine months.

A few months ago, it was time to start thinking seriously about Green Week. We had to fill out the billing paperwork (notice, I didn't say permission slip). This invoked serious conversations at our house along the lines of, "Do we really let our six-year-old go away for a week without us?"

This was balanced against, "He'll have the opportunity of a lifetime with his classmates and teachers; and it's something he'll remember forever." In the end, there was really only one choice. We elected a long time ago to have an immersion experience in Belgium. It just wouldn't be the same if we pick and choose which parts we want to experience. How could we possibly invoke the argument "it's just not something Americans do" and let it win out? It helps that we have an inherent trust and unwavering faith in the school and teachers.

With the decision made, the preparations began. Avery's class began to have daily conversations about Classes Vertes. Every night, he would recap the conversations about where they were going, what they would do, how many kids would sleep in each room. We received a packet of information, including a list of things to pack and I had to send back a form with allergies and his medical insurance card. That made me laugh, as our American medical insurance card is completely worthless here. However, maybe the teachers would be able to get it to work in an emergency. If I ever complained about our school supply lists before, they had nothing on this one. I met a friend for coffee and she helped me decipher everything.

The school did an excellent job of preparing the students (and vicariously, the parents) for their first big adventure away from home and their families.

Last Monday, Avery climbed aboard the bus with his buddies. His suitcase, which was almost as big as he was, was safely stowed below. Moms and dads, brothers and sisters waved and blew kisses in the air as the bus drove away. It was like we were shouting "bon voyage" to a cruise ship. Luke and I even managed to keep Johnny from stowing away with the suitcases below.

That night at dinner, Luke announced, "I love Avery a lot and I really miss him, but isn't it nice that we don't have to worry about him yelling at me?" At home, the week passed quickly. John had an overnight trip to Holland, and by Wednesday, Luke was sick with pneumonia. For me, that meant a break from having to wake up to an alarm clock as I didn't have anyone to get to school in the morning. And even though Luke was sick, it was still good for him to have a change in the family dynamics. He enjoyed the opportunity to be the only big brother of the house.

We received daily emails from the principal reporting on the activities at Classes Vertes. She told us that the theme of the week was "Robin Hood," she told us what they ate for each meal, what their daily agenda entailed (i.e. chasing the Sheriff of Nottingham and his men, shooting bows and arrows with Robin, herding "wild" boars, singing songs around the campfire) and once we even received a photo of the group. We got one letter from Avery, in French: "I love you mom, I love you dad, I love you luke, I love you isabelle," (and my favorite) "Pierre loves Louise" (his buddy, and a girl in their class).

On Friday, we waited at school for the bus (it was late) and collected our very tired and dirty six-year old. All weekend, he told story after story. He bought a snow globe and a tiny stuffed wild boar with his spending money.

We are so very proud of Avery for making the most of this opportunity with his class. We are proud of ourselves for trusting in the school, and in him. He truly had an experience of a lifetime with his classmates and teachers and without a doubt, it's an experience he'll remember forever.

Thursday, July 1, 2010
The Fowler's Family's 2010 Rules for Flying.

1. No talking loud or shouting.

2. No kicking the seat in front of you.

3. You can watch as many movies as you want.

4. You don't have to eat all of your airplane food.

5. If you get hungry, you can eat anything you want out of your lunch box, you don't even have to ask.

6. You can go potty any time you want, if the seatbelt sign is off, but try not to touch everything in the bathroom when you do.

7. You can choose whatever you'd like to drink. But you have to set your

drink in the middle of your tray, not on the edge or in the corner.

8. If you have a question about plane crashes, you have to whisper it.

9. You can't ask questions about bombs (on jet fighter airplanes) until after we land. Because people around us might not know that you're talking about jet fighter airplanes.

Thursday, July 1, 2010
Traveling with a Toddler: Our D-Day.

I woke up yesterday morning with a feeling of dread. Butterflies and worry were rolled up tight and tied into a big knot in the pit of my stomach. The feeling intensified as we drove to the airport in Brussels' rush hour traffic. The last time I had nerves like that, I was sitting for the Bar Exam. Weeks of preparation and anticipation all led to this day, just like way back then. There is this knowing, that it's going to be bad. Really bad. But there's nothing you can do, except get through it minute by minute, hour by hour.

I was right, it was bad. Really bad. But it's over. Thankfully, time is a continuum that doesn't stop, even though it might sometimes feel like it stands still.

Here are just a few "highlights" or should I say, "low points."

Our seats, were five in a row (two boys at the window and Mommy, Daddy, Isabelle in the center). Isabelle sat directly behind the one woman on the plane who probably believes that children should never, under any circumstances be allowed on airplanes—even if it's to visit grandparents overseas.

Isabelle slept for a grand total of 37 minutes between Brussels and Chicago. Of course she fell asleep ten minutes before we landed in Minneapolis.

Our joy at being off the airplane, out of the airport and on our way came to a screeching halt on Highway 494, where we endured stop-and-go traffic for the next 55 minutes. With just minutes remaining in our long journey, Isabelle got car sick and threw-up all over herself and her car seat. "Uh oh!" is right, Miss Belle. And yes, I'm "all done" too.

It's 4:30am. I've spent the last hour watching a dazed and confused toddler wander around my parents' kitchen with her sippy cup of milk and a snack.

But I had the pure joy of gently coaxing her back to sleep by rocking her on the deck under a starry sky and the warm glow of the moon, listening to the quiet waves creep in against the shore. The first signs of dawn are now showing over the treetops and an early bird has started chirping. It reminds me of our first trip home from Brussels, I was on the patio with one kid, while Johnny was on the deck above us with the other. I've decided it's the only part of the last 24 hours that I'll let myself remember.

And now I think I just heard Luke wake up downstairs, so I'd better sneak off back to bed before he knows I'm awake or I'll never get any sleep...

Saturday, July 3, 2010
Culture Shock.

In this, our third trip back to the States since our expat adventure began, I've come to expect certain transitions. I know everything will be bigger: roads, cars, parking spaces, portion sizes, shopping carts. You get ice in beverages, lots of it. Even so, it's always fun to take note of the little things that surprise me.

I sat for three minutes at a traffic light yesterday before I remembered that I could "turn right on red."

My brother and I were talking and he said, "We were watching Jimmy Fallon...." Jimmy Fallon? Wait, what? He has a television show? And it's not Update News from SNL?

I forgot that here in Minnesota, you still need sunscreen even if it's cloudy. Sorry about the sunburn Avery.

I went into the grocery store and I felt naked without my coin for the cart and my stack of reusable bags.

There's a show on television called "Pawn Stars," and I kind of sort of like it.

You can get fresh milk at the gas station. Even if it's only 7 o'clock in the morning.

I got honked at for making a U-turn. There wasn't a "no U-turn" sign and I think my turn was completely justified. The other driver just didn't like it.

Friday, July 9, 2010
The Good with the Bad.

We've had a lot of "bad" the last few days. I've had to remind myself to see the good through the bad and I'm hoping this will help.

The bad: Upon arriving in Northern Minnesota, Avery had a raging fever. Obviously, there was something going on that was more than just the previous day's sunburn. A doctor appointment resulted in the "worst case of strep throat the clinic has ever seen." The good: We got in to a doctor, didn't have to pay cash up front like we do in Belgium, and we could even get the antibiotics from the nifty RX vending machine in the lobby.

The bad: Last night, Luke, seated in the center of the dining room table, spontaneously threw up all over everything in the middle of dinner. The good: I'm not so sure there is anything good with this one. Maybe, no one was in the direct line of fire?

The bad: Miss Belle was awake from midnight to 3am last night. I think it was teeth, but throw in the travel, over-stimulation, jet lag, change in diet and you've got one big hot mess of a toddler. The good: Mommy got to take a nap today.

The bad: Luke woke up at 6am this morning yelling, "Hey!! Someone dumped water all over me! Who dumped water all over my bum?" The good: Once I had a nap, I realized that it was a really funny way to declare that he had wet the bed. Also good, Grandma had the foresight to leave an extra sheet nearby, "just in case."

The bad: I have a black eye. This afternoon, in a battle during nap time, Isabelle wacked her head against my cheekbone and my eye instantly puffed up and now is a lovely shade of greenish-yellow. The good: Ummm....not sure. How about, our family pictures were last weekend and not this?

The good: We got all of the kids to bed early tonight. Isabelle was even asleep at 7pm. The bad: Avery and Luke started messing around. Luke fell and got hurt, resulting in a whole lot of screaming, which promptly woke up the baby. She's still awake as I type this. Oh wait, that one was backwards, wasn't it? The good: The boys are asleep and her screaming doesn't seem to bother them at all.

At the rate we're going, everyone will be on track and settled in within the next week or so...just in time for us to leave to go home. The good news: We're stopping in Chicago to see some cousins and go to a Cubs game on our way back to Belgium.

Ok, and here's some greater good: We have two brand new babies in our family. (Both boys.) We even get to meet them and hold them while they are still brand new babies....and we weren't on the other side of the ocean when they were born!

Wednesday, July 14, 2010
This is So NOT a Vacation.

A vacation should be defined as traveling to see and experience a place. It should be called something different when you travel to see and experience the people.

We feel very lucky to be here and spend time with everyone. We're having a good time and trying to enjoy every minute. We appreciate every second we've had with our families. But we're also completely exhausted and emotionally drained. Every time we hug someone and tell them how excited we are to see them, we know that soon, we also have to wrap our arms around them to say goodbye. Again.

On this trip, our focus has been on our immediate families. We've spent the last two weeks with our brothers and sisters and their families. Our kids get to be with their cousins. What little time we've had with them is never enough.

As always, we've had to make choices and sacrifices. There just aren't enough hours in the day to see everyone we want to see. We are pushing our kids to the absolute limit as it is. We've had to say "no" more often than we'd like.

But this visit is not at all a vacation in the traditional sense of that word. It's something much more.

Monday, July 26, 2010
Recovery and Reflections.

Whew. It's been a tough week settling back in after our visit to the States, but a quiet one, thankfully. Tonight, was the first night that the kids have gone to bed at a normal time. This is a good sign that the jet lag is almost behind us.

To say I'm tired of doing laundry and unpacking is an understatement. We've spent the whole week putting everything back together and it finally feels like we're almost settled. We left Belgium the last day of school, so I also had piles of school supplies to sort through and backpacks to empty. That gives us at least a couple of weeks before I have to think about translating the school supply list and begin my annual scavenger hunt.

The big question after all of this: "Was it worth it?" The answer without hesitation is "Yes, of course." But it will take a while to erase the memory of those airplane flights with Miss Belle. It's also hard to get back from a trip like that and not have regrets about the people we didn't get to see.

But I love this adventure we're having, and I am trying to embrace everything I can during our short time here. Because when it's all over, that's what it will feel like—a short time.

But one of the things that I've always worried about, is what will it be like to leave and move back? I'm not worried about that anymore. During this trip back to the U.S., I was amazed by how quickly and easily we fell back into life there. While we were visiting family up North, I almost forgot how far we'd come to be there. It felt like we could have easily been living back in St. Paul and just drove up for some family time. For me, there is a lot of comfort in that.

It's so easy to judge. It's easy to compare living here versus there and say something is better here or should be different there, and vice versa. But after this last visit to the U.S., I've completely lost the urge—or maybe it's the need—to compare one to the other. It's impossible to compare anyway. It's easier to just say they're both good. Different, but good.

Within minutes of arriving home from the airport last Tuesday morning, I jumped into the car to go to the grocery store for milk. Driving down the familiar street to the store, that's exactly what I noticed—how familiar it felt. And walking through the store to grab a few essentials, show my grocery store loyalty points card and use my Belgian bank card, I was the only one who knew I'd just stepped off a plane from half-way around the world.

It was good to go home, and it's good to be home.

Thursday, August 19, 2010
We Won! A Free Ticket to Disney! Sort of....

There is an interesting competition between the grocery stores here in Belgium. As a marketing tactic, they often have promotions where they give something little away, usually for the kids, with each 10 or 20 euros that you spend.

When we first moved here, it was packs of Smurf cards and stickers. (Smurfs were born in Belgium and it was an anniversary year.) I had no idea what was going on, they just gave me these little packets and for a few months I had Smurf cards all over the house. Smurfs was a cartoon on television when I was little, but I hadn't thought about them in a really, really long time.

Last summer, there was a promotion with Disney cards. We got a little better with that. I bought each kid a special tin box, specifically designed to hold the Disney cards. But by the time I figured out there was a collector's book with special pockets for the cards, they'd run out of them in the stores. It was Avery's first experience with "trading" at school and it was fun to watch. Every morning the kids would get out their books and tins before school and swap their extras. But then the promotion was over and the boxes went onto the bookshelf.

After that, came Nick Jr. marbles. I said a big "N. O." to Sponge Bob marbles. I mean seriously, Isabelle was just starting to crawl. I didn't need to be worrying about her choking on Dora and Diego on top of everything else around here she could already choke on. That was a short-lived promotion anyway.

Next, came the ultimate giveaway: Go-Go's. Go-Go's are little plastic guys, that look like aliens, about two to three times the size of a marble (close to a choking hazard, but not lethal). Each Go-Go came with a sticker and this time around, I was on the ball and figured out how to get the "free" sticker-calendar-thing to "collect them all." Go-Go's were very cool at school. Avery would take a couple at a time to trade and come home with different ones every day. There was some game you could play with them where you stand them up and try to shoot them down with the "shooter" Go-Go.

A close second to the Go-Go's, were the more recent Disney pins. We got the collector's book, and....(drum roll)...we even got the "pin in gold." Getting a pin in gold supposedly means that you win a free ticket to Disneyland Paris.

I went online and entered our "secret code" from our "pin in gold." I chose "French" (over Dutch) as English wasn't an option. From there, I had to enter all sorts of personal information. AND THEN, I had to answer a whole series of questions about the Disney pin promotion. I decided it was like having a pop quiz for my French and I did my best and only used my online translator tool at the very end to read the last part of the instructions. Which turned out to be a message that said, "Congratulations! you have *almost* (emphasis mine) won a free ticket to Disney, we'll review your information and get back to you."

Talk about anticlimactic. But yesterday, we got our certificate in the mail with yet another "secret code." And a list of dates that we can't use our "free" ticket. (Basically, all of the weekends in September and it expires in October before our fall break.) We also have to activate the code by a certain date, and we'll just see if there is another round of questions. I'm not holding my breath. But bring on the red tape! I'm going to see if I (or anybody for that matter) can crack the code to actually get the free Disney ticket.

Regardless, maybe we'll have to play hooky for a day in September and go to Disneyland. And if we're in the area, maybe we'll have to stop in Epernay and taste some champagne on the way back...

Wednesday, August 25, 2010
Dear Check-Out Lady...

Dear Check-Out Lady at Carrefour Express,

Yes, I gave the baby a whole baguette to hold, knowing full well she would start to eat it. Yes, I understand that probably constitutes a faux pas. I realize that it's not good manners to hold a baguette and start to eat it from one end like it's a giant hot dog.

You know that I'm from the other side of the ocean. You know that I've lived here for two years. I have done an excellent job surviving and thriving in a foreign land. My family and I have immersed ourselves in your culture and learned to live here without drawing too much attention to ourselves when we are out and about.

Don't judge me.

I'm an American. I realize I chose to solve my problem creatively at the expense of good manners. Sometimes, getting this toddler through a grocery store requires a little bit of creativity. If occasionally that means my screechy toddler starts to eat a baguette in an inappropriate manner, so be it.

Tuesday, September 7, 2010
Alopecia Aereata

....is what Luke has.

Last week at this time, I was sitting in the kitchen with my mom having a glass of wine. John and my Dad had gone out in downtown Brussels. The kids were all tucked into their beds in anxious anticipation for the first day of school.

Tonight, I'm in downtown Brussels, listening to the sounds of the city below from Luke's hospital room.

On Wednesday, after school, we (John) noticed that Luke's hair was falling out in clumps. That resulted in a visit to our General Practice doctor and then to the Emergency Room (which meant that John and Luke missed Avery's birthday party and dinner with my parents on their last night). That led to trips to the pediatrician and a dermatologist on Thursday. Friday evening, Luke saw a dermatologist who specializes in Alopecia. We've been told he's "the best in Belgium," but whenever anyone says that to me, a little voice always reminds me that it's a really small country.

He confirmed the diagnosis of Alopecia. It's an autoimmune disorder, usually chronic but not fatal, where the body attacks its own hair, causing it to fall out. It's rare to see it in children as young as our almost-five-year old. However, in Luke's case, the doctor thinks that we've caught it early enough for him to respond well to a progressive new steroid treatment. This steroid treatment requires four hours of an IV drip twice a day for three days. It was urgent enough that the doctor worked hard to make sure Luke could start on Monday morning.

And here we sit. After Avery went to school yesterday, Mommy, Daddy, Isabelle and Luke (now minus half of his thick head of hair) spent the day at the hospital. Isabelle and Mommy got to go home, while Daddy stayed with Luke. Tonight, Mommy is on relief duty at the hospital, so Daddy can sleep in his own bed.

A short walk down the hall to stretch our legs after Luke's medicine, reminded me that we're probably one of the luckier families on this floor tonight. A lot of the rooms had cribs. Some had crying babies. Others had weary looking parents who could not have been comfortable sitting on the thin mattress on the floor next to their baby's crib or bed. At least we know that on Thursday, our baby will be able to pack-up the nine million stuffed animals he brought and head home.

Thursday night, we are going to drive to France. Friday, we'll go to Disneyland. (That free ticket worked out after all.) Saturday, we'll stop in Epernay for some champagne. Maybe we'll buy Luke a bottle and tuck it away for his wedding day.

Next week, maybe our life will be back to normal. But then again, it's life. Is there ever any such thing as normal anyway?

Tuesday, September 14, 2010
Tidbits.

In an effort to focus on something different for a minute, here are some other updates:

Isabelle has lots of new words. It doesn't surprise me that one of her first words is "baguette," which she pronounces as "ba-ga." Nor does it surprise me that her other first word is "chocolate," which she pronounces as "ca-ca." Just so you know, "ca ca" is French for poop. Yesterday, when we went through the grocery store, she screeched "CA-CA, CA-CA," all the way down the chocolate and waffle aisle. That was fun. We didn't get ANY stares at all from the elderly shoppers. None. (Yes, there is a whole aisle just for chocolate and waffles. Come visit, I'll show you.)

This morning I got ready to go for a run and went to get the dog. For the first time ever, she lifted her head, looked at me in my running clothes and her eyes said, "You've got to be kidding." Then she laid her head back down in the sunny spot in John's office and I left without her. She was in the same spot when I got back. Our pets are getting old.

So far, we've had two weeks of school and Avery has come home without a new sweater, his lunch box and the new jacket that he got for his birthday. We've recovered everything except the new sweater. If this is any indication, it's going to be a long year. Hopefully, he still has clothes to wear in the spring.

We got a flyer invitation the other day for the annual La Hulpe liberation party that will take place next Friday. A Glen Miller orchestra band will play. They're serving roasted chicken for dinner. I'm sure the location is the equivalent of the American VFW. Johnny wants to go. In the name of the pursuit of any and all things relating to WWII we're thinking of crashing a party of elderly Belgians.

I missed the open house for Luke's class tonight. I didn't even know about it until late this afternoon. John is off to Ireland, so there was nothing I could do, it was too late to get a sitter. It's funny that we've lived here two years and we try so hard to make sure we're on top of everything at school but random stuff like this still happens. Oh well. I wouldn't have understood anything anyway. I'll get my French phrases all figured out so I can apologize appropriately to Luke's teacher tomorrow morning. Or maybe I'll just have Luke do it for me.

And now, it's late. I have to sign-off. Before bed, Avery announced in frustration that we've been late every day this week (it's only Tuesday) so I promised to try to be early tomorrow.

Thursday, September 23, 2010
Fall Out.

For the most part we've held it together around here. But as is with any crisis (I've learned from experience) after it passes there is an emotional and physical let down when it becomes "safe" to do so.

Today was my day.

The crisis, of course, was Luke's Alopecia diagnosis and hospitalization. I stayed strong and held myself together, and then threw myself into several different distractions as life settled back into normal. But then, there was the trigger. The trigger was Luke telling me about some kids at school who weren't nice to him on the bus last week.

Luke's classmates and friends in his maternelle class (the preschool/kindergarten groups) have been great. They've barely batted an eye about his new bald look. But on Tuesdays, Luke's class rides the bus with the first and second primary classes to the swimming pool. Some of the older kids were pulling his hat and hood off his head. Luke never mentioned anything until a week later—I think he was processing it and didn't realize it bothered him.

I had a friend help me talk to the teacher. As it turned out, Luke's teacher has been getting a lot of questions from parents and she hasn't been able to answer their questions. Some have even asked if he's contagious. So together, we decided that I would send an email to the parents and she would go to talk to the first and second year primary classes.

My email was in French, and far from perfect but I was able to tell the story and explain what happened and why Luke is now bald. I received immediate responses, all supportive.

Sigh. Even though it all seems to be working out, we can go ahead and file this under "things that would be easier to deal with in English."

Monday, October 4, 2010
Alopecia: One Month Later.

I really wish people would stop saying, "It's a good thing he's a boy and not a girl." Yes, he's a boy. He can wear hats. But he can't wear hats everywhere, like to church. And boys can't wear wigs. A little girl could wear a wig everywhere, like to church. In fact, she could even wear a hat to church. But little boys are supposed to take their hats off at church and at school and at the table, and his little bald head gets cold.

For the most part, the kids at Luke's school have gotten used to his bald head. The older kids don't see him as often, so there are still a few issues with that. Tonight, Luke told us that some boys in the first primary class told him something in French that translated to "he didn't look pretty." He's doing really well though—he's a tough little guy and I honestly can't believe how thick his skin is. Although, of course we still worry. He shies away from our questions and changes the subject if we try to talk to him.

On Saturday night, we went to church. Saturday night was a tough one for me, it caught me off guard. We had already dealt with the parents and kids at school, Johnny answered the parents' questioning looks at soccer, and when we're out and about in town, Luke often wears a hat. We don't even notice Luke's bald head at home, except to make a few light jokes about it here and there.

But, if there is ever a place that you expect to walk in and feel accepted, it's church. Saturday night, the church in La Hulpe has a service for families. The little kids are all herded into a small room during the readings and homily so they can hear their own edited version and color a related picture. Of course, it's in French, but our boys speak French, and Johnny and I have gotten a lot better at following along so it's all good. And it's three minutes away from our house so we're hardly ever late. Hardly.

Now that school is back in session, Saturday is "Scout Day." On Saturdays, the Scouts are let loose in La Hulpe. There are boy scouts and girl scouts everywhere, marching here and there all over town in their Belgian scout uniforms. They end their day with Saturday evening mass. (A good reminder that there is no separation of church and state here.)

In any event, the church was crowded on Saturday night. And pretty much anyone under the age of 16 spent a lot of time staring at Luke. Some even turned all the way around in their seats—several different times throughout the service—to look and point. A group of boy scouts about nine or ten years old jabbed each other in the ribs as they were walking by us during communion. One boy was staring as he walked but I think he got the message when he looked up into my eyes, with my arm protectively around my bald five-year old, to see me glaring back at him. He looked forward after that. I'm sorry, God, I know that I shouldn't give the evil eye to little boys at church (other than my own) but my innate protective motherly instincts were tuned to high frequency by that point. I couldn't help it.

To my utmost surprise and admiration, Luke seemed completely oblivious to it all.

The reality of Luke's condition hit me like the proverbial ton of bricks on Saturday night. Will he have to deal with stares and unasked questions like this for the rest of his life? If so, he's not always going to be oblivious to the looks and stares. I guess only time will tell. And time will also give us more tools to deal with this each and every day.

In the beginning, I was just thankful that he was alive and I could hug and kiss him. It felt silly, or vain of me, to pray for him to have hair. Now, though, I find myself praying that some day we will get to say to each other, "Remember those few months when Luke didn't have any hair?"

Friday, October 15, 2010
Last Night at Dinner...

Last night was a crazy night at the Fowler house. It's been a really busy week, and this morning, Johnny left for Minnesota for a week in the U.S. for work. The kids were tired and hungry, but it was an important night to have a family dinner. Sometimes when everyone finally sits down to the table, you just know that it's going to be chaos and last night was one of those nights.

In addition, we also had to tell Luke that his doctor wants him to go back to the hospital for another round of steroid treatments. Nothing has started to grow on his head, and he's almost completely bald. His eyelashes and eyebrows are almost completely gone. But his doctor thinks that one more round of treatments will help tremendously. He wanted to start Monday, but as John is going to be in Minnesota and then Spain, that's not possible. We scheduled treatment for the first week of November.

We had to tell him last night. The last thing we wanted was for him to learn about it by overhearing us talk to others, and we also didn't want to tell him right before bed.

It went about as well as could be expected. He announced through tears that he'd rather be bald than have to have the needle stuck in his arm again.

Thursday, October 21, 2010
Our Week Without Daddy.

With John on another continent for the week, we've made our way to the end of the week quietly. I've used up my reserve levels of patience and I'm coasting on empty, but I'm sure I can squeak out another 36 hours. There was only one day this week where both boys went to school at the same time and that was Wednesday, the half-day.

Avery was sick Monday and Tuesday and Luke was sick today and his fever tonight will keep him home tomorrow as well. Belle and I are bored, we're used to getting out and about, especially in the mornings, but I've been able to catch up on a lot of stuff around the house.

Here are some highlights:

Tuesday, Luke's teacher pulled me aside in the morning to tell me that on Monday, he stood up in front of the class (with a big smile on his face) and told them all about how, during the upcoming fall break, he would be going back to the hospital for another round of treatment. That same morning he said to me, "Mommy, I'm not so afraid of the prick (i.e. the IV) anymore. I'm going to be brave and I know I'll be fine." It was incredible to watch him to process the whole thing and go from anger to acceptance all on his own.

The other day I was putting Isabelle down for a nap and I softly began to sing one of the songs I've always sung to her. I was promptly and loudly

"Shhhhhh't" Exactly the same way the Belgians do it – with a loud sharp "shhhh" but with a "t" on the end. Just to experiment, I tried to sing again today and got the same response. So I guess I'm done singing my baby to sleep?!

Tonight is Friday night movie night at the Fowler house. I would hazard a guess that we were the only ones to walk into the movie store up the street to specifically request "Chimps in Space."

Tuesday, October 26, 2010
French Cooking Lessons.

A few weeks ago, I rented the movie Julie and Julia. Julia Childs was a bored expat in Paris and started taking cooking classes because she loved the cuisine. (I never knew that.) And it got me thinking about my own French cooking lessons.

One of my best friends here is from the Alsace region of France. We often have dinner at their house or they come here with their three kids and it inevitably turns into a cultural exchange. One of the first times we invited them here was for an American Thanksgiving dinner. They also love my Mexican food. She's cooked all kinds of wonderful things for us. They introduced us to Raclette, a meal that originated in the Swiss Alps, where everyone melts their own cheese and dumps it over potatoes and bacon and onions. (It's definitely more of a winter thing.)

Once, I made a salad and served it with Hidden Valley Ranch dressing (for all of the sauces served in Belgium, they don't do ranch dressing). I also had a bottle of a mustard vinaigrette that I put on the table for anyone who didn't want ranch. She saw the bottle and with surprise asked, "Don't you make your own salad dressing?" Umm...no. I don't. I mixed the mix from the envelope packet thingy with mayo, does that count? She told me that one of the first things French girls learn how to make is a vinaigrette dressing, and they also make their own mayo. I got a lesson right then and there on how to make mayonnaise.

I explained that one of the first things I learned how to make was Rice Krispie bars. She accepted that with a nod as she loves my Rice Krispie bars. I didn't tell her that the other thing "first" thing I learned how to make "for dinner" as a kid was Kraft macaroni and cheese from a box. I'm sorry but mixing powder orange cheese with milk and melted margarine probably wouldn't count as "cooking" to someone who is French.

Any time I get the chance, I pay extra attention to what she's doing in the kitchen and I've been taking secret mental notes. One Wednesday morning (half-day for the kids) I went over to her house for coffee and she "threw together" a lunch that she popped in the oven when we left to go get the kids. It was pasta. She dumped the noodles into a baking dish, tossed in about a cup of ham (or maybe it was bacon), stirred in some butter and cream, sprinkled some white cheese on top and stuck it in the oven to bake.

Wait just a minute. You mean you don't HAVE to use the jar of alfredo sauce?! Or the hamburger/chicken "helper" meal in the box to make a "quick and easy" dinner?! It really doesn't get much easier and simple than dumping noodles in a bowl and pouring cream over the top.

On a side note, my friend promised to bring me a bottle of her special honey vinegar that she uses in all of her salad dressings, the next time she goes home to Alsace.

She is from a town in France that's only four hours away from where we live, but it's two countries over if you drive through Luxembourg. Like us, she can't find certain products from home in grocery stores here. If you drive four hours from Minneapolis, you hit Des Moines or Madison, neither of which is all that different from where you started. To be four hours away and in an entirely different culture with different products in the grocery store amazes me.

Monday, November 1, 2010
When It Rains, It Pours.

It's fall break. While everyone around us was getting ready to go off on holiday, we were getting ready for the hospital. Sort of.

As it turns out, on Saturday afternoon, I started feeling queasy. By the end of the day, I couldn't eat anything and was beyond exhausted. I went to bed at 9 o'clock and slept for twelve hours with some sort of a stomach bug. The good thing with those sorts of bugs is that they are usually only 24 hours. But in those 24 hours, I was supposed to be getting us all ready for Luke's week at the hospital.

Thankfully, by the end of the day yesterday, I was less dizzy on my feet and able, at the very least to pack up a bag of clothes and activities for Luke. I crawled into bed early and called it a day. Our original plan, was for Johnny and Luke to take the train to the hospital in time to get there by his 8:30 check-in time. I would come with the other two kids later in the day to visit, and maybe take over for the night shift depending on how everyone was doing. The plan changed.

I was up early and feeling much better, but not Johnny. He caught some version of the same virus, but it hit him much worse. This called for Plan B. We didn't have a Plan B.

Let me just stop for a second to say, "Haven't we had enough?" Could we please just catch a break? Any sort of a break? I won't even begin to describe the insurance nightmare we've had with all of this. I think we will probably have cash flow problems for many days and weeks to come until we get it all figured out. We've got a kid in the hospital for an extended stay for the second time in two months. All of our family is on the other side of the ocean. Most of our friends are off on their holidays. We are truly flying solo on this one.

Ok. Enough. I've got to stop going down that road before I fall so far into the pit of self-pity, that I can't get out. Stop. Breathe. Think.

Plan B. Plan B was me throwing a bag of clothes together as quick as I could. I got all of the kids ready to drive Luke to the hospital. John nobly dragged himself out of bed so he could drive us there and the other two back home. He managed to get through the day taking care of Avery and Belle while I took the first shift at the hospital. This was an opportunity for a role reversal, as I am usually the one that has to take care of kids while sick. This experience has taught me that it's just as hard to be the away parent, as it is to be the sick one home with the kids.

I hope tomorrow is a better day. In my haste to pack, I forgot a whole lot of stuff. I hope Johnny is at least feeling better enough to bring us a delivery. I especially need food. As a celiac-sufferer, situations like this aren't easy and I have to scavenge for food. I'm allergic to pretty much everything that Luke gets served, so I can't pick off his leftovers. Thankfully, he doesn't like mashed potatoes. Today was even worse than usual. It's All Saints' Day, a bank holiday in Belgium. Nothing is open, not even the café at the hospital. I found a tiny convenience store around the corner and nine euros bought me some cheese, an apple, a coke and a candy bar, even though I wished for one of the baguette sandwiches. But enough, that's another one of those self-pity roads I don't need to travel right now.

Stop. Breathe. Think.

Addendum: After I wrote this, the eternal optimist in me found a bright spot and silver lining in our day. I really tried not to, I really just wanted to feel sorry for myself. But I couldn't help it. The bright spot of the day was our nurse. She was amazing. And the silver lining was getting to spend so much time with Luke. We played games, read stories and talked, all day. That was really special for both of us, even if I was hungry.

Wednesday, November 3, 2010
Bright Spots and Silver Linings.

As it's turned out, I've had to try to find the bright spots and silver linings all week. More complications have made for a rough week.

Luke came into the hospital on Monday with a cough. He'd been getting over a cough and cold when we arrived. In the middle of the night on Monday night he was getting a round of his treatment, during which he is hooked up to heart rate and breathing monitors. The breathing monitor recorded a drop in his oxygen levels and he needed oxygen.

Here is the visual: A blood pressure cuff on his left arm. His IV in his right. His chest with three electrode stickers to monitor his heart rate, oxygen and something else I don't remember. And then an electrode taped to his big toe, also for his oxygen levels. He was doing all right with all of it. Then the oxygen got hooked up with a clip on his nose, with the tubes hooked around his ears. And that's when he said, "No." The nurse had to tape the tubes to his cheeks so he wouldn't pull it out. My poor, poor little guy. But he got through it. And, well, there's the fact that now he could breathe. Breathing is sort of important, and therefore a pretty big silver lining.

Today, I arranged for Avery to go to a friend's house after soccer and spend the night—his first sleepover. Not to mention something to do during his school break that didn't involve babysitting his little sister or driving back and forth to the hospital while Mommy and Daddy changed shifts. However, he woke up feeling sick, with the same bug John and I had over the weekend. Poor kid. He was supposed to get one fun night but we had to cancel.

Bright spot: Our babysitter called me yesterday to say she was back from her holiday weekend and could babysit anytime. I had already booked her to stay with Belle for the afternoon, so now at least Avery didn't have to drive all over Brussels when he was sick. She'll be back again tomorrow morning, so Belle and Avery are spared from having to drive to the hospital for the rest of the week. John can work uninterrupted until he has to come and pick us up. Please, Lord, please. If there is only one thing this week that goes the way I planned it, please let it be the babysitter showing up to help Johnny tomorrow morning at 9am. If You do, I can tell you I will be so grateful that I will probably cry.

Another silver lining. I think I could probably drive here now (to the hospital) without our trusty GPS. That's a big deal. The hospital is in the middle of downtown Brussels, just a few kilometers from the City Center. Until now, I never felt comfortable saying, "I live in Brussels." A suburb, sure, "I lived in a suburb of Brussels." But now, I feel like I live in Brussels. I feel like I'm more a part of this city than I was before. That's a big deal for a self-declared city girl who has missed her connection to the city life of St. Paul.

Thursday, November 4, 2010
It's Been a Helluva Week.

We're averaging one major thing going wrong each day. I'll spare you the recap.

Today's really bad news: We're still in the hospital. It doesn't get much worse than finding out you have to stay an extra night when you thought you'd be going home. Luke went on oxygen again last night. And his really great night nurse tried everything to keep him off of it. Because, as she warned me, once he goes on oxygen he has to stay 24 hours in the hospital without needing it. But he needed it, and as previously stated, breathing is sort of important.

We had a roller coaster of a day, thinking they would let us go home, and then finding out that we had to stay. It went back and forth several times over the course of a couple of hours. It was a ride made worse by a not-so-great nurse. And while, as a general rule, I try not to add to the negativity out there in the universe, I actually took great pleasure in telling our not-so-great nurse that we weren't leaving until the next morning. She thought she was getting rid of us.

At the end of it all, there was one really disappointed five-year-old and one worn out mommy. We allowed ourselves a few minutes to get mad and sad about it, but then pulled ourselves up and ventured down to the gift shop to buy treats.

Did you know that European hospital gift shops have mini wine bottles right next to the bottles of coke and water? Luke picked out a Scooby Doo magazine and we were on our way. When we returned to our room, he announced that now it was time to go to the cafeteria. Did you know that the cafeterias in European hospitals sell beer and wine along with the coffee? Luke picked out a bottle of juice.

Luke is sleeping soundly now. Fingers crossed for a night of unassisted breathing and high blood oxygen levels every time the nurse comes in to check. At least the IV, tubes and other wires are all gone.

I think it goes without saying that I really, really, really want to go home.

Friday, November 5, 2010
We're Going Home.

We thought we would get to leave as soon as we saw the doctor, but we have to wait until this afternoon so she can complete the paperwork and review the results of Luke's blood work. All of that is worth waiting for, as the more paperwork we have, the better for dealing with our insurance nightmare. I'm interested to see if anything out of the ordinary reveals itself in Luke's blood test.

Luke has been packing for the last 24 hours, and all that's left are a few dirty clothes. He is getting antsy. I finally talked him into going down to the art room for a while to help him pass the time. He stomped down there with a scowl on his face but he likes to paint and they were happy to oblige him so I hope the next two hours will go quickly for him.

Happy Friday. I, for one, am very happy to see this week come to a close.

Friday, November 12, 2010
It was a Quiet Week…

It was a quiet week. A much needed, well-deserved quiet week. The boys had Veteran's Day (Armistice Day) and today off. I think that every week-long break should be followed up with a three-day week. It was great, they went back to school for three days and got a four-day weekend. We needed it.

Luke is doing well, he was really happy to be back at school. Avery is almost over his cough and was happy to be back to soccer this week. Isabelle was at the doctor this evening for an ear infection, but is taking it in stride.

Johnny had fun with a telemarketer today. He answered a phone call and asked the person if he spoke English. They said (in French) that they'd have someone call back. When the person who spoke English called back he asked (in Spanish) if they spoke Spanish. They hung up. That is now my new goal: To make the telemarketers hang up on me.

Tonight, we are making moules frites (mussels and fries, a traditional Belgian dinner) for our Belgian friends which I find rather comical. We should be making them something "American," rather than cooking Belgian food for Belgians, but it should be a fun night no matter what we have to eat. And we're looking forward to it!

A quiet week. A much-deserved, quiet week.

Sunday, November 21, 2010
Will We Ever Have a Healthy Kid Again?

This was one of those weeks that I spread my time and talents much too thin. It's easy to do when you've got three kids, volunteer commitments and a traveling husband.

The best part of the week, will arrive on Saturday morning when my brother and his family step off the airplane in Brussels. But until then, there is a lot to do.

Last Sunday night, John flew to Tel Aviv. Tuesday morning, Luke woke up with a fever and a headache. He was completely miserable. I talked to a few parents at school whose kids were suffering the same specific symptoms and it was easy to determine that a trip to the doctor would be futile with the news that it was a virus. The worst part was having to drag him out of the house every time I had to go get Avery from school.

Thursday morning arrived and John came home from Israel on the red-eye. Thursday night, Luke was feeling much better and I was holding my breath to make sure he didn't start coughing. Friday morning, he was even better and still no warning signs for bronchitis. Fingers crossed. By Friday night, he had a whole new kind of fever, and a wheezy cough. Ugh.

Saturday morning, in lieu of going to his last day of soccer games and award ceremony, I took him to the doctor where we left armed with prescriptions for antibiotics and inhalants to help him get over this new round of bronchitis.

I knew it was going to be a busy week, but a sick kid makes it all the more stressful and chaotic. I only hope that we get some answers for Luke soon.

When lawyers prepare for litigation, there is a whole phase of the process called "discovery." It's during this time that lawyers gather evidence, interview witnesses and prepare their case for trial. I'm looking at this like the discovery phase for Luke. I've gone back and made notes of his health history for the last six months. In December, we have an appointment with a pediatric pulmonary specialist and I'm hoping he will help us figure out what's going on with my little guy.

Tuesday, November 23, 2010
Ryan-itis.

My brother and his family arrived on Saturday morning with their two little ones in the whirlwind of our Saturday morning. I think they've settled in and are doing well with the jet lag.

Luke responded well to the antibiotics and is doing much better. I kept him home from school yesterday just to give him a quiet start to the week and to make sure he was ready to handle school again.

Avery is so excited to see his Aunt Jenny and Uncle Ryan and his cousins. He helped me to get their room ready, and keep it neat while we waited for them to arrive. For days he talked to me about "when his godfather was here," he would do this, that or the other thing.

Yesterday morning, the house was quiet. Avery and I were the only ones up and he was slowly getting ready for school. "Mommy, I feel shivery," he said. "I'm really tired and I have a headache." Hmm. As you can probably imagine, those are words that have come to strike fear in my heart lately. But my trusty thermometer revealed a perfect body temperature. Hmm. "Are you sure you're not just nervous for your spelling test?" He reassured me that it was not nerves.

John took him to school as he had a meeting nearby. Twenty minutes after departing our quiet house, John called to say that Avery slept the whole way to school and was crying about being sick. What? This is not my typical seven-year-old. Negotiations ensued and the outcome was that John would go to his meeting and come back by school to check on Avery before returning home. I hoped that he would get around his friends and classmates and snap out of whatever was ailing him.

John returned home with Avery a few hours later. His teacher said he was pale, not like himself and probably needed to go home.

It's funny how he perked up when Uncle Ryan walked into the room. We all started teasing him about his case of "Ryan-itis." And a tiny smile crept across his face.

While I don't think he was faking it by any means, it's funny how the subconscious mind can help you get what you want—or maybe even need, when it's necessary. Avery got a day off to make sure he wasn't missing anything at home.

Both boys are back at school and Johnny took the Tritz family on a tour of Bastogne. I didn't fit in the car with all of them, so I get a quiet morning at home.

But it's good to catch my breath for a minute. I'm looking forward to the rest of the week, and when Thanksgiving arrives (the official day on Thursday AND our designated dinner day on Sunday) I will be very thankful if everyone in my house is healthy and fever-free.

And a case of Ryan-itis is just fine by me.

Monday, December 6, 2010
Great Expectations.

If there's one thing we've learned over the past few years, it's not to set your expectations too high whenever there is travel involving young children.

In this particular instance, the travel involved my two sweet nephews that came to visit us. Now that they are safely back home and mostly recovered from jet lag, I can say this without jinxing any further travel—they are rock stars. They handled the flights well and settled in here without any trouble.

The trouble came from my camp.

When the Tritz family walked through our front door two Saturdays ago, I was rushing off to a doctor appointment for Luke's bronchitis. By Wednesday, Luke was back to school but by Wednesday night, Avery was sick. (I guess it was more than just Ryan-itis after all.) By Friday, Isabelle and I were both sick too. In other words, at least one of us was really sick the whole time we had our special visitors.

I was so disappointed. While there weren't great expectations for the week since we knew not to plan a lot with all of the little ones, it would have been nice to have healthy kids. It would have been nice not to get sick myself.

But, our visitors never got sick, so that's a bonus. I think they are probably thankful for the flu shots they made sure to get before they came. I think they had fun, we managed to sneak in a few special outings here and there. And I didn't realize the Christmas market in Brussels started so early, we got to go before they left.

In any event, we are very thankful they came so far to see us. And while we wish we weren't plagued with illness their whole visit, we still have some special memories from their time with us and we are thankful for that as well.

Friday, December 10, 2010
A Little Bit Broken.

Today is a dark and gloomy day in Belgium. And my heart is just a little bit broken.

Luke is sick again. With a cough and fever and I don't need to wait until after the doctor appointment he has later this afternoon to tell you that it's probably bronchitis. Again.

His appointment with the specialist earlier this week revealed that he is indeed allergic to our pets and it can only help him if we find them new homes. To see him get sick time after time with the same symptoms, I tend to agree. My heart is a lot broken to see him so sick, all of the time.

Sigh.

I sent an email earlier this week to all of the expat email lists I could think of, pleading for people to help us find a new home for our cat, and maybe our dog.

Today, I received a very kind email from a woman who lives alone and recently lost a cat to illness. Her other cat is desperately bored and she would love to have Athena come snuggle on her lap.

Sigh.

My Athena. The kitty I got in law school to keep me company while my new husband traveled the world for his international sales job. The kitty that has gotten up with me every single time I had to nurse a baby or check on a sick kid. The kitty that begins every evening by snuggling

Avery to say goodnight to him. My heart breaks a little to think about saying goodbye to her. My heart breaks a little more to think about him having to say goodbye to her.

But when you get a pet before you have kids, how can you possibly predict something like this?

I don't know if Athena is going to like a house with another cat. She's a bit crabby about that sort of thing. But I think she'll probably love living in a quiet house, with a lady who loves her cats and isn't afraid to give Athena her medicine every day. I think Athena will be happy to say goodbye to the dog and the two-year-old who tries to carry her around by the tail. I have to trust that fate sent me this angel of a lady who wants to help us out and that it will be a good fit for everyone.

Sigh.

But my heart is a little broken anyway. There's no question though, that if it helps Luke, even a little, it will be worth it.

Sunday, December 19, 2010
Advent, and a Season of Hope.

It has been a long and challenging four months. We entered this Christmas season, adamant about enjoying each other, our three little ones and hopefully, put the sickness and bad days of the last few months behind us.

Last week was a week of doctor appointments. I think someone in our family went to the doctor every single day. Luke had follow-up appointments for his alopecia and allergies. We learned that he has Alopecia Aereata Universalis. Which means he has no hair anywhere on his body. The good news is that he does not have to go back to the hospital. The bad news is that the treatments didn't work and it looks like this is something he will have forever. In some patients, hair does come back for no apparent reason. But there is no way of knowing if or when that will ever happen for him.

After a not-so-good appointment with an allergist in Brussels, we found a good doctor. He was able to use all of the results from the blood tests Luke had in the hospital, saving Luke from further allergy testing. He advised that we send the cat and dog to new homes. Athena went to her new apartment in Brussels this weekend.

It was a sad day for me and Avery, but there are lots of good things to think about. She has a new person who is totally devoted to cats. When we left, the lady asked me if she liked "cat milk." I'd never heard of it, but mostly because I would never go to the trouble of giving her something like that. Athena has roof access in the summer months and she will love sitting on the rooftop watching her busy Brussels neighborhood. She won't ever have to endure a move back across the ocean to the United States.

For the moment, everyone is relatively healthy. We're all looking forward to a quiet Christmas and a long break. And I will be very happy to say "goodbye" to 2010 on New Year's Eve.

Monday, December 20, 2010
Avery's Buddies and Their Playground Chatter.

One advantage to living where we live, for which I will forever be grateful, is to embrace the history of the area and make it real for the kids in a way we could only do with books if we lived in the States. For example, the boys have seen the battlefields of Waterloo and they know who Napoleon is and what he was trying to do.

As I've blogged about before, our family has also developed an immense appreciation and understanding of the events of World War II. We've been to Normandy, France, and we love to take our visitors to Bastogne, and teach them about the Battle of the Bulge and show them the foxholes in Foy. We've also been to the river in Metz, France, where their great-grandfather was killed on a mission crossing the river.

Last week on the way home from school, Avery started telling me about the conversation on the playground that day:

"Mommy, my friend's great-grandpa fought in the war. He pretended to be dead so the Germans wouldn't kill him."

He continued for a while, telling me how all of the boys had been talking about who's great-grandpa did what during the war. I asked him if he told anyone about his great-grandfathers. And he said:

"Yes, I told them about my great-grandpa that was a fighter pilot (my Grandpa Bares) and I told them I had another great-grandpa that gave everyone their underwear (my Grandpa Tritz worked in supplies). And I also told them about my great-grandpa that was killed in the river in France (Johnny's grandfather). I told them that it was a really bad time for him to go swimming."

Which made me realize that even though they know a great many things about the war, it's from a different perspective. Johnny and I explained that his great-grandpa was killed during a mission where the Americans had to cross the river. There is a scene in Band of Brothers that shows the troops going on a mission across the river, and shows the Germans shooting at the Americans as they come back across. There is no blood or gore during this scene, so we let Avery and Luke watch this five-minute part over the weekend. Their eyes were wide and Luke had a million and ten questions, but I think they have a better understanding of their great-grandfather's sacrifice.

It's my guess that there are some really proud great-grandpas looking down from heaven, who got a big kick out of a group of seven-year-olds on a Belgian playground bragging to each other about what their great-grandpas did 65 years ago.

Saturday, December 25, 2010
Christmas Carols.

For the first time in my memory, I haven't gotten sick of Christmas music this year, despite the fact that it's all we've been listening to for weeks. It might have something to do with the fact that this particular iTunes radio station seems to have banned the "Christmas Shoes" song from their play list, which is fine by me.

For now, though, imagine Frank Sinatra's velvety voice, singing my favorite Christmas song from this year, and have yourself a merry little Christmas…

Thursday, January 6, 2011
A Blessed Holiday Season.

We have spent a truly blessed holiday season. The blessings have been easy to count, they are simple and numerous.

We'll start with Luke. He is going on one month of being fever and cough free. He's been sick almost every other week since the fall, so this is truly amazing. It's too soon to know if it's because the cat is gone, but I'm sure that has helped. For the moment, we're holding off on making any further decisions about Jasmine. It's fun to see Luke's sparkly personality re-emerge, which in and of itself tells me that he hasn't felt like himself for a really long time.

John and I each spent a few days with some sort of a virus, but Avery and Luke were spared and haven't spent any of their vacation days sick on the couch. A definite blessing.

Brussels received a snow-filled forecast the week before Christmas. We were in the minority, but the Fowler family counted this as a major blessing. It interfered with plenty of travel plans, but since we didn't have any, we just sat back and enjoyed it. It snowed, and snowed, and snowed. We almost walked to Christmas Eve Mass but decided to 4-wheel-drive it instead.

Speaking of 4-wheel drive, we upgraded our car situation just in time. We traded in our tiny Volvo station wagon for a Chevy Captiva, just in time for the snow. As the snow maintenance plan in Brussels is slightly less organized than Minneapolis, I am truly thankful to have the 4-wheel drive. And we even have a third row of seats!

My parents arrived last week for a New Year's visit and the weather actually served to improve their travel plans. The storm in New York caused their flight to get cancelled, allowing them to fly directly from Minneapolis to Amsterdam. It's not often that cancelled flights actually improve the travel itinerary, but this time it did.

We helped my parents celebrate their 40th wedding anniversary by going on a quick overnight to Champagne, France. We all fit comfortably in the new car, even if we did have our overnight bags shoved into every available nook and cranny. It didn't even matter that the Champagne houses weren't open for tastings, as we wouldn't have had anywhere in the car to put any bottles anyway. (Ok, yes, you're right, we would have figured out a way to make room, I'm sure.)

My parents leave tomorrow and the boys head back to school on Monday. We've really enjoyed sleeping in and have been enjoying every minute of our holiday break, but I'm sure I'll be ready to see them go back to school on Monday. And I'm sure they'll be ready to be back with their friends.

Today, the rain has almost washed away the snow, and it smells like spring. I'm sure we'll see snow again, but I think it's going to be a quick winter....and since I won't ever, ever be able to say that when we move back to Minnesota, I'm enjoying being able to say that now.

Monday, January 10, 2011
One Night at a Chateau in France...

If you follow this blog with any regularity, you'll know that we really don't travel much with the kids. We pick and choose destinations here and there, but we've said all along that we were doing this for the immersion experience, not to travel everywhere every weekend. We're just happy to be here in Belgium.

But when the opportunity comes a' knocking...we answer.

Just such an opportunity knocked last week. My parents came for a visit, during which they celebrated their 40th wedding anniversary. I'd say that's an opportunity. We scheduled an overnight at Chateau du Fere, a castle in a small village in the Champagne region in France. In other words, a wicked-cool place to celebrate an anniversary.

Just two hours and 45 minutes from our house, the hotel is located on the grounds of the ruins of a 13th century castle, in buildings that once housed livestock. It was very much a destination place, dinner was included, (i.e. required) as part of our stay. And not just any dinner, a fancy-shmancy full-course French one. I was extremely impressed by how welcoming they were to us with our three kids. We were given rooms in the center of the hotel, and seated in the center of the main dining room.

There were a few highlights from the overnight, of course.

One of my favorite parts was in the evening before dinner. John, my parents and the boys went off to explore the ruins of the castle for some fresh air while I stayed behind with Isabelle for some needed quiet time. I absolutely loved that I could hear Luke's voice carry up and over across the property from wherever he happened to be "exploring." Through the closed window. (That's my boy!)

My favorite part of the evening was when we arrived in the dining room. My two-year-old was wearing black leggings, a sweater, and matching boots. She insisted on accessorizing with her pink princess purse, packed with her pretend keys, plastic cell phone, chapstick and various other carefully selected treasures. As the waiter showed us to our table, she handed him her purse, and climbed up into the cushioned seat all by herself. She left the waiter standing there holding her pink princess purse, like he was her personal coat hook. She is a princess in a castle, to be sure.

John's favorite part of the evening was when said princess got up to wander the dining room. Mommy's quick reflexes and table maneuvering skills kept her from wandering too far or getting into trouble, except once. Once she reached the bread basket in the center of the dining room with mere seconds to spare before I caught her. She promptly sneezed all over said bread basket. Mere seconds was all she needed to shock the heck out of the fancy French lady sitting behind us. Oh well. I did my best and when all was said and done, our kids did great and I was really proud of them.

Monday, January 10, 2011
Relapse.

The relapse is mine, not Luke's.

One advantage to the quiet peacefulness of the last two weeks is that it gave me a chance to restore my reserves of hope and faith. It's really a rough place to be when those two tanks get low.

Today was busy, but we were ready for it. Compared to our quiet vacation days of sleeping in and having no schedule, jumping back into a busy Monday made for a long day. But we got through it.

Unfortunately, it ended with some bad news. After three weeks, I've learned that Athena is not doing well in her new home. She is not adjusting to the other cat and is clearly one unhappy kitty.

This news breaks my heart all over again. Especially tonight, John's first night traveling, since I had to give her away. It's a night where she would normally be curled up in my lap, making sure that I was ok before she went to bed. I am so sad to know that she is unhappy.

But, I've emailed the one other family who inquired about her. They just returned from their vacation last week, and I'm going to sleep, hopeful that they are still interested. We shall see. If there is good news to report, I'll amend this entry in the morning.

Hope and faith, let something good come of this, and help my kitty.

***

Good news to report: Athena will move to her new home on Saturday. My hope and faith, and general optimism with the world is back. When you put it out there in the universe that you need help, it's reassuring when the universe responds with something good.

A few emails and a couple days later, the first woman who took Athena has already coordinated with the new family who will take her now.

I only wish I could give my sweet kitty a hug and tell her I miss her something terrible, and I tried to fix things as best I could. I hope she will be happy. But I know there is a 15-year old girl who is really excited for Saturday because it means she will have a kitty to snuggle again. I'm sending it out there to the universe that I hope it's a perfect match.

Thursday, February 3, 2011
La Fête de la Chandeleur

So, there was this holiday yesterday that we (or I should say, I) didn't know about.

Here are my three clues that something was going on:

Clue Number 1: Avery came home a few days ago and said he needed to take two eggs to school because his class was going to make crêpes.

Clue Number 2: I noticed a big display at the grocery store the other day that featured every ingredient for crêpes. While crêpes are certainly common here, specific displays at the grocery store with all of the necessary ingredients, are not.

Clue Number 3: Luke's class made crêpes yesterday too.

On the way home from school, I began to ask questions. On the way to and from soccer practice, I asked more questions. (Driving in the car is usually when I get critical information about current events.) Here's what I learned. Per Luke, it was something about the sun and moon. (He likes to make stuff up when he doesn't know the answer to something, so I usually take his information with a grain of salt.) Avery told me that it was the celebration for when Mary and Joseph took baby Jesus to the Temple to present him to the priests.

And voila. An internet search confirmed it.

We've lived here for three years and we are still, completely out of the loop some days. But not all of us. The boys seem to know what's going on most of the time.

Thursday, February 3, 2011
Cheese.

I'm sure you've noticed that my blog entries about feeling out of place have faded away over the years. But every now and then, something happens to remind me that even though we've adapted and settled into our adopted country, some days I'm still most definitely a stranger in a strange land.

Today, we had a teacher in-service day so the boys were home from school. I was excited. It's fun to have a day off when everyone around us is still going about their busy regular schedules. I planned a few outings, including a stop at the library at the Women's Club (for English books). I also had to stop on Main Street in town (pharmacy, dry cleaners, that sort of thing). As a bribe, I promised the kids we would stop by the waffle lady at the market (the fresh market in our town is on Thursday and there is always a waffle lady).

Even though my French is limited, I am certainly comfortable enough around town, using it to get what I need. But today, I had two fluent-in-French interpreters with me. Maybe that made me over-confident. We walked through the market area and I got some things I needed. We were just about to pass the last stand at the market (for artisan cheese) when a vendor waved a plate of samples at us. While the atmosphere was a bit different than the Sample Saturdays at the supermarkets in the states, the effect on three small children was the same.

We all tried the cheese. Wow was it good! Encouraged, the cheese guy swiftly cut sample bites from the next block. Harder, but just as good. When he reached to take the knife to the third, I knew I couldn't walk away without a purchase. I was in too deep by that point. Quickly multiply, three different cheeses times the four of us and he's shared a lot of his daily supply.

After all of the samples were divvied up, and the last cheese declared "stinky" (by Luke) we started to discuss purchases. I guided the cheese man's knife smaller and smaller for each of the first two cheese. He quickly weighed and packaged my purchase and announced the total. Twenty-five euros.

Excuse me? Twenty-five euros for two chunks of cheese? I won't even apply the conversion rate for this scenario.

Looking in my wallet at my 10 and 20, I told him I no longer wanted the second kind. I think he felt bad, about the whole "hooking me in" thing. My new total was 10 euros 26 cents. I handed him my 10, and then counted out 26 cents in five and two cent pieces. (There was no way I wanted him to see I had a 20.)

Sorry cheese guy, I can't pay 25 euros for cheese at the moment.

But the one I did buy is really, really good. And I'm not going to let the kids eat any of it. They can have the cheddar from the British store.

Thursday, February 10, 2011
Egypt.

We decided to cancel our spring break plans to go to Egypt, due to political unrest. Just kidding. We don't travel much. But there are many expats that travel to exotic places from here, because it's a closer trip to plan from here than the U.S. I wouldn't be surprised if someone I know is changing their plans for a trip to Egypt.

We have said that it'd be nice to pick a few exotic destinations that we would never think about once we move back to the U.S., like Croatia or Israel. Now that I think of it, I do remember mentioning Egypt once, but we weren't serious about it. But don't worry, Grandpas and Grandmas, we have no immediate plans to travel to any of these places.

We did start looking at spring break destinations. Luke wants to go to Portugal. (He likes their football/soccer team.) Avery wants to go to Barcelona. A destination that was also chosen for sports related purposes. John wants to go to Florida (for the sun). I think we'll wait a few years for that trip, though. How crazy would that be? The American family, living abroad, that goes to Florida for spring break. It's actually cheaper for us, though.

It only takes a few keyboard clicks on any of the airline sites when selecting "five" under the "number of passengers" to realize traveling gets pretty expensive pretty fast. Five of anything, especially airline tickets, adds up quick. Even train tickets are expensive. Also, in many European cities a family of five needs two hotel rooms. That's a lot of fun with three little kids. (Not really.) You get the idea.

We decided to make a short list of a handful of destination cities, and we're going to watch the airlines for sales. Sometimes, spontaneity can pay off. But don't worry, we'll leave Egypt off the list.

Thursday, February 10, 2011
Political Unrest.

Speaking of Egypt, did you know that I am living in a country of political unrest? Belgium is going on eight months without an active government. If the situation isn't resolved, in March, Belgium will surpass Iraq and take over the world record of "longest days without a government." Who knew they even kept such records? I just hope they don't have a party, because that would be inappropriate.

As someone with a legal education, I've watched with interest. Did you know Belgium has no less than eight political parties? There seems to be two parties that represent the majority opinions, one Francophone and the other Flemish. These are two groups of people that are as different as night and day. But it certainly doesn't help matters when one or more parties come to the table to "negotiate" but refuse to walk away with less than 100% of what they want. No wonder the mediator has resigned twice.

Most Belgians I've talked to believe something will work out eventually. People are beginning to lose patience though. The red, yellow and black flags are flying. But after watching the CNN coverage of Egypt, it's pretty obvious that tactics here are a little different.

Recently, a Belgian celebrity declared that it was time to "grow a beard for Belgium" and proposed a ban on shaving facial hair until Belgium could figure it out. I'm sorry, but this isn't the hockey playoffs. Today, I read a headline that one party leader, from Ghent, declared that the town (presumably everyone in the town) would abstain from sex until a new government was formed. Really? Are you serious? It seems not, as now I've read that she was "just kidding."

A couple of weeks ago, a few students organized a protest via Facebook and thousands of people turned out to march. Thank God for the Facebook march, because I don't think beards and abstaining from sex are really going to do a whole heck of a lot.

I read an article a while ago, about a U.S. reporter (maybe from the Times? I don't remember) who was quoted as predicting that the situation in Belgium could turn ugly. I think he meant a potential for violence. He most certainly was not predicting excessive facial hair and sexual frustration. But violence? No. This is a country that is just sitting back to wait and see what will happen. I'm not complaining of course, I most certainly do not want my adopted country to erupt into violence any time soon. But it's going on eight months...surely there must be something more serious than the beard thing to get things moving?

Wednesday, February 16, 2011
Valentine's Day

Avery informed me last week that Valentine's Day is just for people who are "in love." And he said it in the way a seven-year-old little boy talks about girls and kissing and other gross stuff. I asked him where he heard that and he said from the kids at school.

And it's true. Here, Valentine's Day seems to just be for the people that are "in love." (Read with the same expression as a seven-year-old talks about girls and kissing and other gross stuff.)

Yes, Valentine's Day in the United States is a commercial holiday. On Valentine's Day, I saw articles about how many billions of dollars Americans spend on the mass-marketed holiday. What, I ask you, is so wrong about kids, and anyone else for that matter, stopping for a second to appreciate their classmates, teachers and other people that are important to them? There are worse things.

Right then and there, I decided on a self-imposed mission. Part of my job as an expat, is to not let my kids forget where they came from. For the next week, I told story after story about the little boxed sets of Valentine cards I picked out at Target when I was a little girl. I talked about tiny candy conversation hearts. And how, when I was about seven or eight, I would sit for hours at the kitchen table agonizing over which candy heart to put in the envelope for which classmate.

I told them about the parties we would have at school. And the pink sugar cookies my mom made one year for my class party. Or the frosted pink cupcakes she (or someone else's mom) made a different year.

I gathered up every ounce of mom patience I had last weekend. Inventing a perfect holiday related project or two to keep little ones busy for the weekend that their dad was traveling and the weekend before Grandma came to visit. I made cookie dough. I cut out pink and red construction paper hearts in various sizes. I set markers, glue, scissors and paints out on the table and let them have at it. I tried to ignore when Isabelle painted the table purple (I still can't get it off.) I tried my best to run interference any time she tried to "sign" someone else's Valentine with her black marker.

When all was said and done, the kids had created Valentine cards for anyone and everyone. I had two boxes of frosted pink heart sugar cookies for Luke to take for his class and for Avery to take to his First Communion class, and just a few extra for everyone to eat after dinner for a day or two.

Luke proudly carried his box of Valentine cookies into school on Monday morning. In my best French, I explained to his teacher that the kids in the United States celebrate friendship on Valentine's Day by having a party at school, and that Luke wanted to share cookies with his class.

After school, I anxiously awaited news from Luke about how it went. I asked him in the car on the way home about it, and if his teacher said anything. He said, "Yes." And then buried his head in the seat. Uh oh.

"What?" I asked. "She said that I'm in LOVE (read the same as above—you know, girls, kissing and gross stuff) with my whole class."

Sigh.

The next day I held my breath to wait to see how Avery's First Communion class liked his special treat. Being a sacramental preparation class, I had higher hopes for support from his teacher. But being seven-year-olds, I still wasn't sure.

His cookies fared much better. Especially when his best buddy announced that they were the best cookies he'd ever had in his life. To which I received a text from his mother wanting to know when I'd be bringing her some. (She's a good friend.) Whew. Something from the holiday as I know it, salvaged.

Tuesday, March 8, 2011
A Weekend Getaway.

I think we've turned a corner. Not counting our summer vacations to Minnesota, we took our first airplane getaway as a family since Belle was a tiny baby.

This weekend, we returned to Spain. This time, to Barcelona. The boys are on a one-week break from school (for Carnival). The cheap airfare is because everyone else goes skiing for Carnival break. And while we may be ready to start traveling a bit here and there, I know for certain we're not ready to take a family of five on a ski vacation just yet.

Avery is a big soccer fan and his favorite team is Barcelona. A few weeks ago, John tracked down a few tickets to the match.

We flew in on Saturday morning and stayed in a hotel near the stadium. When we pulled up to the hotel, we parked behind the opposing team's bus. Sure enough, upon entering the lobby to check-in we walked into the middle of a whole bunch of really tall, young athletes dressed in matching warm-up gear.

After a few minutes, there was a small buzz of little boys going from one player to the next getting autographs. There were women (both young and old) whispering to each other, discretely pointing, and smiling. We asked the boys if they wanted to get autographs too and Avery said, "No way." (It was the opposing team after all, he didn't want to have anything to do with them.)

But Luke was all in. That is, until a really hot Russian model girlfriend of the equally hot star player kneeled down to talk to him in Spanish. He batted his eyes and flashed her a bashful smile, and promptly ran to hide behind me. I think he's starting to figure out that his little bald head sometimes gets him extra attention. Usually, he's ok with it. I guess, unless it's a really hot Russian model. (When he's 16, I'll be sure to tell him about how he dissed the really hot model when he was five because he thought "girls were icky.")

We had a fun weekend. The football match was Saturday night. I stayed at the hotel with Belle, (although we did walk with the boys all the way to the stadium before the game). On Sunday, we went to the wharf and the aquarium and Monday we had time to spend most of the day at the zoo before we flew home in the evening.

It was completely new for me and Johnny to experience a city through its activities for children. It was just enough time, too—we were ready to be home last night and now we have a whole week of no school.

What's next? Maybe Madrid? Lukee's favorite player (Ranaldo) plays for Madrid. And I think one more trip to Spain might be enough to get my Spanish back? It's almost there, I came back to Belgium telling everyone "Gracias" and "Hola" which is a good sign.

Monday, March 14, 2011
John's Dad

This is just a short entry to provide a quick update on John's dad.

A little over a week ago, Johnny's dad was admitted to the hospital with pneumonia. This happened while John's mom was here visiting us. She cut her trip short (just by a few days) to go home to be with him. It didn't seem that serious in the beginning, but he wasn't getting better so they made the decision to transport him from Northern Minnesota to the Cities, where there were more resources and be better able to handle everything going into the weekend.

He has a major infection in his lungs, and at that time they had him on oxygen. Now, however, he is sedated and has been put on a ventilator. He is in critical but stable condition in the ICU. As bad as all of this sounds, they do expect him to pull out of this and recover. At this point, we're just waiting for information to come in, taking things one day at a time. He is receiving excellent care and what he needs right now is just for the doctors to keep doing what they are doing. John's mom, Sue, is doing well. She is staying strong and taking things one thing at a time.

This, of course, is one of our worst nightmares coming true. Someone we love so much is very sick, and so very far away. All we can do is wait for the information to come in—but I suppose that's what everyone is doing back in Minneapolis, waiting for more information. It's difficult not to be there with other loved ones, waiting for that information. We've had our own personal experience with this, though. The tables were turned last fall with Luke. That understanding helps make it a little bit easier.

Monday, April 25, 2011
Our Worst Nightmare

John's Dad passed away on Saturday evening, March 27. He passed five minutes before his favorite time of the week—5 o'clock happy hour with Garrison Keeler. Johnny was able to make it there in time, and be there with his family. His lung infection, actually turned out to be an aggressive lung cancer that came quickly and evaded detection until the very end.

I stayed back with the kids, and then we had to figure out what to do next. Would I travel back with all of them by myself for the funeral?

Monday, April 25, 2011
Minnesota.

Never one to back away from a challenge, I took three little kids on a transcontinental flight, all by myself. And I don't ever want to do it again.

But our time in Minnesota was a blessing—precious time with aunts and uncles and cousins that we would never have had otherwise. It was a blessing to see Minnesota in a different season; two actually. We arrived during the winter and flew out in spring weather. Before this, the kids were starting to believe that Minnesota means sun, sand and beach. We even got to watch the ice go out on the lake while we were at my parents' house. I've lived in Minnesota for a lot of years and I've never had the opportunity to watch day by day, hour by hour as that happens. It was incredible.

Upon arrival, one of the most surprising things to me was the lack of culture shock. Nothing seemed strikingly "bigger" or noticeably foreign yet familiar, as in past visits.

Maybe it was because I was operating under a shock of a different kind, thereby numbing any possible culture shock. Perhaps it was a spinoff version of Post-Traumatic Stress Disorder incurred as a result of traveling with three little kids all by myself within 48 hours of learning about the death of my father-in-law?

Or maybe it's because it hasn't been a whole year since we were there last, and John has been making frequent trips back this year. But I think, the real reason is that it's because after three years, we've reached some sort of mile marker. Home is here. And home is there. We are comfortable in both. Our hearts live in both.

Thursday, April 28, 2011
Three Years.

In the midst of our crisis, we celebrated the third anniversary of our arrival in Belgium. Usually, my annual blog update is a running list of reflections of how far we've come within that year.

This year's reflection is different. This was the year that life didn't care we were expats. It came at us with full force anyway.

From Luke's diagnosis of Alopecia, to his hospital stays, to the departure of our pets, to the loss of a beloved father and grandfather, we've had to deal with a lot. But we've learned that support from friends and family knows no boundaries. An ocean in between doesn't mean the love and prayers stop flowing. And our friends here in Belgium have become our surrogate family.

***

Side Note: Yes, I did say "pets." About two months ago, we came to the difficult conclusion that we needed to find Jasmine a new home. I can say with certainty that she has upgraded her accommodations. She has a giant back yard with picturesque weeping willows. She has a doggie buddy (an old black lab that has been depressed since the family lost their other dog about a year ago). She has two girls (ages four and six) who absolutely adore her because she is named after one of the Disney Princesses. The family spends a lot of their weekend time taking long walks in the forest. But it doesn't mean that I don't miss her terribly.

***

Before I had a chance to post this, we've had another bit of bad news. Our good friends are moving back to Strasbourg. I guess that comes with the territory. Part of being an expat and having expat friends includes an inherent risk that someone will have to move. We are happy and excited for them; there are better job opportunities and they will be close to their families again. But we are sad for us, we will miss them terribly.

But the sun is shining, and each day brings the hope of good things. Good news can come just as easily as bad, right? What else can you do but the best you can with what you've got, and have hope and faith that everything will work out the way it's supposed to.

Tuesday, May 3, 2011
Junk Day

I know I've blogged about this in the past, but I just can't resist.

Today is our semi-annual "put whatever junk you want on the curb and the garbage truck picks it all up day." This day is also known as "watch the creepy white vans repeatedly circle through town to scavenge through everyone else's trash."

I put a small pile next to our front door this morning. Then I made sure the front door was locked, and I stayed away from the front windows the rest of the day. Every now and then I would walk into the kitchen and see the head of one of those creepy-van-people pop up into the window after digging through my particular pile and I would jump. (I'm pretty sure I only screamed once.)

It's a perfect form of recycling because nothing ever actually goes to the garbage. Today, my pile included a whole box of coffee maker parts and pieces (apparently, coffee makers here are disposable appliances, and need to be replaced after a few months). My pile also included my Graco infant car seat and base. Although, the handle bar doesn't always lock into place anymore thus running the risk of tossing the baby out on the sidewalk if it isn't properly belted in. I hope no one takes it. There was also a plastic bag filled with sippy cup parts. By the third kid, those things multiple like bunnies. There was also a broken pink and purple princess chair (I should have never tried to stand on it to change the lightbulb) and a broken pair of roller blades, a broken plastic booster seat that was left out in the rain ten too many times, and some scrap wood.

I've been monitoring the pile throughout the day (while trying to avoid the creepy-van-people). The rollerblades were gone within the first hour. At one point, I glanced down from an upstairs window in time to notice someone run to grab some sort of tool. Curious, I watched as they came back to my pile and cut the cord off the coffee maker. Who knew someone would only want the cord? Now, at the end of the day, all that's left is a piece of scrap wood, Avery's old leaky rubber boots and the neglected booster seat.

Maybe an environmentally-clear-conscience is worth a day of the creepy vans?

Wednesday, May 25, 2011
Susan G. Komen Race for the Cure: Namur, Belgium

I try to run two or three times a week, mostly for stress relief. I don't run far, maybe three miles? I used to sign up for a road race here and there when we lived in the States. It was always nice to have something on the calendar because it kept me motivated to keep running. It has been too complicated to sign up for a race here, until now.

A few months ago, I got an email from one of my expat groups about signing up for a team running the Susan G. Komen Race for the Cure in Namur on May 22. It was as easy as replying to the email, so I did.

I was excited. This was always one of the races I ran in Minnesota—usually held on Mother's Day.

On Sunday morning, May 22, I drove myself to Namur (about 45 minutes away). I had no idea what to expect. I arrived early to give myself time to get lost and figure out parking.

I walked up to a sea of pink and white t-shirts and balloons. There was a "warm-up" and a few minutes of Zumba led by a perky French girl. It was cool to see the same sorts of logos and sites that you would see in the United States, only everything was on a much smaller scale. I think I read there were 750 runners? Much less than the thousands of people who participate in the Race for the Cure in Minnesota.

The run itself was unlike any road race I've ever run. We started in a pack but quickly spread out. There weren't that many runners so it was easy to find space.

There were lots of obstacles. In general, I've stopped paying attention to all of the things in Europe that the American personal injury attorneys would scream warnings about, but there were several red flags for my attorney brain. At one point, we ran under construction scaffolding. We also ran along a stone boardwalk next to the river—that didn't have a guardrail or barrier. This was about the time the lead runners had reached the turn-around point and were running back toward us. But the Belgium equivalent of the Coast Guard was hanging out in a boat in the water below, so I guess we were ok?

The whole race was run on cobblestone, and at one point, we ran up a set of stairs. The run was a 6k and the walk was a 3k. The runners started 30 minutes before the walk, and we ran the 3k course twice. It actually worked really well. It was fun to loop around through the start and have all the walkers still there waiting. It was also nice to know we were at the halfway point. And while it was a twisty curvy run in and through the village streets, there were volunteers stationed at every possible turn to make sure we didn't get lost.

I have no idea what my time was. There wasn't even a clock. And I didn't get a water at the finish (I left all of my euros in the car). But at the end of it all, it was really, really fun. They are doing it again in Antwerp this fall (I think because the Wallonians and the Flemish Belgians each wanted their own race?) I will definitely sign up again, and I will recruit a team to go with me.

Thursday, June 23, 2011
Caution: Road Work Ahead

I am going to have to rely on my words to paint the picture for this situation.

The last several weeks, workers have been replacing pipes or something in the street that runs between the kids' maternelle (preschool) building and the entrance gate for the primary school playground.

We've had to deal with an occasional dump truck and construction vehicles driving or parking, or leaving loads of building materials right near the school. Normally, the only traffic allowed on this street is for the homeowners who live next door. Parents have to park about a block away to walk their children down this quaint little cobblestone street. I'm not kidding when I say quaint. There's even an overlook view of a sheep pasture.

But now, the cobblestones are all lying in a big giant pile and the street is one big mud puddle.

Today, there was a backhoe parked in front of the maternelle playground. A trench, roughly ten meters long and shoulder deep on a really tall construction guy (I know this because he was in it) ran the length of the playground, right up to the school gate.

There was also a dump truck, and a construction vehicle with an extended crane-arm-type-thing next to it.

It was 3 o'clock in the afternoon.

The backhoe was scooping dirt and delivering it to the guy in the trench. Parents approached to fetch their preschoolers and primary kids from school. The only way through the mayhem was to walk between the dump truck and crane, UNDER the actual crane-thing that extended over the dump truck, around the trench, wait for the backhoe to get out of the way and THEN go to the maternelle gate.

Are you kidding me?

And I was the ONLY one who thought this was funny. I was the ONLY one who questioned that maybe, it wasn't so safe to let a bunch of kids (ages 2.5 and up) wander around the heavy machinery—THAT WAS IN OPERATION!

This highlights a major cultural difference that I've observed while living here. From playgrounds to school functions, I probably notice it more because of my years of legal training. Here, people are expected to assume their own risk and proceed with caution. In the U.S., after years of ridiculous product liability cases (like the one about McDonald's coffee being too hot) the burden has shifted to the manufactures and institutions. They are supposed to warn everyone about every possible misuse. It's their burden to make sure their products and playgrounds are safe. They are even expected to imagine far-fetched scenarios where people might get hurt and issue warnings.

Here, if you act like an idiot or drink your coffee too soon, it's your own fault. If you don't watch your kids on the playground and say "no" when the three-year old wants to go on the ripcord or the giant structure that spins around, then their resulting injuries are your responsibility. Assume your own risk. Take responsibility for your own actions. There is no one to sue if it goes bad. There are no deep pockets to attempt to dig into, and no contingency fee structures to make it easy to try.

But I think today illustrated that maybe, just maybe, there is a happy medium out there somewhere. I hope that tomorrow morning all of the children in the preschool are present and accounted for, and that none of them fell into the trench or got squashed by a truck on the way to or from school.

Thursday, June 23, 2011
M-I-N-N-E-S-O-T-A! Minnesota, Minnesota!

Yay....Minnesota! Here we come!

We leave on Wednesday for vacation. And we really can't wait! Last year, to say that I was dreading our transatlantic trip was an understatement. (I wasn't dreading the vacation part, just the "getting to the vacation" part.) But, all it takes is one trip back by myself with three kids for unexpected (heartbreaking) circumstances and a new perspective is achieved. Now that it's time to make the trip again a few months later for FUN, bring on that 10+ hour flight, baby!

We're ready for you. Devices such as iPads and iPods will be charged. Books are packed. New puzzle games are tucked away. The two-year-old will have a whole bag of stickers that she can stick wherever the heck she wants to stick them, forehead and window included.

Isabelle has been getting ready. She fills her "suitcase" with all of the necessities (usually her baby doll, purse and a handful of princesses and she waves goodbye and says, "See you later! Going to see Grandma and Grandpa Chips!" (Or, Tritz if you're not two.) "Me take helicopter to see Grandma and Grandpa Chips!" (Honestly, I don't know where the helicopter came from, except that maybe she thinks it's more exciting than a plane.) Then she walks to the front hall, waits it out for a few minutes and makes her big re-entry. "Me back! Me so glad to see you!" And then, everyone in the room gets a hug and a kiss whether they want one or not.

So, Grandma and Grandpa Chips, and Grandma Sue, we'll be there soon, and we really can't wait.

July 26, 2011
Home Again Home Again

Last year, we had absolutely terrible flights back and forth to the United States with the littlest one. It was awful. My one saving grace, the thing that got me through, was to repeatedly remind myself (every second of every minute if I had to) that it was a finite period of time. Thankfully, time does not stand still. The seconds would keep on ticking by until enough of them had passed that the experience would be over. I kept telling myself that eventually, the plane would land and we would be on the ground.

Today, though, time stood still. At one point, I glanced up at that map at the front of the plane that said "Local Time at Departure: 19:03" and "Time Remaining: 3 hours 52 minutes." I think it said that for two hours. I was so relieved when I finally realized the clock had stopped working. It gave me a good idea for a horror movie—the main character is on a plane where time just stops and it goes forever. It would certainly be one of my worst nightmares come true.

This year on our annual summer vacation to the U.S., our flights were much easier. My favorite moment from our flight back to Belgium was when I turned to the toddler and asked her what she was excited to see at her house. She very seriously answered, "My kitchen." And sure enough, when we walked in the door, she made a bee-line for her little pink sink and stove.

My least favorite moment was after we landed and taxied along the runway at Schipol Amsterdam Airport. Isabelle woke up just before landing. It was the "shocked, I don't understand where I am or what I'm doing here" type of wake-up. She screamed. A lot. By the time we began the taxi along the runway—which easily takes at least 20 minutes in Amsterdam—she was in a full-fledged temper tantrum unlike any I've ever seen in any of my kids. Screaming, choking, and gagging sent fears of vomiting rushing through my mind. Her back was arched and she reacted violently to any sort of touch. I rescued her from her seat belt (she had wriggled down and almost choked herself with it in an effort to get to the floor) and pulled her on my lap. I restrained her as best I could. I was proud of myself for keeping calm, for not raising my voice, for tuning out every other person around me (even if most of the stares were sympathetic). I tried to just focus on doing whatever might help my distraught toddler. I also managed to successfully divert her clawing scratches and thumping kicks (not only for myself but on behalf of anyone else within range).

Thankfully, when our plane FINALLY reached the gate, and that all-important "ding" sounded to alert us that the "fasten seatbelt sign" had been turned off, she settled down and realized (between hiccups and shallow breaths) that her temporary nightmare was over.

Exhausted and relieved, we started to pack up our many, many belongings. That was when the guy sitting behind me reached up to retrieve his carry-on from the overhead bin and dropped it. On me. No worries, though, my head and back successfully broke its fall. I'm sure by the look on his face, that his thought process was something like, "Oh my God, of all the people this thing could have fallen on, it was the poor mother who has been restraining the crazy kid for the last 30 minutes." Actually, he did me a favor. It gave me a valid reason to publicly shed a few tears and that was a good release.

We are home now and mostly unpacked. This afternoon I noticed that the top envelope on my junk mail stack was from our local grocery store. The envelope advertised that we could be the winners of a trip to New York City! I immediately threw it in the trash without opening it.

Addendum: It's 6:59pm (18h59). The toddler just shouted down the stairs "Mamma? It bedtime now?" When do two-year-olds ever ask that? It is now 7:40pm (19h40). Every one of my kids crawled into bed on their own and are already snoring. I set each one of them up with a flashlight and a stack of books along with specific instructions—when you wake up in the middle of the night and can't get back to sleep, use your flashlight to read until you get tired again. What do you suppose the odds are that will actually work?

July 26, 2011
My Complicated Relationship with Target.

I hate Target.

Did I really just say that out loud? My Americanized friends here in Belgium are going to be so mad at me for even thinking that, let alone saying it out loud.

When we go back to the U.S., I don't pack any toiletries. Here, toiletries are expensive. (Let me rephrase: Here, *everything* is expensive.) For example, a bottle of Pantene Shampoo or Conditioner costs about five euros per bottle (or more) and is easily half the size of a U.S. bottle of the same stuff. If you figure in the exchange rate, multiple that example by all of the various toiletries a family of five needs regularly and that adds up. But then again, I would never plan to "stock-up" on these products when I'm back in the U.S., as suitcase space is usually reserved for items that we can't find here in Belgium. A happy medium is to not bring any of the expensive toiletries from Belgium with to the U.S., and instead make a Target-run within a day or two of landing stateside.

This year, on our very first morning in Minnesota, I found myself alone returning from the rental car pick-up. The three kids and one ecstatic grandma were happily getting reacquainted at a park. I needed diapers. I swung into one of the many Target stores on my route home to "get a few things."

Do you have any idea how overwhelming it is walking into a Target store after an extended hiatus? In the past I have always mentally prepared myself for this, with a shopping strategy. I don't know why I thought I could go in for "just a few things." Maybe because we had just been in the U.S. in April and I didn't think it would hit me so hard. Or maybe it was because I hadn't even been on U.S. soil for more than 12 hours and the jet lag buzz was still peaking.

But seriously, I needed diapers! And I was alone in the car without the three kids! The stars had aligned. Just a few things or not, it was a chance early in our vacation to knock a whole bunch of "stuff" off of our never-ending shopping list.

I will not even tell you what my bill came to. I will tell you that it included the usual boxes of colored sugar cereals necessary for any good summer vacation, several grocery items, the aforementioned toiletries—including suntan lotion and bug spray (neither of which we need much of in Belgium) and a plethora of children's medicines and topical creams that are unavailable or require a prescription in Belgium. And of course, the handful of random non-essential "spontaneous" purchases that can be found at Target, like a small plastic serving platter with a whimsical summer pattern.

And I know this will come as no surprise, but I almost forgot the diapers.

And I know that this will also not come as a surprise, (and maybe even redeem my reputation back here in Brussels among the expat community) but we've been back home for roughly seven hours and I've already caught myself saying, "I miss Target." I guess I will just have to accept that it is a complicated, love/hate relationship.

July 26, 2011
U2 Baby!

Never in a million years, did I think I would be lucky enough to see U2 live in concert. (Little kids, plus expat experience means concert tickets are really low on our list of priorities.) But last Saturday night, we went to the concert of all concerts with my brother Ryan and his fun wife.

The anticipation in the Twin Cities built steadily throughout the week which proved to be hot and steamy. Saturday morning arrived with thunderstorms that still didn't manage to break the heat and humidity. The forecasts called for showers throughout the evening and the ever-vigilant news media diligently advised concertgoers to pack rain ponchos, as umbrellas would not be allowed into the stadium.

Side note to my Belgian/European friends: The U.S. has a lot of rules and regulations, especially when it comes to public venues and massive congregations of people.

Anyway, back to the forecasted rain. We live in Belgium, so we laughed. If there is one thing I've learned while living there, it's that we don't melt in the rain. It rains all of the time. And it's usually a cold, damp, unpleasant rain. The thought of a rain shower that would follow one of the hottest and steamiest weeks of Minnesota summer weather, sounded just a little bit like heaven.

Here was the extent of *our* preparations: I packed a plastic grocery bag inside my newly purchased, vintage, painted leather purse. The purpose of which, was to keep said vintage purse dry if it rained. We also put a stack of towels and a change of clothes in the car so we wouldn't have to drive home all wet and soggy.

The concert was amazing. An hour into the show, the promised rain arrived and managed to break the sticky humid heat. Everyone around us pulled out their plastic ponchos. I pulled out my plastic bag and safely tucked away my purse, the cell phone and my camera. It poured buckets for the rest of the night, only letting up at the end.

For a few hours, we forgot we lived on the other side of the ocean and left a whole bunch of kids at home with a babysitter…and were just at a rock concert, dancing in the rain.

Sunday, July 31, 2011
American Boys

Usually, our annual trip back to the States is marked by reflections of culture shock and finding humor in what we found remarkable. Just like after our trip in April, I don't have any of the standard cultural shock observations to share. However, in our jet-lagged-fog the other night, I realize I have a few observations of a different sort. A reverse reaction so to speak. I realized that this time, I am noticing how American our children are upon returning to Belgium.

A critical part of this immersion experience is to keep our children, well, Americans. They have adapted so well and immersed themselves in their Belgian school and the European culture, that if we don't work hard to nourish their American roots, that part of the experience—the comparison that provides them (and us) with insight into our own culture by living in another—might be lost. Not only that, on a more basic level, it will make it difficult to readapt and repatriate when we move back. We know that time is coming at some point in the near (or not so near?) future.

Here are two observations from our first few days back in Belgium:

The other night, as I pulled a couple of boxes of American cereal (think Lucky Charms and Fruit Loops) out of duffle bags and put them on the counter, the boys started singing the commercials for each one. They also had at least a ten-minute banter back and forth about a Toucan Sam commercial that doubled them over in hysterical laughter. Considering they are the target audience, I would declare that ad campaign a huge success.

Walking through the Amsterdam airport, the seven-year-old saw the Burger King sign and declared that all he wanted was a burger. (It was 5am local time.) Considering we were at the mercy of jet lag, which causes wacky cravings at random times, and also, no one in my family had eaten a single bite of airplane food the entire flight, we succumbed to Avery's craving. Everyone inhaled their food. Avery declared that it was not a very good burger and we explained that a.) Americans have the corner on the fast food industry and b.) It was 5am in an airport Burger King.

And now, as the jet lag fades, we are slowly but surely easing back into our life here.

Sunday, July 31, 2011
Travel Tips and Water Spritzing

I just came across an article in my fashion magazine about travel tips for dealing with long flights. It emphasized staying hydrated, eating the right foods, and it mentioned something about "spritzing" water on your skin to help with the dry air. I laughed.

Having just completed our recent transatlantic trip, I just can't sit by without comment, having gone what we just went through.

Here's my travel tip to get you through a long flight: Take three little kids with you. No wait. Let's make it easy. Start out with two. If you need a challenge, then add the third. But at least one of them has to be a baby, toddler or two-year-old. Instead of bringing a water spritzer, bring extra clothes. For everyone. The goal is to not get "spritzed" by anything (like spilled drinks) but most especially, by bodily fluids from one of the little people. Pack the extra clothes in one of your ten carry-on bags. Trust me, when you show up at the airport with a gaggle of kids, they don't actually count everyone's carry-on bags.

Just try it once. After that, anytime you fly without kids will feel like a holiday. Even if it's a really long flight, or you get stuck on a tarmac somewhere; it will feel like paradise because you don't have kids with you. You can talk to your spouse. You can read the book you want to read, watch the movie you want to watch or listen to the music you want. You won't have a million pieces of carry-on luggage to juggle while carrying a sleeping child. You won't have to wait at the door of the aircraft to pick up the stroller!

You might even have room to pack the little spritz bottle the magazine mentioned!

Thursday, August 18, 2011
The Longest Line

To break up our summer, we took yet another trip to Disney. The kids are older, and Miss Belle is so much easier, we knew we had to go. After all, when will we ever live three hours away from Disneyland, ever again? Plus, our champagne supply was getting low.

One night, we tried to choose rides we had not gone on. We found ourselves waiting in a really long one, because not many people could go at once. The line was long. The line was slow. It didn't take long to realize, we'd made an excruciating mistake.

But because our littlest one had picked it, we felt obliged. Everything happens for a reason though. While waiting in line, we found another little boy with Alopecia. He was just a few years older than Luke and his bald head was marked by a few small patches of shaved hair. It made me catch my breath.

It was just about a year ago that we were here in Disneyland just after Luke's first hospital stay, and his head looked exactly the same. We started talking to the mother. Through a combination of French and English, she explained that the doctors didn't know what it was, but that they thought it was a reaction to a shock—she herself was a recent cancer survivor. (A common trigger for Alopecia is shock and stress.) Luke pulled off his hat and we explained that he had the same thing and one year before looked exactly like her son. She had never heard the name of it before. Our two boys did the "exploding knucks" anytime they saw each other in line after that.

Something else happened in that long line. About half-way through, I realized there were some kids trying to sneak past us. I refused to let them by. To my complete shock, at the next turn in the line (that went by the exterior wall), I saw their mother join them. She was kind of hard to miss, as she was wearing a hot-pink blazer that should have stayed in the 80's. They had settled into the line too far behind us for me to really care, other than roll our eyes at each other about her gutsy behavior.

And then. About ten minutes later, I noticed her three children were perched conveniently along the wall that would deposit them neatly in front of us, a dozen people ahead from where we stood. The mother placed her hands under the armpits of the first kid. The oldest kid slid sneakily onto the ground, securely in his new place. I grabbed John. I didn't wait for him to do anything.

In my rustic French, I started screaming, "Madame! Madame! Stop, there is a line! Stop, Stop!" Or something like that. I don't really remember. It couldn't have been much more than that, my French isn't that good. All I remember was John laughing and saying, "Ok honey, that's enough." The woman nonchalantly shrugged. She shook her head at the kid still on the wall and pulled the other ones back to their original spot, where they'd already cheated an unearned place.

All around me, people were nodding their heads, saying it wasn't fair. Later, Avery told me that he heard all kinds of people saying (in French) that they were glad I said something. On one hand, I was surprised that I was the only one to speak up. On the other, I was proud of myself for seizing the moment. I'm not usually confrontational. It didn't hurt that we had just come from dinner (which was accompanied by a shared bottle of wine).

My stomach feels a little sick when I think about the lessons that lady is teaching her kids about cheating. I'm just glad that my own kids got to see me stand up to something wrong and maybe be a little bit of a hero, however small.

Thursday, August 18, 2011
The War on Slugs

I hate slugs. They are disgusting little creatures. I'm sure they serve some purpose, but for the life of me, I can't figure out what it might be. Last year, I ran through the grass late at night in the backyard...barefoot. I stepped on a slug. I will never, ever, run through the grass barefoot again, ever.

The last few weeks, we have been caring for our German neighbors' cat. The cat (we call it Tripod because it only has three legs) is a sweet outdoor cat. To make it easy for us, they made a little outdoor shelter for the cat on their patio bench, gave it a huge tank of self-filling dry food and all we need to do is check on it every few days. When I watch this cat for their short trips, she prefers to stay out for days at a time anyway. It's a good set-up for everyone.

However, I realized the cat wasn't eating. I thought maybe she was upset because her people were gone. Every few days I gave her a can of wet food to appease her and make sure she wasn't starving. But one early morning visit revealed the real reason the cat didn't want to eat.

It was damp that morning, and the slugs were out. To my horror, her food dish was covered with giant, slimy slugs. She looked at me and meowed. Ok then.

Together, we declared war on the slugs. I used the food tank to scrape them off her bench. The slugs landed in a pile on the ground, as did about a cup-and-a-half of her food. It was the slimy part anyway. I put new towels down on her bench to cover all of the slime trails. I filled her dish with fresh food. I left the big pile of food on the ground to serve as a decoy. By their very nature, slugs are lazy, right? They won't climb up her bench if there is a pile of food on the ground.

And then I remembered reading somewhere a long time ago that snails like the taste of beer. If you put some in a shallow dish, they climb into it, get drunk and can't get out and die a blissfully drunk death. Maybe slugs like beer too? After all, aren't snails just like slugs, except with a shell? I went home and got a beer and some shallow plastic take-away dishes. I came back an hour later and guess what? There was a slug taking a drink of beer. I found a stick and "helped" him to get a better taste.

A couple of hours later, the five-year-old and I went to check the slug situation. There were lots of them helping themselves to the pile of cat food. I grabbed two (really long) sticks and chopstick-style, we helped them all taste the yummy beer. Tonight, when we checked, there was only one slug on the patio. It turns out, he likes beer too.

I'm not sure how I will explain the dishes on the patio filled with dead beer-slugs to our neighbors. They return in a few days. I know I'm not going to touch the beer-slug dishes.

Current Tally in the War on Slugs:

Me: 13 Slugs.

Slugs: None.

Kitty: 2 Mice. But I'm not touching those either.

My neighbors will find a whole carnage-death scene on their patio when they return. But as long as their cat isn't included in the death toll, maybe they won't care?

Monday, August 22, 2011
The Annual School Supply Scavenger Hunt

I don't know why I keep thinking that the search for school supplies will get easier every year. It doesn't. This year, I have three lists, with varying degrees of complication.

Isabelle's list is pretty easy. It includes markers, crayons (which are actually colored pencils) glue sticks, a pillow and blanket for nap time, and a box for her nuk when it's not nap time.

Luke's list was potentially difficult, but it has only been two years since I bought all of the same stuff for the big kid. The stranger the item on the list, the more likely I was to remember it. Like three little boxes, or a deck of playing cards, or a pair of dice.

Avery's list for third primary was the toughest. This year, I learned what "highlighter" and "protractor" are in Belgian French; "equerre" and "surligneur" respectively. I'm more than a little bit scared for the homework he's going to need help with.

I have developed a strategy, though. I head to the school supply aisle. I get as much as I can by myself. Then, I wait until an unsuspecting employee ventures within a two-aisle vicinity. I pick the most obscure thing on the list, explain I don't speak French very well and have them show it to me. This year, I started with the protractor and highlighter. My employee was patient and helpful. She helped me with five or six other things. There were even a few things that she couldn't figure out, which oddly made me feel better. After she went on her way, I sorted myself out and realized I only had a few things left. I asked an unsuspecting Belgian mother for help and that took care of another item or two on the list and the rest I'll figure out later.

While the lists don't get any easier, my comfort level—and therefore attitude—has improved. Mostly, I've learned to let go of having to do it all perfectly, which helps a lot.

Monday, August 22, 2011
A Play Date.

Our neighbors with the cat are home now. (They were grateful for my slug traps.) They have a daughter who is two years older than Isabelle and the girls like to play together. She was very happy to come play at our house this afternoon, but their play dates provide an interesting language challenge.

Our neighbors speak German at home but their daughter goes to school in French. I speak to the mom in English, but she doesn't understand French. When her daughter comes here to play, I can speak to her in French, and she can tell me what she needs (in French). My daughter bosses her around quite successfully in English (Isabelle won't learn French until she begins school). One day, my neighbor asked me if Isabelle speaks Dutch.

Wait. What?

I assured her that while Dutch has trickled in sometimes with the boys (Dutch class is required at school) there is no reason Isabelle would have learned it yet. She told me that her daughter insisted Isabelle spoke Dutch.

Today, I figured it out. The girls were playing together at our house and at one point, Isabelle jibber-jabbered away in complete nonsense. When I asked Isabelle what language she was speaking, she said French.

When school begins next week, Isabelle's teacher is going to have a lot of fun.

Friday, September 2, 2011
The Laundromat

Now that we have been here three years, it's not often that I experience moments of complete panic. Those moments of panic were common in the first few months. That feeling of walking into a place, with absolutely no clue about what was expected of me or how to do what I needed to do.

Flashing back, I remember having moments of panic the first time I went to the gas station; the first time I had to pull a cart out of the cart corral (here you need to insert the proper coin); the first time I bought produce (here, the customer has to weigh loose produce on a scale and print the price sticker); or even the first time I had to use my bancontact card. It was a fun first week, filled with lots of panic-stricken moments.

I am happy to be beyond all of that. Now and then, though, something comes along to remind me that I don't know everything.

A few months ago, one of the kids threw-up on our king-sized quilt. I rinsed it off of course, but no matter how hard I tried, I couldn't stuff it into our 8kg washing machine. So it sat, in our tiny basement laundry room, taking up a corner on a shelf. There is a laundromat in town, across from the grocery store. I had driven by it a number of times, thinking, "I really should wash our big quilt from our bed." The sick kid expedited this errand.

After a reconnaissance mission, I learned the laundromat had a washing machine large enough for my quilt. I figured out I needed my own soap, and I had to buy tokens from a machine on the wall. I ventured back with my smelly quilt, and was thrilled to find out the large washing machine had a delicate cycle that only took 24 minutes.

Mission accomplished. The other day I realized that the cover for our Ikea sofa was washable, so I returned with confidence to the laundromat.

I know it's a simple thing to be proud of, but I'm proud of it anyway.

Friday, September 2, 2011
Lightning Strikes

Thunderstorms aren't common here. But this last month, we've had quite a few. Last week, a storm in the middle of the night lasted for hours. Another thunderstorm delivered a lightning bolt that hit our building. Everything shook, and all of the burglar alarms started going off. Our landlord requires everyone here to have one, except we (and by that I mean John) talked them into an exemption because we had a big yellow dog that barked at everything.

Burglar alarms here are obnoxious. They are attached to the exterior of the building in an obvious place. Our neighbors have them over their front doors. When triggered, a flood light flashes a pulsing light and a piercing screech screams at a high decibel.

Our power went out. The next morning, it took me longer than I care to admit to find the reset switch in the basement. Ok, let me rephrase. It took me longer than I care to admit to figure out there was such a switch in the first place. I had to hear the vacuum cleaner next door before I thought to ask around about the power loss and what to do about it. (Sometimes, my strategy here is to wait to see what happens. Sometimes, things just fix themselves. This wasn't one of those times.)

A few hours after our power was back on, I realized our brand-new dishwasher was still dead. The flashing lights indicated a short. I called for a repair. The first available appointment was a week away. Today, that coveted appointment revealed the dishwasher needed a part and a new appointment was scheduled for next week. The repairman explained that he has been extra busy because of the recent storms.

Our neighbor's phones and modem were fried. Another neighbor's burglar alarm died a slow, agonizing death, as evidenced by loud, whiney screeches at random, unpredictable intervals. Of course this happened at two in the morning. Our neighbors were out of town and John called the number for the non-emergency police, who told him to call the fire department—who told him to call the police. When the firemen arrived, of course the alarm was quiet and well-behaved. They didn't believe us, until it gave a loud screech just as they were about to leave. The fireman "fixed" it by hacking at it and ripping it off the brick wall.

I've decided we were lucky. Our dishwasher is an appliance that is still under warranty, and our landlord maintains it. And while it's not as convenient, it's not critical. I can use my hands to wash my dishes. Our computers were both were plugged in at the time, running updates but those went unscathed.

Now THAT would have been an expensive, critical loss.

Friday, September 2, 2011
How Many Milestones Can We Fit into One Day?

Yesterday was the first day of school for the public schools in Belgium. It was Isabelle's first day of maternelle. It was Luke's first day of primary. It was also Avery's 8th birthday.

Isabelle was beyond excited. For all of her short life, we've made the walk to the school gates to kiss her brothers goodbye in the morning or greet them after their school day. It was finally her day to march through the gates and wave goodbye and she was all in. On the big kid playground, she was the only child from first maternelle not clinging to her parents. No. She was running in the middle of all of the first, second and third primary boys.

When it was time to go into her play yard and classroom, she skipped. When it was time for us to leave, she was cool with that. When I picked her up, she was wearing different pants. (An accident.) Today, she was a little less excited and there were a few more tears. She cried when I picked her up and she is very, very tired. French immersion will do that to a kid. But she'll be ready to go again on Monday, I'm sure. And no, I wasn't sad to see my baby go off to school. She made it easy for me to walk away because she was so excited. I was thrilled and happy for her.

Luke loved his first day in primary school. Avery was excited for his birthday to finally arrive. He went to school with his arms full of cupcake boxes. The smile on his face was worth the extra level of stress birthday cupcakes adds to the first day of school preparation.

I spent my morning running errands, happily rushing about without dragging a child with me. I even had "freedom" themed songs playing like a soundtrack in my head all morning. Lyrics like: "I'm free, to do what I want, any old time," (Soup Dragons) or "Freedom, you've got to give for what you take" (George Michael) randomly popped into my head throughout my day.

We also celebrated another milestone yesterday. One year ago (the first day of school) we noticed Luke's hair was falling out. A whirlwind of doctor visits eventually resulted in his diagnosis of Alopecia and a three-day hospital stay for a progressive treatment.

We celebrated all of these milestones by creating a new tradition. After school, we took our first family bike ride, without training wheels, to the outdoor patio pub at the Chateau and toasted our day.

Thursday, September 22, 2011
A Voice.

I don't get homesick very often. But I was homesick last week, for something that caught me a little off guard...I was homesick for democracy.

I found myself in a situation where I didn't have a voice. That's not all that unusual, given the language barrier I face daily. (I really should find another French class now that all of the kids are in school.) But that's not what this is about.

The first week of school, the usual calendar of the year's events such as vacations, holidays and class trips came home in a backpack (or three). A tiny detail jumped out at me immediately. This year's Classes Vertes (the Green Week overnight camp) will not include the first primary class.

Ok, yes. I know. If you are reading this and you are an American, you are probably thinking, "First grade is much too young to go away on an overnight class trip, let alone four nights." That's what I *used* to think too. I thought that exact same thing two years ago when Avery was in first primary and his teachers began talking about their spring Green Week trip.

Despite my anxiety about my oldest baby leaving to go away with his class, I didn't want to be the only parent to keep my kid home. I didn't want him to miss out on a bonding experience with his class. We're here in Belgium for an immersion experience.

For the last two years, Luke has watched enviously, waiting for his moment when he could climb on that school bus and go away with his class (and his big brother). Last year, he shouted to the whole world that he only had one more year to wait. He was finally going to get to go to Green Week this year.

An email to the principal and a conversation with Luke's teacher revealed that this year, "Parents complained that the children were too little." Now, I happen to know that parents have said that in the past (I said that) but the Green Week trip was never canceled.

I don't know what happened, I don't know who or how the decision was made. I do know that I never had a voice.

If I had a voice, I would have said, "Yes, I know they are little. Yes, I know it's four days. But the teachers do an excellent, amazing job at preparing the kids for these days away. And somehow, in all of that preparation, they prepare the parents too." I would have also said that as hard as it was to say goodbye to my baby for a few days, the difference I noticed in him when he got off that bus to hug me again at the end of it all, was well worth it. He was confident. He was self-assured. He was so proud of himself. And he had so much fun.

I am so sad that Luke doesn't get to do that. I will be crushed if we are called back to the U.S. before he gets a chance to go. I am sad that I never had a chance to stand up for the teachers, and tell everyone what a good job they did with the children. And how I felt the same way, but even more so because it isn't even our home country. But mostly, I am so sad that I never had a voice.

To be fair, I don't know if this is the way things always get decided in these situations in Belgium, or if it's a quirky one-time thing that just happened at our school. But it made me homesick for the democratic process I would normally take for granted; the process where all of the parents (or at least those who wanted a voice) come together in one room and talk about their concerns. But I know that didn't happen for this.

Sunday, October 16, 2011
An Illegal Alien...Temporarily

Thanks to a snafu with the work permit paperwork, for a week or two, I was an illegal immigrant. The government renewed the children's permits without realizing it, so the kids were fine. John had an upcoming trip to the U.S. so he expedited his paperwork to make sure he'd be able to re-enter the country after his departure. That just left me.

Here in Belgium, they often have random checkpoints. Police blockades. These occur at various hours of the day (not just at night like a DWI checkpoint). It's my understanding that these are employed to look for illegal immigrants, driving under the influence, and other various infractions.

This is another one of those situations where I've noticed the absence of the constitutional protections offered in the U.S. that I would normally take for granted. There is no probable cause requirement here.

I have never been stopped at one of these checkpoints, although I've seen them often enough. I figured it would be just my luck to be stopped at one of these while I was carrying an expired ID. It didn't happen.

I did however, happen upon a checkpoint a week or so after I received my shiny new ID card. In the past, any time I've gone by one of these checkpoints, the police officers are all busy with other cars and I zip by without being stopped. Usually, I avoid eye contact with the officer directing cars over to the side of the road, because who really wants to get tied up in that for who knows how long? This time, though, I looked the officer right in the eye as I drove through the orange cones filtering cars past one at a time. I practically dared him to pull me over. Might as well show that shiny new card to someone, right? And I really wanted to know what happens at these random stops. He peered into my car and waved me by. I was a little disappointed.

It wondered if racial profiling might be standard practice here as well. If my skin had been a different color, would my day would have been interrupted with an impromptu police interview?

Wednesday, November 16, 2011
Holes.

Last month, we noticed that "they" (workers, from the water company, we think) dug a big hole in the street at the end of the block. A day later, there was another hole, about a block away. A few days after that, they dug a hole across the street from us, on the corner of our neighbor's driveway. It makes the turn out of her driveway so tight, that she can't get out to the street without backing up at least once. A week later, they dug one directly across, on our side of the street. These big, deep holes have blue and yellow plastic fences around them. I thought the neighbor's cat fell into one the other night, but it was a false alarm. (Thank goodness, because I didn't really want to climb down into a hole to rescue a three-legged cat.)

Last week, as we left for school, "they" were digging more holes. (This time, I know it was the cable company, he told me when he asked me to move my car.) They dug these holes on our lower sidewalk, next to where everyone parks their cars. They jack-hammered through the cement stones causing quite a ruckus. But by the time I brought everyone home from school, everything was all put back together again. The next day, they were at it again. It was the same—they waited for all of the cars to leave, dug more holes, made lots of noise, and everything was all patched up again by dinner time.

Our front walk is still a mess of sand and dust. But I'm actually ok with that, because it means it hasn't rained in over a week to wash it all away. And a week in Belgium without rain, means we've had a lot of sun, and sun in Belgium makes everything more tolerable.

Today, they are jack-hammering away at the big hole across the street. It has been sitting open for at least a month. (But then again, there were a few bank holidays in there, who has time during consecutive bank holidays to do any work?) I hope they aren't making it bigger.

What are all these holes for? It is almost like they are looking for buried treasure. But I'm sure it's nothing as exciting as that. Just boring old utility work. But trying to figure out the rhyme or reason to it is interesting....

Monday, November 21, 2011
American Football

Football in Belgium (Europe) is soccer. To talk about the sport that involves tackling, passing, kick-offs and a brown pointy ball, it is best to specify American Football.

That's not to say no one here knows anything about American Football. Last month, the two Belgian boys who live next door were playing football in the backyard, and they were using their bike helmets as protective gear. Imagine their sheer delight when John went out to our garage and came back with our boys' purple Vikings' helmets. It almost made it worth the extra baggage fee he paid last fall when he brought them home.

Luke and Avery went out to help teach them the rules, and soon the four boys were running plays, but eventually they were all more interested in the tackling part.

This year is the first year we have an ESPN channel on our local cable package. Johnny no longer has to watch NFL games via the spotty internet. But last night, he had the NFL pass on the computer (Vikings game) and a different game on ESPN. His chair was in the middle of the room so he could watch either. Instead, he was focused on Facebook. At one point, he said, "I'm not even really watching, it's just nice to have it on in the background." And that's true. On the NFL pass, we even get some of the American commercials. This time of year, as we go into Thanksgiving week, I am thankful for those subtle, American customs that sneak their way into our life here.

Monday, November 21, 2011
Football Practice

Wednesday is football day at our house. (The round black-and-white-ball kind of football.) Wednesday is the half-day in Belgium. The half-day gives kids one afternoon a week to devote to an extracurricular choice. Our boys chose football (aka foot for short and/or soccer if you are American).

The boys play for a local team and they play with their friends from school. Luke is in the first year (U6) and Avery is in the third year (U8). There are a few differences I've noticed between an American team and here. Last year, was Avery's first year playing on the local team, and Luke played with the BSA (the Brussels Sports Association, an English-speaking group, mostly for Americans) and John was the coach. Last year (given our one car situation) I often found myself running back and forth between the two games to drive everyone where they needed to be. It was a perfect chance for back-to-back comparisons.

One noticeable difference was the coffee. The American parents always brought their travel mugs and drank their coffee during the match. The European parents waited until after the match, to buy each other drinks (coffee, coke, beer or wine) at the stadium bar (every sporting facility has a bar here, even the pool!) Here, the socializing after the sport is as important as the workout itself. I have to say that I've learned to appreciate the later. Standing on a cold field drinking a lukewarm cup of coffee doesn't compare to coming in off a cold field and drinking a cup of European coffee, or a beer or glass of wine. (I wait until after noon for the beer or wine but not everyone does.)

This has become part of our Saturday morning tradition now. After their matches, we go into the bar with the rest of the parents and wait for our kids. The kids come in with their drink tickets, and we all have something to drink, and maybe a sandwich and/or a bag of chips. I love it. It reminds me of when I was a kid and got to pick a treat from the concession stand after my brothers' baseball games.

Another difference was that it took us awhile to realize (maybe March?) that we had signed on for a full school-year commitment. Who would have thought? In the U.S., kids play one sport in the fall, another for winter and maybe even a third and fourth for spring and summer. Of course, a Minnesota winter obviously doesn't cooperate with the idea of a full school-year of outdoor soccer. Avery was a bit tired of foot by the time the season ended in the spring. But he spent the summer with a soccer ball attached to his foot so we signed up again for this year, knowing full well (this time) what the commitment entailed.

This brings me to his little brother. Luke signed on as well, and is incredibly happy to be on a local Belgian team of his own.

We did have to have a talk though, last week.

The boys have different practice schedules on Wednesdays. I pick them up from school at 12h30. I take one of them for a practice (the field is right by school) at 14h30/2:30pm, and he's done at 15h45 (3:45pm). The second kid has practice from 16h (4pm) to 17h30 (5:30pm). I drive back and forth to school on Wednesdays at regular intervals no less than five times. One such Wednesday, I dropped Avery off and looked for Luke. I walked all over—out to the back fields, around the clubhouse building—everywhere. I could not find him anywhere. While I was starting to get a little bit anxious, I wasn't in a panic just yet. And then I checked the bar. There was my kid, kneeling on a bar stool, belly-up to the bar chatting it up with the bartender drinking free cherry-flavored water. Because he was thirsty. Of course.

After a reprimand, he promised never to mooch free drinks from the bartender ever again. I was left with the incredulous realization that I had just told my six-year-old that he can't hang out in a bar and order drinks all by himself. He's six. I thought I had at least another 14 years before having that conversation. But then again, it is Luke. He's ahead of his time.

Monday, January 19, 2012
Shortcuts

The kids went back to school today, after two weeks of Christmas vacation. I think it was the first time we haven't had visitors from the U.S. during the break. Grandma Sue came before Christmas, for three weeks, including Isabelle's birthday, but was home in time for Christmas Eve.

We loved every minute with Grandma, and really appreciated the time we could spend with her during those special weeks in anticipation of Christmas. When she left, I realized that having a visitor right before Christmas means those few days before Christmas become jam-packed with last minute holiday preparations.

Not to brag or anything, but I breezed through those last couple of days without stress, thanks to the shortcuts. Upon reviewing my mental list, I realized there just weren't enough hours left in the countdown for the cookies I wanted to make, presents I wanted to wrap, food I needed to prep for both Christmas Eve and Christmas Day dinners.

Go skating, at the rink in town with the family? Of course! Who wants to miss out on that? Go to lunch with a good friend? (That, by the way, was supposed to be a back-to-school lunch date and was pushed back all the way to Christmas.) Of course!

Thanks to the shortcuts.

I took shortcuts wherever possible. Knowing my patience level with baking in general, I only mixed a half-batch of dough. Just when I was sick of rolling out dough, I was done.

My dinner prep shortcuts worked as well. I whittled down my Christmas Day dinner list to the bare essential turkey trimmings—potatoes, vegetable, stuffing and gravy. I was glad that I froze a cup of cranberry sauce leftover from Thanksgiving, and I was even more glad I remembered that it was in the freezer.

All in all, we had a wonderful Christmas. For the most part, I felt free of the stress I usually shoulder, trying to make everything "perfect." I was happy to settle for "adequate" in the preparation details, and because I was happy, everyone else was happy too.

Monday, January 9, 2012
Holiday Hangover

On Saturday night, we were invited to a neighbors' house for happy hour. Happy "hour" turned into several hours and at 10 o'clock (22h) our kids were finally home and tucked into their beds. I should have expected as much. After all, we were with an Irishman. The next morning arrived with evidence that I cannot actually "drink champagne all night" like I originally boasted early on Saturday night.

It turned out to be a good metaphor. For the last week, my entire family has suffered from holiday hangover. It was next to impossible to get out of bed in the morning. No one felt like doing much of anything all day, every day. It required extra effort to go outside, even if the sun was shining. We ate what was left of the Christmas cookies. We made frequent visits to Frite Guy. We recovered, but it took the entire week.

Today, the kids went back to school and John left on a work trip. We all dragged our feet this morning, but everyone was ready, sort of. We never reached that point where we made each other so crazy that we looked forward to today. It was more like it was just time to go back to our regular lives. And we did.

It was a pretty awesome vacation doing absolutely nothing.

Sunday, January 29, 2012
There Once Was a Little Old Lady...

Have you ever noticed those little moments when your life intersects with another person—a stranger—on a regular basis? The first time I ever noticed it, I was a child. I would stare out the school bus window and see the same people every day going about their own daily routines. In high school, my carpool drove by a certain bus stop on the way to school and the same three people were always waiting for the same bus at the same time. I never knew who they were or where they were going or anything about them at all, but they mattered to me because I saw them every single day in the same place.

When that started to happen here, it made me feel as if we belonged. We were no longer outsiders looking in. This was our home, our town, our people. When I leave to pick the children up from school, I can tell if I'm early or late based on where the old man who walks his dog is on his route. Every Sunday morning, the same husband and wife walk by our house with their walking sticks, clearly on their weekly hike to the chateau. There are two old Shetland ponies that live somewhere on the other side of town. Their owners take them for walks and they just passed by our kitchen window.

There is one little old lady who I see regularly, and she has become a hero of sorts. She is short, but not too short. She is not fat, but she's not thin either. She has glasses and short, gray curly hair, but often, it is covered with a rain scarf just like my grandma used to wear. I usually see her on our route to school, about halfway between our house and the school. She is usually dressed in a skirt, with nylons, black short "sensible" boots and a gray trench coat. Sometimes I see her walking, pulling her grocery tote along behind her. I've seen her hitchhiking once or twice, which makes me smile and think of my Great Aunt Rosella who used to hitchhike from Belle Plaine to bingo at Mystic Lake Casino. My absolute favorite sighting of all, is when I see her on her white motor scooter. She wears a matching white helmet that fits perfectly over her black glasses. And she honks the little "beep beep" horn at everyone she passes along the way.

I've decided that when I'm 80, I will get myself the motor scooter my parents refused to allow when I was 16. I will ride around town and "beep beep" the horn at everyone I see.

Wednesday, February 1, 2012
The Swan.

The Ugly Duckling was a poignant story from my childhood. What awkward pre-adolescent doesn't identify with the poor, lost swan, ridiculed and laughed at by the other ducks? When the ugly duck actually turns out to be the graceful swan, and the envy of all the others...who doesn't hope for that? It made the swan a mythical creature for me.

Swans are regal, graceful. We see them a lot here, usually in pairs, off in the distance on a lake. They float with ease, their necks curved in elegance. They demand attention. If I passed by and saw them on a certain lake, I always found myself looking for them again the next time I passed by the same place.

During the holiday break, Isabelle and I took frequent afternoon walks around the lake (which is really more of a pond) at the Chateau. A walk gave her a chance to relax in the jogging stroller and provided an exercise opportunity for me. Fresh air and a break from the boys was good for both of us. We always brought our stale bread for the ducks and after we walked around the lake Isabelle would feed the ducks.

There are Mallards here, and also some cute, but rather mean little black and white ducks. We are partial to the Mallards, Isabelle likes them because she can tell which ones are the mommies and which are the daddies. I like them because they are Minnesota ducks. The black and white ones peck at the mallards and steal bread right out of their beaks. I know, it's nature and survival of the fittest and all of that, but I don't care for rewarding that kind of behavior, even if they are only ducks, so whenever possible we find duck-feeding spots that only have mallards.

One day, there were two swans, right in the middle of all of the ducks. What an amazing opportunity to see a swan up close, right? I was happy that we brought bread that day. That is, until the swan tried to eat my three-year-old. It hissed and made noises that I've never heard a bird make before. It stomped on all of the other ducks in its path to try to get closer to us. We threw the bread and ran.

I know that "hate" is a really strong word so I choose it very carefully and use it sparingly. But now I think I hate swans. I hate that something could look so beautiful and graceful from afar, and up close be so nasty that I feared for my daughter's life, just because she happened to be holding a chunk of crusty, stale baguette.

This encounter made me think. How many times in our lives does something look so beautiful, so desirable and covetable from afar, but up close it turns out to be ugly and nasty? Watch out for the swan, I say.

Thursday, February 9, 2012
A Minnesota Winter

We are in the midst of a deep freeze here in Belgium. It is Minnesota winter weather, no question about it. Glorious sunshine during the day, but below freezing temperatures. The daytime temperatures are sub-zero (in Celsius). We haven't quite reached daytime temps of sub-zero Fahrenheit, and I pray on behalf of the handful of little kids at school who still aren't wearing hats or mittens, that we never do.

While the cold makes it harder to get out of the house in the morning, I appreciate that we have a break from the outdoor football practices and matches. Yesterday it was nice to bring the children home at lunch and just let them play away the afternoon.

Up until a week ago, we were on track to skip winter altogether. The bulbs were already starting to grow. I even saw flowers growing at school just after the break. It was so strange to see crocuses about to bloom in January. We hadn't had a single snowfall. But last weekend, it snowed and we got to use our snow boots, snow pants, snow shovel and sleds at least once for the year. But I'm pretty sure the little flowers at school aren't faring so well. My autumn pansies finally froze.

Strangely enough, this weather has made me homesick for Minnesota. I'm not exactly sure why. Maybe it's because John is heading there for work this week. Or maybe it's because we just booked our tickets to come back for a visit during spring break. Or maybe it's the rare stretch of extended winter sunshine during what is usually a dark and gloomy month.

I have learned to take the weather here in stride. Often, I deal with the dark and rain by telling myself that at least it's not cold. But this week, I am dealing with the cold by being thankful for the sunshine.

Thursday, February 9, 2012
Boots.

When I first arrived in Belgium, I was in awe of the fashion. I noticed that women always looked pulled together, in an effortless manner. Even the moms who I knew stayed home, were wearing skirts with boots, or jeans with pumps. It's not just moms at school. It's women of all ages everywhere, in the grocery store, running errands or going about daily routines.

I let their fashion sense be contagious. I observed and realized it's all about the choices. In the morning, I choose my dark jeans over the old faded ones. I choose any pair of jeans over (cue the embarrassed whisper) sweat pants. I choose an oversized sweater instead of a sweatshirt. I choose my tall boots over my running shoes. I throw a scarf around my neck. I realized it doesn't take that much effort and the clothes are just as comfortable. Nothing even has to really match. In fact, it's almost better if it doesn't.

The result is a haphazard, effortless fashion. Personally, I noticed I felt so much better about myself. There is a confidence that comes with taking a minute to be conscious about my appearance. It is well worth the minute.

Sometimes, though, I wondered: what would happen if you put Belgian women in the thick of a Minnesota winter? What would change about their apparel choices if they had to dress for snow and ice? Does necessity require that fashion be sacrificed?

With this week's cold spell, I had a chance to answer my own question. Yesterday, I made a point to look at everyone's feet. There was the usual variety of suede, faux fur boots, and most of them were fashionable, yet practical. But I saw one kind of boot that I hadn't seen for a while—hiking boots. This morning I dug out my own pair of hiking boots from the storage box in the basement. I am happy to report that they are excellent for slippery cobblestones, and they still look nice with my dark jeans and sweater.

Wednesday, February 15, 2012
A Belgian Winter

After the longest cold spell since the winter of 1941, our frigid temperatures have turned into a Belgian winter. The cold here is always described as different than the cold in Minnesota. A zero-degree Celsius temperature reading here (32 degrees F) feels different than a Minnesota 32 degrees F. Until now, I haven't been able to figure out a good way to explain it.

On Monday, we woke once more to the freezing cold temperatures we had been enduring for more than a week. I went about my day and by afternoon the temperatures were on the rise. I sat in my kitchen next to the heater and as the temperature outside rose, I got colder and colder. A chill came over me. It was a chill that I hadn't felt in weeks. No, I wasn't getting the fever that's going around. My body was readjusting to the Belgian winter. The dampness set in. It is a completely different kind of cold: Bone-chilling. Even though it is warmer outside, it feels cold all the time and the sun is gone.

It makes me sad to see all of the dead pansies and crocuses everywhere. It's like Old Man Winter (whom we haven't seen at all this year) is saying, "Ha. You thought spring was almost here but I am having the last laugh."

Today, we've had fits of rain. We get rain in a solid downpour for ten minutes. Then it stops and the sun might come out for a minute or two, just long enough to taunt and tease. Then it will sleet or rain again. It's Wednesday, so the boys have soccer practice. It was cancelled for a few weeks during the subzero temps and frozen field, but now the fields have thawed. I fully expect Luke to come home with three layers of mud, one for each layer of clothes I made him wear.

I hope Spring arrives soon. We haven't had the pleasure for very long Mr. Winter, but I'll be happy to see you go.

Friday, February 17, 2012
Superior French Parenting

I read an article last week that claimed similarly situated American parents found parenting "more unpleasant" than French parents. As an expat mother in a francophone culture (I am careful not to say French because France and Belgium are very different) this made me think.

It made me wonder how French and American parents could possibly be similarly situated. It is easy enough to say it is so, but even if you are looking at working mothers in the same income bracket, there are inherent cultural differences that make them not so "similarly situated."

Here in Belgium, working mothers make up a good percentage of the workforce. Here, the work culture is quite different. People work fewer hours, take longer lunches and have more vacation. Family comes before the job and there is a better work-life balance. I suspect that working mothers here in Europe also experience less job-related stress than in the U.S.

But let's compare stay-at-home moms. I know more about that anyway. Here—and again I mean Belgium, I don't know about France—children begin school at age 2.5. There is structured, early childhood education.

Children learn routines, they learn to listen to a teacher, they learn to take direction from other adults and follow rules outside of home. They learn independence, but so do their mothers.

I think it is much easier to be a stay-at-home mom in Belgium than in the U.S. I remember my early days as a mother in Minnesota, being shut up in the house with two young children. My husband traveled a lot, or worked late hours. Any activity we did, required me to organize it. My life was my children because it had to be. I was frazzled and worn out. I was overjoyed when Avery started preschool at age three, and that was two mornings a week for a couple of hours. It was just enough time for me to run a few errands with just one baby. Here, having Isabelle at school full-time at age three opens up new worlds for me. I have time to volunteer. I have time to pursue my own interests, and more important, she loves it too. We have a better balance and I am a better mother for it.

Now let's talk about housework. The only moms that I know in the U.S. who have cleaning ladies are the ones who work. Cleaning ladies are really expensive. Here, everyone has help (well, everyone except me that is, but I have control issues). And it's not just a cleaning lady, but more of a housekeeper. It is affordable and tax deductible. Housekeepers do more than just clean the house. They help with laundry, ironing and special house projects. Having someone to help around the house on a regular basis, in my opinion, would also relieve a lot of stress on those American mothers.

Like I said, I know about Belgium, not France. But I suspect the French are culturally similar to the Belgians for this example. I argue that French and American mothers could never be considered similarly situated. And that makes comparing their parenting styles like comparing apples to oranges. For working French moms, take away their housekeepers and give them a cleaning lady. Add an extra ten hours into their work week. For the stay-at-home moms, take away their housekeepers. Keep their children home until age 5, with just a few mornings of preschool thrown in for a break. Give them an extra month of kids home on summer vacation, and take away a week of vacation. Then report back to me about how pleasant they think parenting is, and I'll listen.

But maybe a better idea is not to take anything away from anyone. Maybe a better idea is to acknowledge that there is a better way to balance work and home, and well...parenting. Maybe that's something in which the French are superior.

Saturday, March 10, 2012
The Culture of Food.

Is there really anything more cultural than food?

In the United States, in general, food is casual. We are also a culture that "is on the go," so our food is also, "on the go." There is an emphasis on doing things fast. For example, the aisles in the grocery stores are filled with quick dinner ideas and "minute meals." There are many fast food options, some more healthy than others. Even sit-down restaurants encourage diners to eat within an hour so as to "turn over" the table. I know, I used to be a waitress.

After watching a few seasons of Mad Men, I think sometimes, U.S. advertisers want us to think we need to have all sorts of specialty products to make a fast dinner. After living for a few years without some of those fancy products, I've realized that cooking something fresh, even all from scratch, can be just as fast.

I've noticed that meal-time here is more formal. Restaurants never, ever rush people through a meal. In general, dinner is late, so families can eat together once everyone is home from work. The focus is on sitting together, having conversation and enjoying the food. Wine is almost always served at dinner (not just for special occasions or on the weekend) and it's also not unusual to have wine or beer at lunch. It's not that we don't have special family dinners together in the United States. But in my family growing up, we were often on the go during the week and focused on our family time (and enjoyed our dinners together) on the weekend.

At lunchtime, meals are typically smaller here. Usually, I send a sandwich, juice and a piece of fruit. The lunch boxes here are half of the size of those in the U.S. But the children also take a snack to school, to eat in the middle of the morning. I usually send something fun, like a waffle or cake - which reportedly is what all of the other kids bring for snack time. They also have a snack in the afternoon, and again, it's usually a time to have cake or something sweet. This doesn't really spoil dinner, because again, dinner is served much later. In general, portions are smaller (in part because food is more expensive) and children are encouraged to clean their plates. I was raised on the clean plate theory, and with prices here, I more than understand the concept of not wanting to waste food.

But how does one take the best of both cultures, and use it to be a better parent? Personally, I try to take some of the best ideas I've observed and learned from living in the culture here, and apply it to our family life, with the idea that we are still Americans, and some day we will again live on U.S. soil.

If I send something sweet as a snack for school in the morning, then usually the dessert in their lunchbox is a piece of fruit or applesauce (which is also considered dessert here). Once a week, the kids have hot lunch at school so they can get used to eating something different, under different cultural requirements (i.e. they usually have to clean their plates).

I never require my children to clear their plates at home. Our rule is that they have to try at least one of everything. If we were going to live in Europe forever, I would be a card-carrying member of the clean plate club. But I know that someday we will probably be living back in the U.S. With the giant portion sizes in the U.S., I really want my children to learn to listen to their bodies, and be able to recognize when they are full and stop eating. So we don't always clean our plates here, and I don't feel the least bit guilty about it.

When John isn't traveling, we always try to eat as a family, even if it's a little later than we are used to. We are lucky, because with John working from home, his "commute" home is a walk down the stairs. Although, that time in the evening (between 4 and 6pm) is usually his busiest due to the time difference, and it's the best time to be on phone calls to the U.S. Sometimes it's hard for him to break away. We try to have dinner between 6 and 6:30, sometimes it's even later.

But the later we eat, the crabbier my kids get if their bellies are hungry. Besides, as Americans, in our to-go, non-delayed gratification culture, we LOVE our snacks. I don't want to give that up. And again, if we are going to eventually move back to the U.S., then my kids need to learn responsible snacking. So at our house, the kids have an after school snack, like yogurt, or maybe a cookie…especially if they had fruit in their lunchbox. As we get closer to dinner, the healthier our snacks: sliced apple, cucumbers, an orange or piece of cheese. The closer we get to dinner, I offer them snacks that could actually be for dinner.

We are doing our best to balance both.

Saturday, March 10, 2012
An American Girl Goes to a Concert in Brussels: Wilco.

I've been to my fair share of concerts and Minneapolis has always been a great music venue. But concerts here in Belgium are unlike anything I've ever experienced.

Last week, John and I went to see Wilco. I've seen Wilco preform before. One of my top ten favorite concerts of all time was Wilco's Yankee Hotel Foxtrot Tour.

I've decided that anything at the Ancienne Belgique easily makes it onto my top ten list. It's a club venue but they often host American bands that play larger venues in the U.S., and aren't as well known yet here.

We've found the best vantage point at the AB. There is a balcony that looks directly down to the stage. From our viewpoint, we were twenty feet away from the band and had a bird's eye view of the entire floor.

I know I've blogged about this before, but I am fascinated by concerts here. The audience is conservative, almost stiff. No one mushes up together to try to get closer to the stage. People practically stand in straight rows. Personal space is completely respected. No one moved, they just watched. Not very many people sang. That's not something this Minnesota girl relates to. They clapped and cheered, of course. And after an hour or so into the concert, when Wilco front-man Jeff Tweedy asked if everyone was having fun, people shouted out a few different song titles, but that was about it.

I'm not out of control at a concert, but I hopped around a little, and I definitely sang along. I sang some of the songs more loudly than others. During the brief pause before the final set, I turned to the Dutch man next to me and asked if he had ever seen them before. Twice, he answered. And then he said, "You obviously have."

As an expat, I am thankful for a lot of things. On that night at the Ancienne Belgique, I was thankful for the chance to see a favorite American band, in a small European venue. I was thankful to have a good babysitter which meant we could venture into Brussels for a night out.

But I was mostly thankful that the lyrics were in my native language and I could easily sing along—which was something I'd never even thought about before.

Saturday, March 17, 2012
A Heavy Heart.

My heart hurts.

Earlier this week, there was a horrific accident. A bus crashed in Switzerland. It was filled with Belgian students, returning from a school ski trip. More than half of the people on the bus were killed, and 22 of them were children. Twenty-two. I can hardly even think about it without tears filling in my eyes.

This is such a small country. That's a lot of kids. They were 11 and 12-year-olds (sixth graders) from two small catholic schools in Flanders. All of the adults perished, two bus drivers and four teachers. The tragedy hit the entire country, but it's impossible not to know someone who was personally affected. John plays hockey with guys from Heverlee, one of the villages where the children were from.

I know that it's not easy for Americans to relate to school trips like that, especially for younger students. I never, ever went away for a school trip, except for a weekend retreat and that wasn't until high school. It's just not something that American kids usually have the chance to do.

When I take the kids to school in the morning, Isabelle and I usually walk Avery and Luke down to their playground. Luke often requires assistance. On Tuesdays, his class takes the bus to the swimming pool first thing, and a few weeks ago when I didn't walk him all the way to his classroom, he forgot to take his swim bag to the pool. On Fridays, his class puts on their muddy boots and walk across the pastures to the recreation center up the road for gym class and he needs to remember his gym bag. Anyway, after we help Luke get settled, Isabelle and I usually sit on a bench and watch the big kids run and play before we walk to her building.

This week, I sat and watched the oldest kids at our school, the sixth graders, on the playground. I could hardly do it without crying. There are probably only 22 kids in the entire sixth grade class at our school. I cannot even imagine what it would be like to have them suddenly gone.

These faces. While I don't know all of their names, I've watched them grow up the last four years.

My heart breaks for the parents and siblings of the lost children, for their schoolmates they left behind, and for my adopted country of Belgium.

Heaven has 22 new angels. I wish they hadn't been called away so early.

Saturday, March 17, 2012
Four Years Ago Today...

Four years ago today, an American family of four arrived at Midi train station with a lot of luggage and a cat. In hindsight, the train idea was not very smart, but we got here eventually. A few weeks later, our dog arrived (jet lag and all) and we settled into our home in La Hulpe.

Now, four years later, we've had to say goodbye to the dog and cat (Luke's allergies) and we've said goodbye to his head full of hair, but we have an extra kid. And while she may not be Belgian by nationality, she is Belgian at heart. Miss Belle's first words were chocolate (ca-ca) and baguette (ba-bette) and they remain her favorite foods to this day (along with frites). I refuse to let her try a sip of her daddy's beer, because I'm sure, by deduction, that would become a favorite too.

While we might have to work a little harder than we thought to keep them American, our children have embraced life here. They love their soccer teams (their own, of course) but they also cheer for Barcelona and Man-U (Manchester United) and know all of the players in between. They speak French much better than their parents (even Isabelle) and often serve as translators for their parents when the need arises. Last year, Avery sat in on his little brother's parent-teacher conference to help us out.

Despite the challenges of cultural differences, language barriers and homesickness, we will be forever grateful for this amazing opportunity and the life lessons we've learned in our short time here. We are especially thankful for the life-long friends we've made along the way.

Sunday, March 25, 2012
It's a Mad, Mad, World.

It's a Mad, Mad world, and I'm mad, mad, mad. This is a reference to a favorite movie on the Pilarski side of the family. To say that it's not my favorite is an understatement.

The other day, I was almost home from school with a car full of kids. I even had an extra one (the neighbor). A car approached head-on, driving the wrong way (our street is one-way, but sometimes people cheat). We were at a section of the road where only one car fits at a time, I was already passing through that spot when the other driver insisted on coming straight at me.

The driver was a young adult male, about 19 or 20 years old. (Can you tell that I occasionally watch police procedure dramas? And don't forget I'm currently working on my second mystery novel.) He was wearing a baseball cap and driving an older dark-gray or black sedan. There were at least three other boys in the car. He sped up and as he did, the back end of his car clunked into the back end of mine. I immediately put the car in park and jumped out but he stepped on the gas and sped away as quick as he could. I squinted into the sunlight but was unable to read his license plate.

I came home and called the police (actually, I made my neighbor do it for me, with my poor French and all) and the police said it would have been nice to have the license plate number (no kidding) and to come in to file a report if my insurance needed it. Sigh.

And then my neighbor said, "I wonder if it's the kids who play basketball at the park?" And come to think of it, I have seen a dark gray/black vehicle parked there on a regular basis. The boys play basketball at the park around the corner. They always block the drive to the entrance, so it's easy to remember seeing the car there.

I spent the rest of the evening being mad about it. I was mad that there are people who think rules don't apply to them. I was mad that I'm a good person and this happened to me.

And then I turned on the news. I've been watching the local news lately because it's a good French lesson and as expats it's easy to get stuck in a bubble where we don't know what's going on locally unless we make an effort. The lead story was about the terrorist in Toulouse, followed by coverage for the joint funeral of six of the children from last week's bus crash. That's enough perspective for me not to care in the least about a dent in the back of my car.

Friday, after school, I made Avery come with me to the police station to file a report. And guess what?? On our way to the police station, we saw a dark gray/black car pulling out of the driveway parking spot at the basketball court. He thought I was kindly letting him out of his parking spot, when really, I was trying to find a pen and paper to write down his license plate number.

After an hour-and-a-half at the police station Avery and I successfully filed a police report. We had a close call and almost got turned away, when the flustered desk officer didn't want to take a report that wasn't in French, but we prevailed. I am grateful that I have a personal interpreter in the form of a really cute eight-year old. While Avery was initially excited to see what the new police station looked like, I'm sure the novelty wore after the first ten minutes. But I couldn't have been more proud when, after an hour into the process, he turned to me and said, "Mom, I can see why you made me come with you."

The car will get fixed and maybe the irresponsible teenager will get a good lesson in owning one's actions. And now Avery and I can add "visit police station" to the long list of "Things We Did in Belgium."

Friday, May 4, 2012
Overtimulated and Overstimulated

This year, we took our annual trip back to Minnesota at Easter break, instead of summer. We want to experience more of Europe while we have the chance, so rather than spend time and money to travel to the U.S. this summer, we decided to take our trip to Minnesota at Easter, leaving a wide-open schedule (and budget) for us to travel somewhere warm and vaction-y here this summer.

The kids are older, our transatlantic flights were much easier. This trip was the first time since we've lived here that I was actually more excited than nervous to go. That was a good feeling. We all appreciated the fact that we would be there to celebrate a holiday that we usually celebrate alone, here. We figured that we could manage it during the school year and the kids would be able to handle it. What we didn't think about was the reality of trying to fit our visit into a two-week period, when we usually have a month.

We focused on family and overall feel like we did a good job with the schedule.

Isabelle had a little trouble. It didn't take long to figure out that our three-and-a-half-year-old just needed to have a temper tantrum at least once a day to decompress. We never knew when it was going to hit. Once was in the middle of the night (sorry Fowler and Roberson families, the girl has a set of lungs and she knows how to use them). Another time was after a big outing (Tritz and Morrison families, you missed a doozy after we got home from Easter dinner). One night, when

John was traveling for work, the only way she would sleep is if she had one hand on my back the entire night. By the end of the trip, I was just as overtired and overstimulated as she was. It's hard to be a good mom when you are so far away from home!

We got through it though, and had a wonderful time with our families. And now we have a summer vacation to look forward to, and a wide-open calendar for anyone who wants to book a visit....

Friday, May 4, 2012
Spring Has Sprung

Spring is arriving slowly to Belgium. Over the last few weeks, the weather has started to change from the random fifteen minute cycles of rain-sleet-sunshine to mostly sunshine with enough rain mixed in to remind us that we are indeed still in Belgium and shouldn't get too excited about it.

When we were in Minnesota, we took the boys on a tour of the catholic school they would have attended if we had stayed there. It was impressive.

The purpose of our tour was to show them the school because some day, our time here will come to an end. The boys are already nervous about it. Since we were in Minnesota during the school year, we took advantage of the timing to provide them with a visual image of school in the United States.

During our tour the assistant principal turned to Avery and said, "Now we're going to go see the big gym." Avery replied, "The little gym is already a lot bigger than the one we use." We explained that the children walk approximately 2km through the cow pastures, rain or shine, to the community sports facility for their gym class. After visiting the fancy computer labs, science, art and music rooms, we couldn't help but wonder if our kids are getting the same quality of education in Belgium.

About ten days ago, Isabelle and I were waiting for the boys after school (her class sometimes gets out before the boys). We stood at the fence overlooking the pasture below and watched the sheep. We noticed a tiny little lamb. He poked his wobbly legs into position and stood for the first time. His little tail wagged as he tried to figure out how to eat. His mama started the long process of trying to clean him up.

When I told the boys about the new baby lamb, Avery said, "We already know. We watched it being born at recess. Christophe was the first one to see the legs come out." Huh. I guess that's a pretty cool thing to see at recess.

This week, we've watched the daily progress of preparation for the annual spring school party, fête du printemps. Our family is beyond excited for tomorrow's party. This is the first year where all three kids get to be in the spectacle, and Isabelle even showed me her entire dance routine last week. (Girls are so different...neither of the boys have ever come home and actually practiced their dance routines for fête du printemps.) This morning, we arrived at school to an assembled stage and sound checks. This turned into an impromptu DJ/dance party with songs that were heavy on the base and lyrics along the lines of "steal all of the booze from your mother's liquor cabinet..."

I should mention that English lyrics aren't censored here, and my kids often look at me with wide eyes while listening to the radio. More than once, Avery has reprimanded a friend on the playground for singing lyrics that are laced with swear words.

As I walked out of school this morning, my excitement and anticipation for tomorrow's festivities matched the same level as my children. We are so lucky to have found this school, we are grateful that the families accept us as their own, and we are happy for the chance to celebrate spring.

Friday, May 4, 2012
Hollaback Girl

Over the years, I've taken up running as my form of exercise. My free-time is precious and my workouts need to be easy. I lace up my shoes, turn on my iPod, go out the door, get my heart rate up and approximately 30-40 minutes later I'm home again and in the shower. Et voila! Workout accomplished, allowing me to indulge in Belgian delicacies such as saucisse (sausage), frites and of course, chocolate.

This spring, I decided to add a little bit of mileage. Nothing much, I just want to extend my workout time to about an hour, three times a week. I'm thinking about signing up for a local 10k race this summer, and maybe, just maybe attempting a half-marathon at some point next year. Ok fine, I'll admit it. The half-marathon I'm thinking about is in Paris. If

I'm ever going to do a half-marathon, how cool would it be to do it in Paris?!

In any event, this morning I took the kids to school, and with a whole sunshine-y day ahead of me, I headed out for my run early. Incidentally, the road in front of our house is a complete mess. Multiple road work crews are tearing it apart to make a bike and walking path. Hopefully, it will also be impossible to drive the wrong way thereby improving the traffic situation. Meanwhile, it's a pain-in-the-you-know-what to use it for anything, running included. But it's the route to the trails at the chateau, so away I went.

By the time I got to the end of the road, I was the embarrassed recipient of at least a dozen catcalls and jeering remarks. As a mother of three approaching 40, I'm not sure what to make of that. Should I be proud, that I can still turn heads? I wasn't. Should I be embarrassed that I'm out enjoying a much-needed workout? No way José, that's not my style. I settled on being proud to be an athlete.

This got me thinking. Running is primarily a male sport here in Belgium. I haven't noticed or thought about it much before. I have the luxury of being an American woman born in one of the first generations that can take Title Nine for granted. But now that I think about it, nine times out of ten, the runners who pass our house are men. And while it doesn't happen very often, I've noticed that when I do pass a male runner because I'm faster than they are, they don't like it very much.

As I ran my 7km route, I thought about one of the greatest experiences of my lifetime. In college I competed on the varsity co-ed swim team. In the pool, we were one team. We all swam the same workout, regardless of which type of swimsuit you were wearing. We respected each other as teammates and fellow athletes. The friendships born in that old stinky pool have endured through the years as some of the most precious and valuable of my lifetime. And as a result, I don't even think about differences in men's and women's sports, especially running and swimming.

As I approached the home stretch of my run this morning, I braced myself for the looks, pulled my baseball hat down over my eyes and set my iPod to the ultimate girl-power song, Hollaback Girl by Gwen Steffani. I turned up the volume and sprinted the last 500 meters to my house, grateful and proud to be an athlete. And from now on, I will have to resist the urge to high-five other female runners here and shout, "You go girl."

Saturday, June 16, 2012
Jinxed.

I don't think I should blog about running anymore. When I do, it seems I jinx myself and end up with a running-related injury that puts me on the injured reserve list for six weeks. This time, it's a stress fracture in my left foot.

My immediate family will be the first to tell you that running keeps me sane. When I'm not in a regular running routine, I get cranky. Quickly. Last week, I did what any former swimmer would do, I found a pool.

One of the many things I appreciate about Belgium, is the easy access to community sports facilities. (It reminds me of St. Paul, where there are lots of options for open swim times at any one of the four universities in a two-mile radius.)

I paid my three euros and gimped my way into the pool. The swim lanes were less crowded than last time. I settled myself in a lane with only three other swimmers, stroked through my first lap uninterrupted, and without pain in my left foot which was a good sign. Over the next 1500 meters, I learned something new about Belgium.

Swimming in Belgium is a lot like driving here. The lanes are smaller, thus the risk of colliding infinitely greater. Also, different rules of etiquette apply. For example, there doesn't seem to be a yield-to-the-swimmer-coming-into-the-turn before-pushing-off-the-wall-to-start-a-lap-of-kicking rule.

Forty-five minutes later, muscles that I hadn't used in years and forgot I even had, screamed in protest. But I was proud to have completed a swim workout for the first time in a really long time. (Of course, now I call it a "workout." Back in college, it would have barely been a "warm-up.")

Two days later, I went back to the pool. It was even less crowded than the first time. I recognized a swimmer from before; she had a nice even back stroke and was doing flip turns, a telltale sign of a more experienced swimmer. My muscles creaked. It occurred to me that there might be some benefits to cross-training my running with a low-impact sport like swimming.

When I got out of the pool, the swimmer I admired stopped me to tell me that my swimming was beautiful. After feeling so sore and stiff, and well, broken, the last few days, this actually made me laugh out loud. I explained to her I hadn't swam in a long time. She told me she swims every day. I don't think I can manage every day, but I will certainly try to make swimming more of a regular thing.

Wednesday, June 20, 2012
Sticks and Snails, and Puppy Dog Tails...

What is the old rhyme?

Sugar and spice, and everything nice, that's what little girls are made of. Sticks and snails and puppy dog tails, that's what little boys are made of.

Luke's health has improved significantly. An entire year without antibiotics of any kind (knock on wood) was worth having to find new homes for our beloved pets. I think he only missed one day of school this year with a stomach virus, and managed to stop using his asthma inhalers altogether.

We still really miss our big yellow dog, Jasmine. But when we visited family in Minnesota and stayed with dogs, Luke started wheezing again and needed all of his inhalers. It took six weeks after we came home for him to get over it. It confirmed we made the right choice.

Luke is a little boy who loves Nature. Both our boys are the perfect age for a dog to be their best buddy and partner in crime. But there will be no fur or feathers for our house anytime soon.

Last Friday, Luke came home from school very excited. He and his friends spent their recess time hunting for snails. He found a clear plastic container and with his little sister in tow, set out to the back garden to hunt for his new pet. They came back empty handed and disappointed. Another attempt the next morning was equally futile.

Luke took his snail house to his friend's house after school. His friend has a giant garden with all sorts of wildlife. His friend's mother said Luke was welcome to take as many snails as he wanted, as they were eating all of the vegetables and strawberries in her garden. I told him his quota was three.

His friend's father brought him home. With a sly grin, he drove away. But not before he could pass along a cryptic message, "The snails are your problem now."

I didn't even know that snails could grow to be the size of baseballs. (Maybe it's not quite that big, but it is definitely bigger than a golf ball.) Luke named him "Super-Size" and argued that the two baby snails "didn't count" towards his quota of three, bringing the grand total to five.

Probably, Luke's new pets would be happier if their container was on the patio. We put a table next to the back window so we can watch the new pets from inside the safety of our house.

I have to admit, Super-Size was kind of fun to watch. He was a giant. He moved all over his new home, exploring his container. And also, it seems, looking for escape routes. We caught him pushing the lid off the top. We quickly secured the lid with a potted plant and added a slice of plum to their new home to keep them happy.

The next morning, there was nothing. No movement, nothing. As the day went on and the snails were silent, I worried that the potted plant had blocked too many of the little air holes. It appeared as if we had killed the whole lot of them. We opened the lid to look, and didn't bother to secure it again. I felt bad that we had deprived them of precious oxygen.

The next day after school, Luke and I went out to the patio to deal with the dead snails. There, sitting next to the container, was Super-Size himself, tucked up in his shell taking a nap. Huh. It appears he wasn't dead after all, and took advantage of the open container to escape. Not only did he escape, but he came back to eat the basil from the potted plant. Being the size of a golf ball, he's not exactly inconspicuous. We let him sleep on the table and took the container to the edge of our driveway to dump the contents by the forest and put in new leaves. When we dumped the container out, the other "dead" snails promptly came out of their shells and made a break for it.

It was nice to know we didn't kill them after all. We cleaned out the snail slime and added fresh nature. We fed them some basil leaves and named the rest of them. Luke returned Super-Size to his new home and secured the lid. Today, Luke made a "to-go" container and chose "Speedy" to take to school with him for the day. He is under strict instructions regarding his snail quota. It's only half-day today, which means there's less time at recess to hunt for snails. Fingers crossed.

Friday, September 14, 2012
Rats.

And I mean that literally.

I saw a rat once in New York City. We were standing in Central Park trying to decide what to do next when a big, giant rat ambled out from under a bush, looked at us, blinked and leisurely crossed the path to another bush where he disappeared. After that, I never needed to see another rat.

Then I moved to Europe. When an American thinks about Europe, images of castles and cobblestones often come to mind. Romantic lands rich with history have been teasing our imaginations for years and years until one day, maybe we are lucky enough to come see part of it for ourselves. (Even after more than four years of living here, I still have to stop and pinch myself sometimes at the unbelievable opportunity to actually get to live here.) But there is good and bad with everything, and the Black Plague was a pretty ugly point in European history.

When we had the dog and cat, we didn't have to worry about rodents. But we've been pet-free for a year now, and over the winter, we started seeing signs. What's that they say? Something like, for every one that you see there are hundreds you don't? One day, I saw a dead rat in the road. Once, there was an unexplained rustle in the bushes on the back patio. There was a sighting in the neighbor's garden and another in the garden on the other side. But surely, there was a force field bubble around OUR garden, right? That's what we told ourselves.

It wasn't just in our neighborhood. It appears to be an epidemic this spring. There were others on the road in other neighborhoods. At school one day, the children were looking through the fence at the pasture below, watching one die (its bloated body had clearly been poisoned).

As part of my duties as the Vice President of the American Women's Club, I am required to sit on the board of the ISG (International Study Group). The ISG ladies are wonderful. They are an older group of women dedicated to educating themselves by bringing in monthly speakers to lecture on a variety of topics. They also like to have lunch, so our board meetings were at each other's houses, and the hostess is required to serve lunch. The ladies on the board remind me of my Grandma Bares—classy, and dressed to perfection. Potentially intimidating and certainly not afraid to demand certain standards, I knew making them lunch would be nerve-wracking, but at the same time, an exciting culinary challenge.

My lunch was in February and it was cold. I made wild rice soup and pecan pie. We started the meeting with coffee, finished lunch and I was on my last coffee service when I saw the rat. I was seated at the head of the table, with a view of our patio and garden. A large brown rat, took a leisurely afternoon stroll across our top patio step from one set of bushes to the other. A few minutes later, another one followed behind. They were clearly mocking me. As if by their actions they were saying "*So you thought you would try to serve a proper ladies' lunch? We'll see about that (cue wicked laughter) Mwaahaahaa....*"

Thankfully, the ladies never noticed and the only thing they have to talk about from lunch at my house was this Minnesota girl's wild rice soup. A few days later, our neighbor came to the rescue and brought over some rat poison. (We can get it for free at the commune, and he had extra.) John was out of town and still teases him about bringing his wife rat poison on Valentine's Day. I never wanted to consider poison an option, but with thoughts of the Black Death in the back of my mind, on that particular day it was a present I was happy to receive.

The poison got eaten, and the sightings (both dead and alive) stopped. Early this summer, though, our bushes were invaded by a new rodent. There were teeny-tiny little mice with big giant ears and little bodies, but they were very bold. One night, we were having dinner on the patio when no less than five of them came out of the bushes to see what we were serving. We don't have screens on our doors. If we wanted to be able to open our doors at all this summer, we had to do something before they moved themselves right on into the living room.

About the same time, our neighbor had similar sightings, and his son claimed to have seen another rat. "No way," we all said, just little mice. But the poison went out, got eaten and we waited. One morning, Luke and I went outside. There, right at his feet, was a dead mouse. I screamed and turned. But there, just a few feet away in the other direction, was another dead one. I screamed and turned again, and there, lying in the middle of the backyard, was a large dead rat. That scream brought my entire family (and probably most of the neighbors) out to the patio.

Our garden had become a land of rodent horror.

The remedy was swift and quick. Composing myself, I scooped up the dead bodies with an old shovel and dumped them in a bag. That was that. Hopefully, the message was sent loud and clear to future generations: You'd best be advised to move elsewhere.

Saturday, September 15, 2012
Fifteen Minutes.

I just saw a man die.

Well, I don't know exactly when he died, but I was the first to arrive after he did. It was just another Friday. We are in our second week of school, the routine is already beginning to settle in. I picked up the kids from school and we went to our swimming pool for swimming lessons, just like we've done every Friday for years. Only this time, the lesson was for Isabelle and the boys had to get ready for their respective Friday night soccer practices. I was going to drop them off at the field on our way home. We left the small parking lot and turned down the tiny street towards the intersection leading to the busy street. There, in front of us, was a motorcycle lying in the middle of the road. Something was obviously very wrong.

By the time we got to the end of the tiny street, we could see a man lying just beyond, and the largest dump truck I have ever seen was parked a little further away. The man in the road wasn't moving and the driver was pacing in the street yelling into his cell phone. We were the first car to arrive on the scene. It had probably happened just a minute or two before.

I threw the car in park, told the kids to stay and ran into the street. My mind raced. What do you do at that moment? Do you try to help the lifeless body lying in the road? Talk to the driver? I was afraid of the body and my French isn't good enough to offer anything to the distraught driver. By now, the driver was off the phone and he told me that the motorcycle man had turned out right in front of him, he couldn't stop. I think I asked if the man was dead but I don't remember.

By this time, other cars were stopping. A lady who had pulled out of the parking lot behind me was on her phone, calling the emergency numbers I was sure the driver of the truck had already called. Other witnesses stood around. No one knew at this point if the man was alive or dead, but it didn't look good. No one seemed to know what to do and there weren't any sirens to announce the arrival of anyone who would know what to do anytime soon.

The dump truck was parked in the right lane. The man was lying just behind the truck. Two men moved the bike out of the road. Traffic was starting to back up. Cars that couldn't see what had happened honked impatiently. One lane was blocked by the truck and driver but the other was passable, but it was a corner and hard to see oncoming traffic.

I couldn't just stand there. This American girl threw up her arms and started directing traffic. I stopped one lane of traffic, just like I've seen police officers do a hundred times. I waved about ten cars or so through from the opposite lane and then I stopped the next car and ran fifteen yards or so to the other side and waved about ten cars through from the other direction. One of the drivers was a nurse and she pulled over to try to help the man. Back and forth, back and forth I ran, telling cars where and when to go. It felt like I did this for an hour. But really it was probably only for about five or ten minutes. I tried not to look at the man and his helmet that was cracked in a million places. I yelled at cars to slow down if they were going too fast. I tried to stand in front of the man to block everyone from staring. I guess I also wanted to make sure no one ran over him again. Eventually, we heard sirens. Then, the police officers were there.

The ambulance parked in the open lane and traffic was blocked in both directions. It didn't matter anymore about directing traffic. I had to move my car so the little street was passable. But I didn't want to leave in case I needed to tell someone something. And I really wanted to know if the man was alive...or not. No one was moving very fast, so I think I already knew the answer.

I asked one of the other early witnesses. He didn't know for sure either and he switched to English right away. I told him I was the first one to arrive and he went with me to talk to the officers. I didn't see the actual accident, they didn't need me to stay.

I asked my question. "Is he alive?"

The officer shook his head and said, "His head..."

I told him I would never let my children ride motorcycles when they grow up. Not that they would want to after seeing this anyway.

Then, the officer gave me a small smile that I will never forget, and he said, "Thanks for your help with the cars." I think I just shrugged. I hadn't realized until that moment that I had even done anything. It hadn't been intentional, I just reacted to a situation.

I walked back to my patient children. As hard as I tried, I couldn't hide the tears that had started falling. Avery said to me, "Mom, it was pretty cool that you were able to help."

When I looked at the clock, I realized that the entire interruption in our routine Friday afternoon only took about fifteen minutes. That fifteen-minute interruption is nothing compared to what some nearby family is experiencing as they learn about the loss of a loved one. It's nothing compared to what the poor truck driver must be going through. My heart goes out to all of them.

I have this need tonight to tell anyone and everyone: Life is precious and fragile. Don't take it for granted. Each day is a gift.

RIP Motorcycle Man. I didn't know you, but I will never forget you.

Sunday, September 23, 2012
The Braderie

The end of August always brings with it a little bit of regret: We love going to the Minnesota State Fair and we miss it. The Minnesota State Fair is always the last week in August. It lasts for ten days and ends on the American Labor Day. This is our fifth year in a row that we've missed the "Great Minnesota Get Together." Every year, we look longingly at photos posted by Facebook friends of the fun we are missing. The KFAN podcasts of the "Live at the Fair Broadcasts" filter though our iTunes to remind us that we're here, not there.

For my Belgian friends, State Fairs are time-honored traditions. They began as a showcase for agriculture and livestock, where people throughout the state would compete to win the title of the best of the best in any number of categories from pumpkins to pigs. Still today, there are agriculture and livestock displays. But there are also rides and concerts and markets to shop, and lots and lots of food. There is something for everyone. When we were younger, we went for the rides and games. As we got older, we went for the music and beer. With little ones, we went to wander the streets with the stroller, and teach the American tradition to our toddlers.

But La Hulpe does offer us a consolation. Each year on the cusp of our State Fair disappointment, we start to see signs for the annual La Hulpe

Braderie. Here, our "braderie" is basically a big town garage sale/street fair. They close off the main street of La Hulpe, and sell spaces along the storefronts. The shop owners and restauranteurs each get a spot. Most of the food shops (like the meat market) and the bars or the restaurants set up tables and sell food and drinks. In between everything, local residents sell garage sale stuff. There are rides and games and music. It is definitely more like Grand Old Day (in St. Paul) or BBQ Days (in Belle Plaine) than the State Fair, but we miss those events too so we will take what we can get and not complain.

One nice bonus about Europe: you don't have to keep your alcoholic beverages in a beer garden. You are free to roam about, mojito in hand, which is exactly what we did last night.

This year's braderie marked a new milestone for our little family. We did not need a stroller, and we went at night instead of the daytime. We saw friends from school, older kids from the neighborhood and people we know from around town. It was a beautiful September evening. Our kids went on rides, we sipped a few drinks and ate dinner via street vendors. Afterwards, we came home and tucked tired children into bed, with bellies full of junk food. We love our little town.

Sunday, October 14, 2012
Clonkers.

Autumn is here, with chilly nights and fresh, crisp, sunny days. There is the occasional rain shower of course, it is Belgium after all. We don't get the same vibrant colors on our trees here as they do in Minnesota, but it's still beautiful.

It's also a great big mess. The other day I was at school, waiting to pick up the children. I arrived early, so I had a few minutes of silence in the car to collect my thoughts. It was a blustery day, and as the treetops waved back and forth, leaves and sticks dropped down all around. A giant gust of wind rattled the trees. And my car was attacked by chunks of tree branches and...Clonkers.

Have you ever seen a real chestnut? Before I moved to Europe, chestnuts were only something you sang about "roasting on an open fire" every year at Christmastime. I'd never actually seen one, and if I had, it wasn't in the full shell fresh off the tree. It was prepackaged in the grocery store.

Right off the tree, these nuts look like an organic instrument of torture—something Mother Nature invented on a day when she was feeling particularly moody. Chestnuts are round, and can be range in size between a golf or tennis ball. They are green, with spikes the size of sewing needles shooting out every which way. They are also heavy.

That day, several split open upon hitting the cobblestone street and/or my car. I don't want to know if they put dents on the roof—probably they did, it sure sounded like it. But it's not like I could call my insurance agent here and ask about chestnut damage. All around me on the ground were perfect brown nuts, two to a shell.

After living here for several years, I've learned that there are two different types of chestnuts—the ones you can eat and the ones you can't. I decided to do some research, and figure out which was which. If these things were falling out of the sky clonking me on the head, it would be nice to know if I could at least roast it on an open fire.

The internet is amazing. Within five minutes, I learned that, first of all, they are aptly nicknamed Clonkers. The ones you can't eat are called horse chestnuts. I don't know why, I can't imagine horses actually eat them. The way to tell which is which is easy: The horse chestnuts have short spikes that are spaced wide apart. The ones you can eat are covered with long needle spikes. The website made a joke about figuring out how to get them open. Both types of chestnuts have two nuts inside. The ones that attacked my car were horse chestnuts. Bummer.

Later that week I went for a run. I was almost home, when there in the road before me, was a round green spikey ball, with needles the size of a sewing needle. A real chestnut! I tried to pick it up. It poked me, drawing blood. Forget about opening them, how the heck do you even collect them? Very carefully, I picked it up by the stick part that was still attached and carried it home. I went online again, and confirmed by pictures and descriptions (of the shell, needles, leaves and everything) that this in fact, was a non-poisonous chestnut. All I needed now was an open fire. Provided I could get the thing open.

The next day, Belle and I walked down the road with a basket. Very carefully, we filled it with chestnuts and took those spikey little balls home. The basket sat on the counter for a week, while I worked out a strategy for what to do next. The excitement in the house grew. "We get to roast chestnuts," everyone said. That week I saw chestnuts in a big pile in the produce section at the grocery store. With a smug grin I thought to myself, "I don't have to buy those, I collected my own for free, right off of my street."

Last Saturday morning I was feeling ambitious. With the BBQ tongs in one hand, and the sharpest knife from my drawer that most closely resembled a saw in the other, I set about opening them. The nuts inside were tiny and wrinkled. But this far into my task, I wasn't about to give up. An hour later, I had filled a small bowl. The ones at the grocery store looked better, not to mention bigger. I think the sign said that they were from Italy.

Do you think my family would notice if I buy the ones at the grocery store and we roast those instead? Apparently, Italy grows better Clonkers than we do here in Belgium. I would hate to see how long the needle spikes are on the Italian Clonkers. But that's the beauty of a grocery store, isn't it? I'll never have to know.

Tuesday, January 8, 2013
Cutting the Last Tie.

I love American reality shows. Especially the originals like Survivor and Amazing Race. Bravo also has excellent reality shows, like Project Runway and Top Chef. There is something about watching creative competition that is riveting entertainment for me.

We've always found these shows online. But last year, some sort of computer/internet legislation went into effect in the United States. My reality television shows completely disappeared. Now, links for everything like clips of interviews on a news channel, are completely blocked to users outside the U.S.

My last little window to American pop culture has been slammed shut. The last bridge closed off.

After it happened, I went through withdrawal. It was mid-season Top Chef, and a new Project Runway was about to begin. However, it would have been worse if it happened mid-season of Survivor. Speaking of Survivor, I tried to watch the French version. But really, I'm sure it's more entertaining to watch your own countrymen battle it out in a social game like that. For me, French survivor only seemed to illustrate all of the French stereotypes. And seriously, if you are from Paris, just stay in Paris. There is no need to try to be the last person in a game on a deserted island. In any event, my reality television addiction trickled quietly away and now I don't really miss it at all.

In an effort to cut expenses, we switched our cable package. John bundled our cable together with our phone and internet and now we have a new provider. Our new provider has an employee that is a genius. This genius recommended that John order the Dutch cable channels, because most Dutch television isn't dubbed over, but rather left in English with Dutch subtitles. We have the History Channel! And National Geographic! (File this under: Things I Wished Someone Told Me Four Years Ago.)

But now, I have new favorite television shows! Storage Wars and Pawn Stars! I wonder if Bravo has a Dutch counterpart....

Friday, August 16, 2013
My Real-Life Story Problem...

Last spring, when the weather was cold and rainy, we never knew if we'd have football practice or not on our half-day Wednesday afternoons. But nevertheless, every Wednesday afternoon, I become a chauffeur for the Fowler family children.

On one particular Wednesday, I survived a scenario that rivals a word problem typical to the LSAT (the Law School Entrance Exam). If you read through and can answer the questions at the end correctly, then you may want to consider applying to law school.

Here we go: Isabelle went home with Victoria, so that Victoria's mother Isabelle could take Victoria, Isabelle and Pauline to Alice's birthday party. I planned to bring Nico, Avery and Luke home for lunch at our house, but then Luke went home with Sacha, who lives across the street from us. Soccer practice was not cancelled, so I fetched Luke from Sacha's house, took Luke, Avery and Nico to the field, where I only dropped off Luke. Then, I took Avery and Nico with me to pick-up Isabelle, Pauline and Victoria from Alice's birthday party in Rixensart. On my way back, I dropped Nico and Avery off at their practice. Then I drove to Isabelle's house (Victoria's mom) to drop off Victoria and Pauline. I went back to the field to pick-up Luke. I brought Isabelle and Luke home to start dinner and make Luke take a shower (he played goalie at practice and it was muddy). Then, Luke, Isabelle and I went back to pick-up Avery.

Question 1: How many kids did I have to make lunch for? Question 2: What was the most number of kids I had in my car at one time?

Bonus question: Who ended the day by sitting in the kitchen with a big glass of wine and a good book?

I don't know how to make this next part type upside down, or I would try.

Answers:

Question 1: I only had to make lunch for two and it was very quiet.

Question 2: The most kids in the car at one time was five, the three girls after the party and Nico and A.J. before I dropped them off at practice. The three girls were all sugared up and giggled the whole way home.

Bonus Question: Me. I was the one in the kitchen at the end of the day with a big glass of wine and a good book.

Wednesday, August 21, 2013
A Summer of Slugs.

We remind ourselves all the time that slugs are better than mosquitoes. Yes, they are gross and ugly and leave a nasty trail of slime and ooze behind them wherever they go, but they are harmless. You just don't want to go barefoot in the back garden at night or morning. Or maybe ever. Just in case.

Slugs are a novelty for our American visitors, especially those who hail from the Midwest. When our cousins from Apple Valley came to visit the first week of summer break, of course we had a Belgian BBQ and enjoyed a mosquito-free evening on the patio. This BBQ stretched into the late evening hours. And then the slugs came out.

At first, it was funny to see a big, fat, slimy slug trailing ooze across the patio. The teenagers laughed, and my kids remembered that not everyone has slugs in their garden. However, when our slimy intruder invited his siblings, grandparents, descendants and best buddies, it stopped being funny.

I went outside after everyone went to bed to cover the grill and straighten the patio. I'm glad I remembered to turn on the light, because there were at least fifty oozy invaders having an after-party. Had I stepped in the wrong place at the wrong time, I would have brought a whole new meaning to the word "busted."

We've never had slugs like this before. What was once an occasional slug in the garden, had turned into a full-fledged infestation. We didn't have much time to worry about it. The same day our guests left us to go find more excitement in Paris, we departed for on our own holiday. As a last-minute attempt to make a dent in the slug slime, I poured a can of beer into two bowls and placed them strategically in the garden. By strategic I mean, easy to climb into, hopefully not so easy to climb out when that beer buzz takes effect.

We returned from our holiday and to my surprise, my beer-bowl strategy worked. There were twenty drowned enemies in both bowls. Yuck. If I thought the living slime balls were bad, the drowned, fermented, decomposing ones were worse. But one thing was sure, the population had dwindled. I patted myself on the back for a job well-done.

I filled new bowls and went for Round Two. While I hated to waste the Belgian beer, I felt ok with it morally. Yes, I was intentionally killing a living creature, but from the slug's perspective, it had to be a good way to go. It's not like I was dumping poison everywhere. Beer bowls in place, we sat outside one evening after dinner. It was fun to watch the grotesque creatures hone in on the beer like a beacon was calling them home. They fell in, lolled around and got clearly, stinking drunk. By the time we called it a night, there were at least twenty drunk slugs.

The next morning, I went out to deal with the carnage...and they were gone. As in, not in the bowl. I assumed they were probably tucked in their little sluggy beds somewhere nursing very big hangovers. If our intent was to open the most popular slug saloon in town, we succeeded.

Wednesday, August 21, 2013
The Battle of the Slugs, Continued.

The beer bowls worked but didn't really make a dent in the backyard slime population. Plus, we realized we were just providing free booze to the neighborhood creepy crawlies.

I'd rather not use poison if I can help it. It's definitely not the first tool I grab for an infestation situation. (See a previous post somewhere back about rats.) But I've learned to never say never, and sometimes, you just have to do what you have to do to take back your garden.

And it was time to take back my garden. I sprinkled anti-slug bits around and it actually smelled good. Let's see what happens, I thought.

Um. The next 24 hours revealed carnage I never thought possible.

Whatever they ingest, causes extra slime trails. Our patio, was a spiderweb pattern of crystalized slime trails.

And.

For some reason (I think it's a conspiracy) they prefer to live out their last moments in wide-open space. They come out to die onto the patio, or the bald patches of dirt in front of the boys' football net. And this, mind you, is an extra-oozy, disgusting, writhing death. (I felt bad. Really, I did.)

We had to implement a Slug-Removal Squad. Yep. That would be me with a shovel. I go around and flick the slimeballs into the bushes before anyone will go outside to do anything. I've been doing this all summer.

We thought the situation was under control. But the other night we had to do another round of chemical warfare. The next morning, there I was flicking dead sluggy critters into the bushes.

Sigh. This is what my life has become.

But then. An amazing thing happened. My three children—who up to this point had been whining and complaining about something or other (for sanity purposes, I stopped listening to the whiney voices sometime last month)—banded together.

Somehow, they came up with a system of water and buckets and they worked together. Just let me pause for a minute and say that one more time. They worked TOGETHER to clean-up the crystalized slime trails all over the back yard.

I did what any good mother would do. I took that as my cue to retreat into the house, unnoticed. I left them to collaborate and use their imaginations to fix the backyard.

And it was beautiful.

Wednesday, August 28, 2013
Car Trouble.

Once a car reaches a certain age, it has to pass an annual test. Last spring, our car was due for a "controlle technique." John's travel schedule was hectic, so I volunteered to handle this whole process and cleared my schedule to do so.

I went to the test center. I waited, I spoke French. Although, it was automotive words, so I didn't speak enough of it. After the mechanics figured this out, they stopped talking to me. I was waved through the test and pointed to the office to pay the bill. It was only after a big red document came off the printer that I realized I'd failed.

The people in line behind me tried to help me understand what the problem was, but the information was vague. There was something about the headlight alignment, and something else about the parking break. Bottom line, I had two weeks to fix the problems and get the car back to the testing center. I drove straight to a mechanic's shop with my paperwork, where I secured an appointment for the first available spot, which was the following week. They assured me they could fix everything to retake the test and pass.

I went to the appointment, and was surprised to be finished within the hour. My bill was only 15 euro for something to do with the lights. "But what about the break?" I asked. "Oh, we don't do that here, you'll have to go to the dealership," they said. Hmm. I drove straight to the dealership. I had to beg for an appointment for some time that week.

Then, I told them I would wait with the car. They hate when people stay with the car. They always want us to drop it off and then it usually takes them three days.

I had one day after the dealership to get the car back for my retest. I went to the dealership, prepared for a long day. To my surprise, the car was fixed before lunch, with enough time to get the car retested. And this time, I passed.

Did I mention it was done before lunch?

Sometimes, the little things are big things here.

***

The following week, the car began making a "clicky-clicky" noise that usually means one of the turn signals needed a bulb.

Sigh.

When I took my driver's ed class, I think we learned basic car maintenance, like how to change a lightbulb. But now, when I pop the hood of our Chevy, the inside is so complicated, I can't even see how to open anything near the headlight, let alone change the bulb.

On the way to school, the boys tutored me in all the ways to say "light bulb" in French. I drove back to the garage that fixed the light alignment. They were my buddies now. Feeling more confident with my automotive words, I asked for them to change the lightbulb. I used every word that Avery taught me. Me and the mechanic, we both nodded at each other. He even had time to fix it right then.

Later, back in the car, I turned out of the parking lot and heard the "clicky-clicky" noise again. I turned back into the lot and went back into the shop. This time, they got the guy who spoke English. Turns out, the original guy (the one that nodded and smiled a lot) thought I meant I had a leak in my tire and he tested the tire for leaks. There weren't any. No kidding. They said they'd be happy to fix the lightbulb, but he didn't have an appointment for that until later that afternoon.

Are you kidding me? How many Belgian mechanics does it take to change a lightbulb, anyway?

I drove home, handed the keys to John and said, "I give up. You're in charge of getting the lightbulb changed."

And guess what? Just yesterday, the same lightbulb started making the clicky-clicky noise again. I think it's a conspiracy.

Sunday, September 1, 2013
P-R-O-C-R-A-S-T-I-N-A-T-I-O-N.

Procrastination: P-R-O-C-R-A-S-T-I-O-N. Procrastination. The putting off of something that should have been done a long time ago. Such as... buying school supplies for three kids. In French. My annual scavenger hunt.

This year, I procrastinated. I didn't even look at the lists until last week. But this year, I had a new plan. First, I had Avery sit down and read the lists and help me figure out what everything was. Then, I took all three kids to the store with me. I handed the older ones their lists and pointed them in the direction of the school supply aisles. Divide and conquer, I thought. Not really. It was a lot of me yelling "Focus" and, "No, Isabelle, you don't need [a stapler, whiteout tape, file cabinet—insert whatever-other-obnoxious-item-she-was-holding-at-that-particular-moment.] In the end, I never needed to call any sales staff for assistance. I was proud.

We still needed a few things, but I knew that Dreamland would have the grid paper both boys needed (specified 1cm squares) and a few other things. My confidence restored, we saved that task for later in the week.

Later in the week at a different store, I found myself staring at an empty shelf. I asked a clerk about the paper. She took me to the shelf I'd just been staring at, shook her head and said "pas encore" (no more) and then she ran. I'm not kidding, she ducked away from me before I could ask for anything else. I hadn't planned on asking for help with anything else, but she never would have given me a chance. I spotted her a few minutes later, hiding in a different aisle checking her watch. (It was almost lunch time.)

I guess it isn't just the moms that dread the back-to-school shopping.

This year's statistics so far: five different stores, two items to return/exchange and a couple more to get. I'll figure it all out. Eventually.

Even after all this time, I still miss Target.

Monday, September 2, 2013
Rocket Fuel.

File this entry under: Things that would never happen in the U.S.

Last spring, Luke's class finally got to go to Classes Vertes.

Each time they go, there is a theme. The first year Avery went, the theme was Robin Hood, and everything they learned was centered around the theme. This year, Luke's theme was science, and the first day the kids built a laboratory in the woods. They did all sorts of nature experiments and even learned basic chemistry.

One of the projects was to make a rocket using of a 2L bottle, fill it with a naturally made gasoline of some type, and then shoot it off into "space." Keep in mind that we weren't actually there, so this is all hearsay, but that's the extent of what I understood.

A few days after they got home and we were settled back into the routine of school, Luke told me he needed to bring a glass jar to school. Luke never remembers anything like that, and I was proud that he remembered something on his own. I was so proud, in fact, that I forgot to ask him why he needed a glass jar in the first place.

A few days later, he brought home his glass jar. It was filled with a strange purple liquid. "Be careful with that," he said, when he saw me pulling it out of his backpack. "That can't touch skin."

"Excuse me?" I said, "What do you mean by 'it can't touch skin'."

"Well," he explained, "my teacher said that if it touches our skin, we have exactly five seconds to wash it off with soap and water, and we don't want to know what happens if we don't."

"But what is it?" I asked.

"Rocket fuel," he answered. "I want to make rockets and fly them at home."

Huh. *And this came home with you in your backpack?*

The jar of purple liquid sat on a shelf for six weeks. I was afraid to dump it down the drain for fear of contaminating the general population's water supply. I assumed this was the very reason the teacher distributed it among the second graders. Every time Luke asked about flying a rocket, I had a million and ten other things for him to do instead. Mr. Wizard, I am not.

Luke has long forgotten about flying rockets at home, and so the mysterious purple liquid is now safely disposed of, along with its container. And next time Luke tells me he wants to take a jar to school, I will be sure to ask why.

Monday, September 16, 2013
Perspective

We've anticipated a move back to the U.S. for a while now. I think it's just something an expat learns to live with—that uncertainty that at any moment the phone could ring and life as you know it will change. I deal with it the way I deal with a lot of things—I live in the moment and enjoy and appreciate what I have while I have it.

In the back of my brain, the wheels are always turning and planning by getting rid of stuff I know we don't need. Besides, with a small house, everything in it has to be worth its weight. I've been good about cycling the stuff out while we've lived here.

Last spring, I discovered the beauty of an organized boot sale. Boot, meaning "trunk" for those of us who speak American English. Last spring, I purchased a parking space at the American Women's Club for 25 euros. In it, I could sell whatever I wanted. I made my entrance fee back with the sale of a stroller.

The next boot sale was on a Saturday at the American school. I took two car loads to that sale and I came home with less than half a car.

Of course, it is typical to chat with your neighbors when there aren't a lot of shoppers. My neighbor at the sale was a teacher at the school. She thought it was interesting that I wasn't a parent from the school and asked me a lot of questions about our expat experience in Belgium.

I explained that we were in the country indefinitely and when we arrived, the children were the perfect age for immersion so we chose a local French school. We wanted them to be able to play with their neighbors and join the local sports teams so we didn't always have to do everything with Americans. (Also, it was never an option for us because we couldn't afford the tuition anyway. But I didn't tell her that.)

I did tell her that we had a great experience in Belgium, we loved living here and our kids were happy and well-adjusted. She too was an expat (from another European country, I won't name it as I don't want to contribute to any stereotypes in any way). She had lived in Belgium for a long time and they had raised their family here. I explained we were anticipating a move in the near future. She proceeded to tell me how awful that would be for the children. It would be horrible to "rip" (her word) them out of the world that they knew and put them in a culture they didn't know or understand.

Ahem. Excuse me?

I explained to her that we felt very strongly that the value in our experience as expats was two-fold. The most valuable enrichment for the children would come after we moved back to the U.S. After they learned to live life in another country, they would better understand their own. After all, I explained, if we stay here, they will only be European, they won't have the other culture to compare it to. The comparison of both cultures provides the enrichment, the value. My husband and I have that, because we knew one first and then the other. The kids don't have that, yet. They only know one. The easy choice would be to stay here. But the growth will come from going back.

I also explained that one of the reasons we loved living here so much was because we knew that precious timer was ticking down and we wanted to enjoy it and appreciate it while we had the chance. Her response was something to the effect of, "Yeah, but that will suck."

At that moment, I heard my mother's voice in my ear and it said, "Only if you let it."

Tuesday, September 17, 2013
Perspective, Continued.

Following my "experience as an expat" conversation with the lady in the space next to me at the boot sale, I was glad I brought my laptop to work on edits for my book during the lulls.

At one point, she asked me what I was working on. She wondered if I was able to concentrate with everything else going on around me.

I explained. I was working on a mystery novel, and while the creative part (the writing of new words) needed quiet and solitude (or at least a cozy coffee shop) I had learned to edit amidst a plethora of distractions. I have three children, after all. I often have to do a lot of things admidst a plethora of distractions.

She asked if she could read my books anywhere yet—everyone always asks that when I tell them I am working on a book. I explained that first, I had to find an agent. Then, the agent had to sell it. (I've come to learn that writing the book itself is actually the easiest part of the process.)

She looked at me, and I could almost see a thought bubble above her head that said, "You are insane."

I got more of her wisdom. Essentially, she told me I was doing too much work for something I might not ever get paid to do. (I so want to tell you her nationality right now, but again, I won't contribute to stereotypes.)

I patiently explained that writing was something I did because it was my passion. Something I lived to do. Something that, if I didn't do, I would probably explode. I explained that most days, I would rather write my own stories than watch television or read a book.

She looked at me skeptically and raised a single eyebrow.

I smiled politely, opened my laptop and got to work. I was so very grateful I had remembered to bring it.

At the time, I was annoyed I had to explain myself to her. I even felt sorry for this lady, who obviously held a narrow view of the world and her place in it. Now, though, I look back on the conversation and I am grateful for it. Because now we are living the reality of an upcoming move, and I am receiving one rejection letter after another. The days have brought more discouragement than not. But I think back to this conversation and it reminds me why I'm doing what I am doing.

Anytime we have a chance to stop and reflect on our purpose, it's a good thing.

Thursday, October 3, 2013
Unbelievably Lucky.

I feel very lucky today. Well, I feel lucky every day I wake up in Belgium. But today, I feel even luckier.

Today, I took the kids to school, and tonight, they will all stay with friends overnight. I feel lucky that we have friends here who are willing to take our kids for an overnight. I feel equally lucky that I know our kids will behave and not be too much trouble (hopefully). Luke was a little weepy this morning when I left. But I handed him off to his third-grade teacher who had managed to turn his tears into a smile before I even walked away. I feel lucky that Luke has such a good teacher this year, even if it's just for a few months.

After drop-off, I drove to the La Hulpe train station and boarded the train to Brussels. I feel lucky to live in a city with trains. At Gare du Midi, I cleared customs and boarded a Eurostar train to London. I feel lucky to live close enough to London that I can take a train and get there before lunch.

I am going to London today, because fifteen years ago, I married a guy, who had a passion to see the world as well as a gift for talking to people. Specifically, he has this amazing talent for connecting with people from other countries and cultures. This guy took me to London for our honeymoon and it was our first trip abroad together. I remember riding the train into London from the airport, watching the gardens and houses rush past, thinking, "I could live here someday."

For the past five years—one third of our marriage—that dream came true. Tonight, I'm meeting John in London for a date night. We have tickets to Les Miserables, a show (my favorite) that we saw on our honeymoon.

I'm on the train now, and everyone around me is talking about where they will go first when they get to London. Which museum? Which neighborhood? The Italian guys near me have a map spread out between the four of them, and their conversation is intense.

It occurred to me, that this is the first time I will go to London, and I don't want to "see" anything. The first thing I'm going to do when I get to London is go for a run. I've always wanted to run the loop around the bridges between Covent Garden and Big Ben. But I've never brought my running stuff because there is never enough time. Or we walk too much and I'm too tired.

Today, I feel really lucky I'm going to London just because I can. I feel lucky that John and I can celebrate our anniversary in a city that is so special to us. When I get there, I don't need to "see" anything, and I will have time to go for a run.

Sunday, October 20, 2013
Roadways and Roundabouts – Revisited

When we first moved here, learning to navigate the roads with all the obstacles, roundabouts and speed bumps was challenging.

As you might imagine, Saturday and Sunday mornings sometimes reveal carnage from the late-night drivers from the night before: tire tracks in the flowerbed of a roundabout; pieces of a broken headlight combined with a missing chunk of cement from an obstacle; or even a fallen streetlight. In all fairness, if you aren't familiar with the streets, the roadblocks aren't always easy to see in the dark whether you've had a few drinks or not.

On our house-hunting trip almost six-years ago, I remember feeling like I was riding with Jason Bourne. My husband zipped our little rental car up and down the side streets like he was being chased. He might have had fun weaving in and out of roadblocks, and bouncing over speed bumps, but I remember gripping onto my seat and yelling at him to slow down.

It's funny, as we get ready to move, I am coming face-to-face with a lot of new expats just arriving. After all, I have to sell everything in our house that plugs into a wall, and new expats are buying everything for their house that plugs into a wall. It's a symbiotic relationship. Part of me is jealous that they are just beginning their experience, as ours is coming to a close.

The other part of me feels the way I felt when I was a college senior—it was fun while it lasted, but it is time to be done. Connecting with new expats also provides me with a fun reflection on my thoughts and feelings when we first arrived, as compared to now.

A recent Facebook post from a new expat friend reminded me about how scary it was to drive here in the beginning. Last week, there was a morning where everyone got out of the house without drama. Everyone remembered lunch boxes, swim bags, and we were even on time. That morning, I slowed down to the perfect speed to go over the speed bumps and no one hit their heads. My car wove in and around the roadblocks in perfect sync with oncoming drivers. I waved my gratitude to the cars that paused when they were supposed to yield. I zipped around the roundabouts at a smooth pace so as to be considerate of Luke's sensitive tummy.

It felt like I was in a fine-tuned choreographed dance. One that is soon coming to an end.

Monday, November 4, 2013
Trick-Or-Treat: Halloween Fun from Abroad...

We have learned that there are three American holidays that are particularly painful to celebrate from abroad. This is mostly because the rest of the world goes about their lives as if it is just another ordinary day, while we, as expats, know it shouldn't be. You can probably guess the holidays: Fourth of July, Thanksgiving and yes, Halloween.

We've solved the dilemmas of Thanksgiving and Fourth of July. Fourth of July is easy, we just make sure we are on holiday (usually to the U.S.). Thanksgiving is the most painful, but we've solved it as well by celebrating with a big turkey dinner on the Sunday before or after, and we usually invite friends who have never celebrated Thanksgiving before (Belgian friends, or our British neighbors). Thanksgiving Day, the kids have school but John usually has the day off. We've created our own tradition which involves a lunch date and some major Christmas shopping.

Of the three, the expat community rallies the hardest for Halloween. While trick-or-treat night is never on Halloween there are two neighborhoods that host trick-or-treating the week before. We usually choose the one closest to us. The houses are closer together and we can cover the neighborhood quickly, knocking on about fifteen doors within an hour or so. (Yes, I said fifteen.)

This year, after our trick-or-treat outing, Avery held up his little sandwich-sized bag of candy with a big grin on his face and said, "Look at how much I got!"

I laughed, and said, "Just wait until next year." He didn't believe me when I told him he'd have to bring a pillowcase.

Wednesday, November 6, 2013
Full Circle, Part One

We haven't done much traveling around Europe with our little family. John and I traveled Europe before we had kids, before we moved here. We have always said that our move here was about the experience of living in Belgium. That said, we still had a short bucket list of places we wanted to take the kids. When time and the tight budget allows, we try to choose destinations that the kids will remember.

One of the destinations forever on our list was Austria, and more specifically, Salzburg. When my husband, John, was in college, he worked hard to earn himself a place in the study abroad trip to Salzburg, Austria. He stayed at the home of an older couple, the Peskas, with three other friends. At the time, they were 70 years old. It was there he learned to speak German, just by talking to them at their kitchen table. He fell in love with Europe and discovered a passion for connecting with people from other cultures.

Salzburg is an eight-hour drive from Brussels, which seems really far with little kids. We pushed it to the bottom of the bucket list, in favor of other destinations: warm, sunny Spain and easy-to-get-to London. But here we are, with a time-clock ticking, and one last week of precious school vacation. We threw together a six-day road trip adventure (cue the music from the Chevy Chase Vacation movies).

We rented a minivan and drove to Salzburg. My husband has seen a lot of the world. There are not many places where he walks around in awe. One of the first times I saw his eyes gloss over in amazement was at the Rock of Gibraltar. Another time was in Tel Aviv. After arriving in Salzburg, he walked through town that night in complete wonder, with a look of nostalgia in his eyes.

We went out for dinner and by the time we returned to the hotel, it was obvious John needed to wander around by himself for a while to reminisce. I happily volunteered to stay with the kids. In his wanderings, he emailed and called some friends from his study-abroad group. He learned that his "house frau" might still be alive.

The next day, we hopped on the bus, and rode the route he used to take home from school. We walked down a little street and around a corner. John rang the bell on the gate. There, we saw an old woman peer out of the window of the little house. She opened the door. Upon seeing John, she threw her arms to the heavens and said, "Johann. My Johann." She is 93 years old.

It was pretty cool.

We followed her into the house and she gave each of the kids a bottle of soda. She cut up a cake (that the kids later said tasted like cardboard). She made us coffee, and insisted Johann drink a beer. She talked to us in German. The children listened to their daddy tell stories that we had heard before, but meant so much more sitting in the house where they happened.

For all of us to get to meet Kathe Peske in person, and see the kitchen table that sparked a passion in John that grew into an expat experience for our little family, was priceless and worth every hour we spent in the car last week.

Friday, November 8, 2013
Full Circle, Part Two

When it comes to World War II history, we make all sorts of necessary exceptions to our travel budget.

WWII is not something many Americans think much about anymore. But it has always been a big part of our family history. John's grandfather was killed crossing a river in France. We live in what was an occupied country during the war, and we are only an hour's drive from where the Battle of the Bulge was fought. Add the phenomenal HBO series, The Band of Brothers, to the mix and you've got yourself a bucket list of WWII sites.

The Eagle's Nest, Obersalzberg, just outside of Berchtesgaden, Germany, is where Hitler went to relax and kick his feet up. It's up in the mountains, not far from Salzburg. It's also a place John had never seen (which is rather unusual these days) and, it's featured in an episode of the Band of Brothers. We decided to go there before checking into our hotel in Salzburg. The town itself was beautiful, and we took our time wandering around before finding the road to Hitler's famous hideaway.

We wound our way up and up and up through the rain and clouds until we got to the parking lot. We found the ticket booth, and watched, as a bus pulled away and headed up the mountain. (You have to take the bus or hike, they won't let cars drive the whole way.) The "kind" (and I use that term loosely) woman at the ticket window told us we had just watched the last bus drive away. When John pointed to the times on the boards and asked her about the bus at 4:35 (in German) she "kindly" explained that what was supposed to be the last bus, was cancelled due to weather conditions. We looked at our watches to see that it was 4:15. Maybe there was a big blizzard coming in the next seven minutes that we didn't know about?

Ok, no problem. We would be in Salzburg for a couple of days, we would come back on our way out of town. The day we left Salzburg, was gloriously sunny. The view from the mountains was incredible. We dressed in our hiking boots and filled our backpacks, planning to park and walk up to Hitler's palace. When we got to the ticket booth, we were told by another "kind" employee that we missed the very, very last bus, two days before by five minutes (the one that we saw pull away). She also explained that the house itself was closed for the season, it was a three-hour hike, and that they were doing dangerous tree work in the mountains and she couldn't guarantee our safety. So instead, we went to the museum (mostly because we all had to use the toilet).

We've seen a lot of WWII sites throughout Europe, but this was our first from the German perspective. We didn't like it much. After walking through the doors, the very first photos were graphic, confirming that we will never go to see a concentration camp. The story boards that lined the halls to the bunker, highlighted propaganda and made me sick to my stomach. Something that struck me immediately was that nothing, nothing at all, was in English.

With the exception of the Charter of the United Nations. I took out my phone to take a photo, to Avery's horror. (He pointed out all of the "no photo" signs and the video camera.) "Ok, thanks," I said, and moved to an angle so as not to be seen by the overhead camera. "Let them try and make me delete the words of the United Nations."

I'm not an American who expects everything to be in English. We work hard to try to speak the language of the country we are visiting. Between John and myself, we can cover French, German and Spanish and we encourage the kids speak a few words of Flemish if and when we need it (to their utter embarrassment). But most of the war sites we've visited have paid tribute to the Americans using English captions. Not here. With the attitudes of the "kind" employees and the lack of English, I was starting to feel like our little American family wasn't very welcome.

In the end, I think it was good that we never made it to the top. I didn't need to see Hitler's golden elevator or hear any more about the riches he pilfered.

Friday, November 8, 2013
What Do You Mean We Can Eat Those?

The last stop of our big European road trip was Strasbourg, France to visit our dear friends who used to live in Belgium but moved back to Strasbourg. They have become our adopted family; their kids are like the cousins we don't have here. We wanted, no, needed, to visit them one last time before we moved back to the U.S.

We love our trips to Strasbourg. Whenever we go, we always get to do something we've never done before. Once we took a hike to the sacred site of Saint Odile. Another time we made tarte flambee (flat pizzas from Alsace) in an outdoor oven while the children played along the river. This time, we went on a hike in the woods to hunt for mushrooms.

We went to the secret spot known within their family to be a good place to find mushrooms. The children have all studied mushrooms in school, Isabelle has been talking about different kinds of mushrooms for weeks. But John and I had no clue what we were looking for. I'd always been told, "Don't ever touch a mushroom in the woods, it's poisonous." This whole outing was a little out of my comfort zone, But I trusted my friends and their knowledge of edible wild mushrooms.

We didn't find much within the first hour. Every single mushroom I pointed out was deemed poisonous, thus reaffirming my original strategy: don't ever touch mushrooms in the woods. But then we found a bunch of good ones growing out of a stump—little yellow ones with the right caps—I can't remember now if they were curved in or out—it makes a difference. And we found others, known as "pieds du mouton" (translation: sheep feet) said to be very expensive in the grocery store.

By the end of our outing, we had bags filled with edible mushrooms. We ate them all for dinner and they were wonderful. That night I had nightmares about mushroom poisoning and dreamt that we woke up dead. But we all woke up just fine the next day, so there was really nothing to worry about.

However, I don't think I'll ever go foraging for mushrooms without a trusted expert. I will start buying some of the more exotic mushrooms in the grocery stores.

Friday, November 8, 2013
The Hills Are Alive...

My first trip to Europe was a backpacking adventure with Sally before law school and Salzburg was one of our destinations. I had just begun dating John, and he probably would have broken up with if I was planning a trip to Germany and Austria without making a stop in his favorite city.

We had another reason for visiting Salzburg on that trip: The Sound of Music Tour. When I was a little girl, The Sound of Music was on television every year at Christmas and it was always a special night. I was allowed to stay up late. I remember acting out the scene where Gretal sings the goodnight song and falls asleep on the steps. As I got older, I daydreamed I was Liesl singing with her boyfriend. (I cannot believe that I just admitted that, but it's true.) Here's a fun fact from the Sound of Music Tour: they've had to close the gazebo to tourists (you can only see it from afar to take photos) because they've had too many people get injured trying to re-enact the dance. Apparently, I'm not the only one with that particular daydream.

Anyway, we've had the movie here for years, and we've always meant to watch it with the kids but never did. In anticipation of our Salzburg trip, we planned a special family Sunday afternoon movie day.

Isabelle was in awe of the singing and dancing. The boys liked it much more than they (and I) expected. But then again, they have a much better understanding of the Nazis than I ever did as a kid.

On our European road trip adventure, after Munich and before Salzburg, temperaments among the passengers were beginning to waver. In a moment of mischievousness, John and I pulled out the movie soundtrack. I laughed to myself thinking about how we had given the kids the perfect "remember when we were driving into Salzburg and mom made us listen to the soundtrack for the Sound of Music?" Seriously, though, I double-dog-dare you to listen to that music and NOT start singing along and feel better about being in the car. Especially if you are driving through the actual hills themselves.

In the end I was so glad we thought to show them the movie and bring the music in the car. Isabelle skipped her way to dinner the first night singing, "I am 16 going on 17..." And when we walked through the park where "Doe A Deer" was filmed, even though it was dark and rainy, she shouted, "This is where they jumped up and down the steps singing!" I was grateful I took the cheesy tour so many years before, and could point everything out.

She watched the movie on my laptop no less than five times throughout the entire week. What a great movie to have on a road trip—it's a long one.

This last vacation was one we will remember forever.

Wednesday, November 13, 2013
One Thing After Another...

We began last week with cash flow problems. Getting paid in one part of the world and getting the money to a bank account in another is something we've learned to deal with while living here. But on November 1, something at our bank changed with respect to international wire transfers (either a law or an internal bank rule, not sure which). When John tried to make his regularly monthly transfer, he was told, "It might take us a few weeks to sort through the new rules." His reply was something along the lines of, "No it won't."

It turns out it wasn't such a good idea to rent a car and leave ours home for the week. We live next door to a forest. I'm not kidding, there is a twelve-foot hedge along the back drive, and behind it is a forest. If you look up our address on a map app, you will see a giant estate, complete with its own chateau and private lake. It belongs to a wealthy Belgian citizen, and is home to an abundance of critters that don't usually cross the threshold of their kingdom.

The wildlife here is mysterious and keeps to itself. In Minnesota, you can tell a lot about the wildlife by the roadkill—squirrels, deer or an occasional skunk. That doesn't happen as much here. For one, there aren't as many animals (I think they were hunted to the point of near extinction long ago.) Also, there are many fences, tall hedges and walls that keep the wildlife fenced into a certain area, minimizing the roadkill quite nicely.

One animal we've heard about, but have never seen, is a type of weasel-ferret-thing that lives in the woods. We've heard about them because they supposedly likes to climb into car engines and eat the wires. That always sounded like the sort of thing that happens "to someone else," so we filed it away under the category: "stuff not to worry about." We didn't think twice about leaving our car in our back driveway for a week. We should have…

By Tuesday last week, all of the electrical power went out in our car and it wouldn't accelerate. A quick peek under the hood revealed that some critter had quite a feast at our expense. We had to have the car towed to the dealer Tuesday morning. On Tuesday night, John left for a quick trip to London.

By Wednesday morning, I felt like I could get a job as a delivery service dispatcher. I sat in my kitchen, and with my laptop and phone managed to coordinate all of the comings and goings of my children. I managed to get everyone—not just to and from school—but also to most of their extracurricular activities…without a car.

Mid-morning, my neighbor asked if I needed a ride to the grocery store, which I happily accepted. When I got back, a mouse walked into the kitchen as if it were asking me to make him lunch. My scream sent him scurrying away, somewhere into the living room. I settled down enough to sit down at my computer in the kitchen, and that's when I looked out the window to see the large rat amble down the sidewalk as if he were out for a midday stroll. Obviously under siege, I ran back to the neighbor's house and he promised to take me to the hardware store for traps as soon as Avery got home.

I bought a little wire cage-trap, with a spring-trapdoor and two sides. The trap lets you catch two mice at once, without killing them. And while this is the more humane option, I bought it because I didn't want to deal with seeing carnage on top of everything else. Plus, my neighbor promised to help me set them free if I caught anything.

That afternoon, Avery and I locked ourselves in the kitchen and strained our ears trying to hear the trap go off in the other room. We kept watch out the front window for the larger vermin. Our wait was in vain, and our trap sat empty through the night. The next morning, I sent the kids off to school with a neighbor, and went down to start a load of laundry. I startled a mouse who scrambled into a dark corner. Excited, I got my trap and put it in the corner. An hour later I had two mice. By Friday morning, I had two more. I named them Eeny, Meeny, Miney and Moe and they have been resettled at an internment camp somewhere in the woods near the creek behind the rugby field. Thanks to my neighbor.

By Friday night, the traps remained empty, and we had our car back. My neighbor's cat needed shelter from the rain (did I mention the rain didn't stop once last week?) so I happily let him sit in my kitchen to wait for his people to get home. I was up to the double, if not triple digits, in counting my many blessings. One of which was the borrowed cat. I also added "ferrel cats" to my list of "reasons I'm excited to move back to St. Paul." Sometimes, the bad stuff has to happen so we can see how good we have it. Friends and neighbors step forward to help. You get through it and are glad when it's over. Peace settled on our house once more and all was right with the world.

For about ten minutes.

Thursday, November 14, 2013
When It Rains, It Pours...

Do you ever feel like the Universe is messing with you?

By the time John picked up the boys from football (soccer) practice on Friday night, he could barely get the car home. The electric went out again and the car wouldn't accelerate (not good, but especially not good in a town with a lot of hills). The dealership had closed thirty minutes before, and the mechanics wouldn't be in again until Tuesday morning. It was a holiday weekend (Armistice Day). We spent a long rainy weekend waiting, looking out the window at a car we couldn't drive.

On Sunday, two more mice showed up in the kitchen. We've since figured out their traffic pattern—they come in from a small hole under the dishwasher, and disappear through a similar hole under the refrigerator. It appears as if our kitchen is a mouse super highway. Yet the trap in the corner remains empty. These mice seem smarter than their predecessors, and if we hadn't seen them for ourselves, we would have no way of even knowing they'd been there.

Tuesday morning arrived with more rain and a tow truck. It was the same driver from last week. One of the blessings from the list I mentioned in the previous post? The emergency tow service John signed us up for last year. (Unlimited FREE Towing, equals huge.) With a confused look, the tow truck driver said (in French), "This seems familiar." "No kidding," was my answer.

When John arrived home from taking the kids to school, we discovered that our internet was down. We began to feel like Belgium was sending us a message: "Get Out."

I eavesdropped for the next several hours as John tried to work out the internet issue with various online assistants. I try not to complain about customer service here in Belgium. I don't expect Belgium to be the same as the United States, and I have learned there are cultural differences that translate to different expectations, especially with customer service. Also, as with everything, sometimes people are helpful while others are not no matter where you are in the world.

This particular company is notorious for poor customer service. With everything else we've been dealing with lately, I was impressed by the patience my husband managed to find throughout the day. (I heard a few random, loud swear words, here and there, but never when he was on the phone, which, when you read further you will know would have been justified.) We reached a point during the afternoon, where there was nothing to do but laugh and ask each other, "Is this really happening?"

Here are a couple of my favorite excerpts from those eavesdropped moments to customer service:

1. "Ok, I've got a stack of bills here from the last six months with multiple passwords and codes, but not the e-code that you are asking for. Is there any other way I can prove to you that I am authorized to access this account?" (The answer was no.)

Side note: After that particular call, I heard ten straight minutes of really loud Led Zeppelin coming from John's office.

2. After driving to Waterloo in search of a new modem, the store manager announced to the six people waiting with broken modems, that they were out of modems. John called the service line again, to suggest that the service tech bring the necessary modem to the appointment the next day. The agent, instead, suggested that John drive to a store in Antwerp "to see if they had one." (He did not.)

By the end of the day, the internet was back up and running (thanks to John's patience and perseverance). Today, the sun is shining. A phone call to the car dealer revealed that they think they know exactly what is wrong with the car, finally, and we should have it back tomorrow. While I'm not holding my breath, it's a more hopeful answer than we've had in the past ten days.

Belgium, if you are trying to make it easier for me to leave, I appreciate your efforts. But it's too late. I have loved every minute of living here, even when those minutes seem like they are trying to teach me something. Nothing you do now will change that.

But I would appreciate it if you'd stop trying.

Tuesday, November 19, 2013
The Kitchen of Death.

Catchy title, huh? I bet it made you want to jump right in and read this blog post.

I figured out what happened to the MIA mouse/mice.

My first clue came from the horrific stench coming from the cabinet under the sink. And by horrific, I mean, one of the worst smells imaginable. It started small, and grew, and grew...and grew some more.

I first noticed it on Thursday. Let's see, that's about four days after the last known mouse or mouse poop sighting. My mystery writing research has yet to lead me to a search for "decomposition rates and factors" but if Law & Order/CSI episodes count for anything (which I'm not sure they do) four days would be about right for a stench like that? I really don't have any idea, I just knew that it smelled and it had been awhile since we'd seen anything scurrying about.

By Friday, I was compelled to pull everything out from the cupboard under the sink, just to make it stop. With trembling, plastic-covered hands, I pulled every bottle out of the glass recycling. I replaced the PMC recycling bag. I took the paper and cardboard out of the recycling box, piece by piece. My theory (at that point) was that the mouse crawled into one of the containers and got stuck. My oldest watched in amazement and told me I had a lot of courage. So, I guess there's that. But to both my horror, and relief, there was no dead, stuck mouse.

Huh.

The mouse poop told me that a mouse had been there, but was long gone. I cleaned everything with bleach laden products and put everything back, stumped. How does a mouse just die?

And then, my mystery-writer-lawyer-fact-finding-brain figured it out. You see, a few years ago, we got a new dishwasher. And when they installed it, the holes for the screws didn't line up with the holes in the wall in exactly the same way. Unconcerned, the installers said, "Meh, don't worry about it, it will be fine." (But in French.) When we had to have the dishwasher serviced a few months later (because a bolt of lightning shorted out the electric) the serviceman said the same thing. When my cousin, who grew up on a farm and is a descendant of my grandfather, (which means he can fix ANYTHING) looked at it and said, "There's no way to fix it."

We gave up. The result, is that when the dishwasher is really full, when the racks are open, the entire dishwasher tips forward, just a little, sending the plates crashing into each other.

Back to my theory. One day, when the dishwasher was really full, it tipped forward with the loud crashing noise it makes when it does this. Any little mousy critters hiding underneath, found themselves in the relatively open space, and scooted back up against and under the dishwasher. When the dishwasher was shut and therefore straightened back into its rightful position...well. You can probably guess. The mousy critters got squashed. Which elevates my personal philosophy that "everything happens for a reason" to a whole new level.

This leads me to my next question. How long does this horrid stench last? An internet search revealed interesting information. One post said that a dead mouse smells like "death." Um. Yeah. Thanks, that helps a lot. But I guess now I know what death smells like. The consensus seemed to be that one tiny mouse, supposedly, equals two days of smell (longer for more, or other, larger dead things). Um....let me just point out with a big shiver that we're going on Day SEVEN here. Another post said the only way to get rid of the smell of a dead mouse in the wall was to cut a hole and find it. Hmm. Go ahead and ask me how excited I am to yank the dishwasher out of the way to retrieve the seven-day-old decomposing carcass of one (or probably more) dead mice (or possibly other large rodent-type-animal that starts with the letter "R" and I won't let my kids say out loud in my presence). Go ahead. Ask me.

Another poster replied that if a mouse dies in the wall, you could feasibly end up with ten or more holes in the wall because there is no way to know for sure if you have the right spot, and it's better just to wait. A big shout out to that voice of reason! Ok, let's just assume, for all intents and purposes, that there is no possible way to reach the dead rodent.

Some tips for getting rid of the smell included heat and candles, they help to dry out the rotting dead thing and burn the odor out of the air. My radiator in the kitchen is set as high as it will go. I pulled out every candle I owned and have kept a candle vigil going in the kitchen for the last 24 hours (but obviously only when we are home and awake). I don't need to start my kitchen on fire.

As I write this, my kitchen is about 100 degrees and smells like a melding blend of cornflower-blueberry-cinnamon-apple pie-vanilla-pine tree...and let's not forget...death.

Sigh.

At least I have my car back and I can leave to go get takeaway for dinner?

Tomorrow is another day. And I hope that one of these days, I can stop saying that.

Thursday, November 28, 2013
Our Very Own Turkey Trot.

I have vivid memories from my childhood of my mother before Thanksgiving. She would pour over recipe books, trying to find something new and special. She would make multiple trips to the grocery store in search of the perfect ingredients and fill the refrigerator with all sorts of strange and exotic things.

I love going to John's family's house before a big holiday, I like seeing all of his mother's lists everywhere. One of my favorite holiday memories at their house was realizing that his mother was checking her list just before we all sat down to eat, to make sure she didn't forget anything.

Last Saturday was a typical Saturday. There were football (soccer) matches to coordinate, household tasks to catch up on, that sort of thing. I went for a run between matches, and when I got back John said, "Maybe we should do Thanksgiving tomorrow?" I stopped and stared.

Of all of the holidays, Thanksgiving is the hardest to replicate in Belgium. John had been traveling all week. We hadn't talked about Thanksgiving. I didn't plan for a dinner and I just assumed our Thanksgiving dinner would be next weekend.

During our time here, I've learned that when you really want, or desperately need to find something at a grocery store in Belgium, it's almost guaranteed you won't be able to find it. We don't exactly have Butterball turkeys lining the cooler cases here, if you know what I mean. Ocean Spray cranberry sauce? Not on your life. Stove Top? Nope. The last two items are usually a non-issue. These are always premeditated, and this year were imported on John's last trip from the U.S. That left the most critical element to fate. Oh, and don't forget, stores here are closed on Sunday. There would be no second chances.

I felt like I'd been handed my very own Amazing Race challenge: Find a turkey in the grocery store, somewhere in Belgium in the next 45 minutes. Ready? Go.

It might have been the sports labels I was wearing that made me say this, but I turned to John and said, "Ok, let's do it." I called Luke into the kitchen. "We're leaving for your football match now, I have to stop at the store first." I called to Isabelle, "Let's go," I said, "We're going on a mission!" We all hurried out the door.

I need to stop and explain something else. Here in Belgium, women do not wear workout gear to the grocery store. Ever. I was committing a major fashion faux pas by leaving the house in my running clothes, and *gasp* baseball hat. But it was all in the name of pulling together a major American holiday. I figured I was wearing the perfect outfit.

There are two grocery stores in La Hulpe. One was recently remodeled so I ruled it out immediately—ever since they moved everything around, I am completely confused when I go in there and I can't find anything. I didn't want to waste precious minutes trying to find a turkey. We tried the other store and got our potatoes. I found turkey, but it was a small breast. And get this (I'm warning you, don't choke) it was 10 euros for .3 kg. (Don't miss the decimal point.) In any event, it would work in a pinch. If I found nothing else, I could come back and cough up a lot of money for a tiny piece of "dinde" (French turkey) and maybe throw in some chicken pieces for good measure.

We dropped Luke at the field for his warmup, and synchronized our watches. We had approximately 30 minutes to get back to La Hulpe before John needed the car to go back to Luke's match. We headed to Waterloo, the neighborhood of the American school and home to a lot of expats. If we were going to find a turkey within a time limit the weekend before Thanksgiving, I knew it would be there. Holding hands, Isabelle and I ran into a store. We saw a friend from school, "We can't stop to talk," we gasped, "we're trying to find a turkey for our Thanksgiving dinner!" No turkey at that store.

We went to the "big" store. Way in the back, we found what would be our Thanksgiving turkey. But it was all in bits. I spent 20 euros on a breast, and two leg parts. But we had turkey. Isabelle and I high-fived each other and went home to share the good news. We had managed to "piece" together Thanksgiving in 45 minutes. That has to be some sort of expat record.

Sunday, we had our turkey dinner. With the leftovers planned for dinner tonight, I am thankful for so many things in my life. But I am especially thankful for this experience, the perspective it has provided, and how much I appreciate the little things I never thought to think about before—like having turkey to eat on Thanksgiving.

Tuesday, December 3, 2013
I Want my Two Stamps. Please.

Loyalty programs and points are a big deal here. I roll my eyes when I think about how much money I have to spend before I earn a bonus certificate worth five euros. But, here, we can buy wine at the grocery store. And here, five euros can buy a decent bottle of French wine. So maybe it's ok to get excited about a little bonus if it means free wine.

One day not long ago, I went to the information desk at the grocery store to claim my free wine. I mean, five euros. A mother and her little girl were in line in front of me. Whenever I am in line at the grocery store, I eavesdrop. (In the name of French practice, just to see how much I can understand.) This woman was in a polite argument with the store clerk. It was about how the ad posted a savings of 56 cents (or something similar) and the receipt showed that she had just paid full price for the item.

You might say, "Are you serious?" Is it really worth the 56 cents to stand in line and argue about it? But the thing is, this happens all of the time here. I read an ad, I chose a product at the store based on what I read on the ad, only to realize later that I paid full price. Or the little sale signs that are posted throughout the store? I've learned that I ALWAYS have to check the date in the fine print on the sign. Frequently, it's a promotion that ended the day before, or for a special that starts the next day. I was raised to be a bargain hunter and I like a deal (and they don't happen often here). But I don't like to be tricked into buying two of something.

When this mother gave me a small, apologetic smile for how long it was taking for the store clerk to check the ad, I smiled back and thought, "You go girl. You get your 56 cents in the name of all of us who have ever been scammed in the same way." Which is, actually, all of us.

Last week, I had my turn. I know I am dating myself as a child of the 80's, but do you remember the movie "Better Off Dead" and the kid on the bicycle? The one who runs around for the entire movie yelling, "I want my two dollars?" That was me last week only I wanted Christmas tree stamps. One of the grocery stores is doing this promotion for

Christmas. If you spend 20 euros you get a Christmas tree stamp. And after you save 25 stamps, you get five euros off your purchase. Please don't tell me the math equation because it's all just too ridiculous for five euros. But not for free French wine.

Anyway. Last week, I only needed two more stamps to fill in my Christmas tree card. We are trying to clear out our cupboards, so I haven't spent a lot with each trip to the grocery store, making those two stamps a challenge. But when I went through the store for a few quick things I noticed that if I bought a pack of the bottled water I usually buy, I would get two stamps. I read the fine print. AND I even pulled out my phone to double check the date. Yep. Two stamps, coming my way.

When I paid for my groceries, and didn't get any stamps, I asked for them. (Because that's the other thing they sometimes do, not give you your stamps unless you ask for them.) The clerk looked at my ticket and said, "Sorry, you don't get any stamps," (but in French). I politely explained, "But the sign on the shelf said I would get two stamps if I bought this today (only my French wasn't as good as hers, but she understood).

Then, she made everyone wait (she was the only open check-out lane) while she got out her weekly shoppers and read them. All of them. That's when I gave everyone in line my polite apologetic smile. She didn't find it and shook her head, probably hoping I would go on my merry way. But dang it, I was right, and I knew it. That doesn't happen very often to me in Belgium. So I said again, "But the sign said two stamps." She called for back-up and started ringing up the next customer.

The guy answered her page, she quickly explained "the problem." He went all the way to the far back corner of the store to look for the alleged sign. Several minutes later, he returned and held up two fingers with a nod. (I did an imaginary fist pump in my head. *Yes! I was right. I knew it!*) She tore off two little Christmas tree stamps from her roll of about 320 and handed them over.

Sometimes, you just have to fight for it when you know you are right.

Tuesday, December 17, 2013
'Tis the Season...

'Tis the season...for a transcontinental move.

A few weeks ago, I had to go into Dreamland (a local store that is sort of like the best Target departments: books, games, toys, school supplies and seasonal stuff. I needed a birthday present. The parking lot was cram-packed, and when I walked through the door, a quick glance at the check-out lanes revealed lines of 15-20 people.

Yikes. What the heck was going on?

I realized: It was lunch hour, and it was the week before Saint Nicolas Day.

Saint Nicolas Day seemed like such a minor entry on the list in my jumbled head, I almost forgot all about it.

As I've explained, in Belgium, children get their presents from Saint Nicolas on December 6, instead of Santa Clause on December 25. When Isabelle came home from school this year, with a Barbie house on her Saint Nicolas List, I explained the Christmas territory concept. (Saint Nicolas brings presents to the kids in Belgium, Santa brings presents to the American kids). She looked at me like I had three heads. I added in the fact that Saint Nicolas knew that we were moving before Christmas and any gifts he brought would have to be small enough to fit in a suitcase or else she would have to wait for our cargo shipment (six weeks) to get to play with it.

Whatever. Saint Nicolas brought us a bunch of French books and CD's this year, and everyone was disappointed (except Avery who is suddenly into French Pop music).

But it got me thinking about how the meaning of Christmas was going to be very different for our family this year. And how maybe, I could make that a good thing.

Wednesday, January 1, 2014
The Meaning of Advent....Fail. Or Maybe Not?

I knew all along that Christmas would be different this year. With the movers arriving on December 10, we wouldn't even have our own tree. Childhood goes so quickly. The boxes of decorations and ornaments stacked in the basement would go a whole year without being opened.

Part of me worried we were stealing a year of Christmas memories away from our kids.

The other part of me rallied to make the best of it. I repeated the lesson of the Grinch: Christmas isn't about the wrappings, it comes anyway. (Only Dr. Seuss was more eloquent and rhymed it better.) I looked at those boxes and decided that our focus this Christmas would be on Advent. We would bring the Advent calendars with us in our suitcases, and count down the days to Baby Jesus no matter where we were.

We have three advent calendars at our house. We got off to a good start. The movers arrived on the morning of the 10th and everything turned into a whirlwind.

Before they arrived, I thought our pack-up would take forever. But these guys were even better than our American packers. They were Flemish. And organized. They arrived at our door at 7:30 in the morning, smoked a cigarette and came right inside and got to work. That first day, I made John take the kids to school so I could keep an eye on them and finish our suitcases.

I learned a lesson with our first move: make sure you have the suitcases packed before the movers show up. Otherwise, the important stuff (like maybe your underwear drawer) might accidentally get packed into the container. I vowed not to make that mistake this time. However, no matter how many times I told Johnny to pack *his* suitcases, he still hadn't. "How can I think about what I need to pack for the next six weeks?" he said to me every time.

Before he got back that morning, I called him to say, "You'd better figure it out quick because I can't keep track of all these guys at the same time and one of them went upstairs and I don't know what he's doing."

In all of that chaos, I forgot the one thing about Christmas I was going to salvage—the Advent calendars. All but one got packed when I wasn't looking. I did save the candy filled Christmas tree. That was good. We weren't allowed any sort of food items in our shipments. That would be all we needed—for our container to get flagged at customs thanks to a few pieces of chocolate and gummies in a Christmas tree box.

In any event, the suitcases and boxes all got packed. Soon, we were on our way in a journey that would end up taking a long time, with many emotional ups and downs. We shifted our focus ahead to Christmas. Not to the trimmings and trappings, but to our family. For the first time in six years, we would get to spend Christmas with our families. That was our anchor through the next few, very difficult, weeks.

Wednesday, January 22, 2014
Moving Out.

In Belgium, when you move out of a rental property, you have to leave it in pristine condition. And by pristine, I mean sparkling. The good news, is that the designated life of a paint job is six years (which we were short of by just a few months). We already knew they wouldn't be able to charge us for all the places that Isabelle wrote her name in crayon. (As long as it was on a wall.)

Over the years, we had heard plenty of stories from neighbors that had moved on, to know that our landlords are very, very difficult at the final walk-through. Their goal is to try to keep your entire deposit (which is double, if not triple a standard deposit in the U.S.). We already had a relocation agent to assist us with everything we needed to do to leave the country. We were also advised to hire an expert to attend the walk-through and to hire a professional cleaning company that specialized in a move.

We had quotes from cleaning companies. Jeesh. I could think of a lot of other ways to spend that kind of money in Europe before moving. But we also knew we didn't want to spend our last weekend in Belgium scrubbing sinks to make them "shine like the top of the Chrysler building."

I saved. And I saved, and I saved—all of the money from everything we had to sell. There were lamps, appliances, a washer and dryer, all kinds of stuff that plugged into a wall. It was also a good time to get rid of any furniture we knew we didn't want to move back across the ocean. Fortunately, the expat community is efficient. I knew all of the sites to post everything. I negotiated. I "bundled" items together to get rid of more and give someone a deal. I sold it all, from the espresso machine to the iron and the toaster to the television. Confession: I sort of enjoyed it. John called me "his own personal Turkish trader." And since he's been to Turkey several times, I guess he would know.

Every euro I earned by pawning off our stuff went into the "cleaning fund" envelope that I had squirreled away. On Saturday morning, when John stopped by the house to let them in, I made a cup of coffee and scrolled through my Twitter feed. It was worth every single cent.

When the walk-through came around on Tuesday, we were feeling confident. It was one of the strangest moving experiences I've ever had. We sat in the kitchen with the landlord, while our expert walked through the entire house with their expert. They bickered back and forth about every little nick, dent and beautifully colored surface (thanks again Isabelle) in the entire four-stories (including the basement). They went into a room, shut the door and negotiated how much each nick, dent and scratch was worth, as subtracted from our damage deposit.

In other words, had we not had our cleaners, our relocation agent and our expert we would have been utterly and royally exploited.

In the end, we got enough of our damage deposit back...(drum roll please)...to pay our boys' catholic school tuition for the rest of the year at their new school.

Cue the big sigh of relief.

Sunday, January 26, 2014
Our Nomadic Journey, Part One: Saying Goodbye

On December 12, we moved to our temporary apartment.

We knew our "pack-up and move-out" would take about four to five days. We knew this would be exhausting. We also knew that at the end of that, we didn't want to wake up in the morning, get on a plane and fly away. We planned an "in-between" week. We needed a way to transition ourselves out of Belgium.

A key factor was location. We needed somewhere nearby so the kids could finish off their last week of school, and we could wrap up whatever was needed as we wound everything down. We found the perfect place.

It was a furnished apartment, advertised as a bed and breakfast. It was halfway between our house in La Hulpe and the kids' school. It was perfect. It was a loft apartment above a garage, with one bedroom and a room with a kitchenette and a pull-out couch. We told them we wouldn't need the breakfast service. I don't think they knew what they were getting into when they agreed to rent to us for the week. You should have seen the look on the guy's face when we pulled up with nine suitcases.

We settled in. As sad as we were to be out of our home, we were happy to have one of the hardest parts of the process over, and a quiet place to live out our last week.

We took the kids to school in the morning. We finished off the last of the football practices. With the cleaners hired, and football (soccer) practices behind us, that left us one last weekend to be tourists. We took a day trip to our favorite Belgian town in the Ardennes (La Roche en Ardennes) and Sunday, we went to the Christmas market in Brussels.

We celebrated Isabelle's birthday on Monday with her favorite dinner (saucisse and frites), by temporarily stealing back the grill we had given to the neighbor and grilling at our apartment. Tuesday, we rented the upstairs party room at the local pub and really confused our Belgian friends with the idea of an open-invite happy hour. I didn't have my class lists, which meant we couldn't send a mass invitation email. We had to rely on word of mouth, which ultimately put the kids in charge of the invites. We had a great turnout and a fun night. Although, I didn't expect all of the going-away gifts! Having to find places for more stuff in our overflowing luggage just about threw me over the edge of my fragile sanity. Thank goodness John had reached his rainbow-gold-sparkly status at Delta and it no longer mattered how heavy our bags were.

That left us one last day of school, and one last night in Belgium. We went to a dear friend's home for dinner. She helped drive us to the airport in the dark the next morning.

Of all of the trials and tribulations I have ever faced living as an expat in Belgium—the last day and night I spent in my beloved adopted country, was one of the most difficult days of my life.

It will be a long, long time before I can think about all of those goodbyes without tears running down my face.

Wednesday, January 29, 2014
Buzz Kill.

The flight went as well as could be expected. There were lots of movies to watch, and everyone was tired and worn out enough to sleep a little.

I've learned a lot about traveling with kids over the years. A long time ago, I realized that it's best to pack every kid a box of (mostly healthy) stuff I know they'll eat, and let them eat what they want whenever they want. It's so much better than having to rely on the airplane food choices. They can of course eat airplane food if they want, but this way, they don't have to.

So yes, Ms. Flight Attendant, I am perfectly fine with my ten-year old son refusing the meal. Please save your judgmental looks for someone else. Not that it's any of your business, but he ate his peanut butter sandwich when we got on the plane, because that's when his body told him it was time to eat. I am also fine with him refusing your hot-pocket-type-pizza-sandwich-thing and only accepting the ice cream cup during the "snack" service. My kids aren't familiar with that sort of gooey cheese goodness (yet) and let's not forget, that it is almost midnight Belgian time. He might not be that hungry.

We got off the plane in a jet lag stupor, and got ourselves through customs. Not being our first time re-entering the good ol' U.S. of A., I knew that one of my biggest jobs as a mom of three was to get rid of all of the forbidden foods before we got off the plane. That meant we had to dump all of the cheeses, uneaten salami sandwiches and fruit. I didn't feel the least bit bad about throwing it all away as most of it had come from our refrigerator before we moved and it had served its purpose well.

We dragged tired little bodies through the line at customs, and each child even answered the agent when spoken to. And not one word was mentioned about our extra bottles of wine. All was good. Avery was in a pile against the wall while we got our NINE suitcases. "You'll be ok," I told him. "It's just the jet lag. We just have to get on the elevator and through the door and Uncle Ryan will be there to take us home."

We shuffled ourselves through the last customs agent. Balancing two carts, wheely carry-ons, backpacks and tired kids, we pushed everyone just a little bit further. "Just get to the elevator," we said again. "Uncle Ryan will be there when it opens to help us."

Only, when it did, there was no Uncle Ryan. There were all sorts of "welcome home" signs for the study-abroad kids we met on the airplane, but no Uncle Ryan. It was kind of funny, to see all of those families waiting with signs and balloons for the college kids coming back after six months abroad. I had to dig out my Belgian phone to text and say, "We're here!"

In all fairness, our flight arrived ahead of schedule, we needed two cars to pick us up, and it was the middle of rush hour on a weeknight the week before Christmas. That's a lot to ask of anyone, but especially of two working parents with little kids. It was enough for us to know we were going to their house, and their house was close to the airport.

Thankfully, my cell phone still worked and we had plenty of luggage to sit on while we waited. We were on our way to their house soon enough with our pile of luggage and backpacks. In our exhaustion, we didn't even really notice or remember that we had to wait a few minutes—it all became a blur in our memories anyway.

The Fowler family was home.

In the end, it turned out to be a good thing Avery didn't eat much on the plane. Somewhere along the way he picked up a stomach bug and spent his first 24 hours in the U.S. with a high fever and unable to keep anything down. Thankfully, it passed quickly and we were just happy it didn't hit any earlier than it did.

On to Christmas!

Friday, January 31, 2014
Our Nomadic Journey, Part Two: Christmas Vacation

The second phase of our trip was all about Christmas. (At this phase of our move, I was still thinking about it like it was all a big "trip." I think I needed a coping mechanism.)

We spent the first weekend with my brother and his wife (Uncle Ryan and Aunt Jenny). We were so happy to be there and catch up, and let the kids get reacquainted with their cousins. We snuck over to our new/old house to leave some luggage, and have the wireless internet installed. (We call it the new/old house because it's the same house we left behind six years ago.)

Then, we were on our way "up North" for a good old-fashioned fun family Christmas with John's family.

It was the second week since we'd been out of our house in Belgium and it really felt like we were on a much-needed vacation. The cousins played. The grown-ups ate and drank. It was wonderful to hold the nine-month-old baby we'd finally gotten to meet, and take time to "be" with everyone. Words can't express our total and complete appreciation for our families and loved ones who were there for us in those first few weeks.

We hadn't had much of a chance to "get ready" for Christmas. But thanks to internet shopping, we had enough to suffice. If there was ever a year not to worry about it, this was it. This was the year that Christmas was all about our family in a way that it had never been, nor probably will ever be to the same extent, ever again.

Tuesday, February 18, 2014
Our Nomadic Journey, Part Three: Let's Just Be Done Already.

Can we please just get these blog posts about the move over with already?

Yes, I know. At this point in the whole process, I was ready to be done with anything and everything having to do with a move.

But, there was a slight problem. We still had to wait for our furniture. In the middle of everything, we experienced a weather phenomenon the weather experts are calling "the polar vortex." From what I understand, that's just a fancy way of saying, colder than hell. No wait, bad analogy, hell is supposed to be hot. Whatever. All I know, is that Minnesota experienced temperatures that rivaled the North Pole, right at the same time we were trying to move in and get settled.

We were already living in our new/old house but without furniture. We had mattresses, a table and chairs from storage, and a camping chair. We also had a newly purchased giant television. I probably don't have to tell you about the arguments over who got to sit in the chair. Although, our new/old house has a fireplace, and laying on a blanket in front of the fireplace was a pretty good alternative to the chair. We felt like squatters.

Meanwhile, school kept getting cancelled because the temperatures were so cold, it was too dangerous to go outside. I was happy that our air shipment contained our Wii, and that Santa brought Isabelle "Just Dance" for Christmas. Unfortunately, this weather also meant delays for our container. It was coming from port via rail to Minneapolis, and the sub-zero temperatures meant the rails were too frozen to operate.

We finally got word that our furniture was here, but because of all of the delays, the company had a difficult time finding a driver to deliver it. They finally scheduled us for a Friday at noon. Of course, we had six inches of snow the night before, and it was a snow emergency. For my Belgian friends, that means we had so much snow, the city needs to plow all of the streets. To do this, there are rules about where you can park your car at night, and then different rules for the day. Of course, during the day of a snow emergency, there is no parking on the street in front of our house. And yet, we were about to have a container delivered. Right there. Thankfully, my genius of a husband thought to call the City to ask. It was a good thing he did too, or we would have had a $500 fine.

I felt physically ill watching this truck pull up to our house on a Friday afternoon. I was there when they packed it. I knew exactly how many boxes were in that container. I knew what our house in Belgium looked like the day before the container came, with stacks of white boxes everywhere. And even though our house here is almost the same square footage as our house in Belgium, the rooms are very different. There was no way, they would be able to unload that truck in four hours without a whole lot of chaos.

Our movers here had never seen anything like it. Every single piece of furniture had been taken apart and put into a box. Our couch, was in six different places. The same was true for our beds, dressers, dining room table and shelves—everything. If our movers in Belgium could have taken apart our mattresses, they probably would have.

I fought hard against the Type A personality that dictates most of my life choices, and opted for Plan B. I left. John and I had already agreed that under no circumstances, were the movers going to be allowed to leave until we at least had beds to sleep in that night, and a couch to sit on for the weekend. I knew I was leaving the house in good hands. I picked up the kids from school and we went to my sister-in-law's house for the rest of the afternoon. We hid. In the end, that choice was probably a better one for my marriage. We got back to the house in the evening and the movers were still getting the last of the boxes in the house and shoving them into whatever tiny spaces were left.

It took all four of the mover guys to figure out how to put the couch together. And I don't think I've ever been so happy to have a couch before.

In this whole chaotic moving mess, we just keep trying to find the good where we can. And it's usually the little things that have counted for the most.

Thursday, February 20, 2014
It's Official.

We still have a few boxes here and there. Ok, a lot of boxes. But I am officially calling this move "over." Funny, I just looked at the date today. February 19, 2014. Two months ago today, December 19, 2013, we flew from Brussels to Minneapolis, to our new/old home.

It is a little strange, but also comfortable to be back in the same house. As I put stuff away into the very cupboards that I emptied six years ago, I feel like I have a chance to make good choices—better, wiser choices. Some of the stuff is going back into the same spot. A lot of stuff is going out the door and not coming back. If there is one thing I learned living in a sparse house for five weeks, we just don't need all the stuff we thought we needed.

I made it official today. I changed my location settings on all of my social media forms—Twitter, Facebook and here on this blog. My heart has this dull ache that comes and goes, and it has been particularly strong today. For six years, my location, Brussels, has been a primary defining factor of my identity. That's what I was doing, that was my purpose.

It's the same feeling I had when I finished college, or even law school. That feeling like you don't exactly know what's coming next. There is all kinds of uncertainty and apprehension. And it's different now too, because we've got little people. My focus has been on them, making sure they are doing ok. It doesn't leave much room for figuring out what's next for me.

But if history has taught me anything, it will be something. A new challenge. Another reinvention, there is something, just around the corner. It will be hard to top the last experience. But I have a lot of faith that I will figure it out.

EPILOGUE

While the previous post was a perfect way to end, I can't help but share some of the funny observations we've had as we re-acclimated to our native culture.

Saturday, February 22, 2014
First Impressions.

It has been fun to watch and observe the reactions of the kids. They pay attention to everything, and they've had several insightful, and sometimes funny, observations about America.

For example, Isabelle noticed the toilets. (Keep in mind she was born in Belgium, and the last time she'd been on U.S. soil was almost two years ago.) "Mommy!" she said. "The toilet flushers here are so cool, they are little handles!" (In Belgium, most of the toilets flush with a button on top.) It's something, I don't think I ever even noticed until she pointed it out. That was followed a few days later with, "Mommy! The toilet paper here is SO soft!" Ahem. Apparently, I should have invested more money in my toilet paper purchases there.

I could do an entire post about American commercials. During the first week of living in our house, Avery said, "Mommy, the commercials here say really important things about life, but then it's for something stupid like toothpaste."

We are also watching a lot more commercials here than we ever have. Back in Belgium, the kids watched a lot of shows on DVDs. But even the shows they watched on television seemed to have less commercials than here. Luke calls them "previews." "Mommy," he said. "There are just too many previews, I don't like all of the previews." It took me a minute to figure out what he was talking about. And one day, he tracked me down where I was unpacking boxes, to tell me, "Mommy! Did you know you can buy a vacuum without cords? I saw it on TV!"

We are not yet used to tuning out the previews yet. I would guess that most American kids have figured out that commercials are the time to run to the bathroom, at least that's what I always used to do during the commercials. Not my kids. My kids are completely riveted to the commercials. Entranced. As a result, I've found myself having to explain a lot of things that I never expected to explain—like erectile dysfunction and vaginal dryness. Why does every product in the pharmacy seem to need its own commercial?

One day last week, Avery came home from school, very excited. "Mommy," he said. "Today, I learned how to open my milk." Mental head slap. I've tried to anticipate and preempt some of their challenges, like explaining the Pledge of Allegiance. But opening his milk carton is not something I ever would have thought to show him. But of course, they didn't have milk cartons in Belgium. They don't drink milk with lunch in Belgium (only breakfast) and anyway, milk is in bottles there, not cartons.

One morning, it snowed. Our short drive to school took exactly the same amount of time as it always did. And the kids said, "Mommy! The cars are driving! In the snow!" I answered, "Yes, I know. It's Minnesota."

Friday, February 28, 2014
Buffalo Wings, Chocolate Torte and Chameleons

Lately, John and I have been enjoying one of the best parts about being back in Minnesota: Grandma Sue. Grandma Sue has been coming to town a lot lately to see all of the grandkids. When she does, she divides her time between us and John's sister. She is happy to stay with the kids while John and I enjoy a quick night out. It helps all of us deal with the monotony of a long winter.

Last night, was just such a date night. We usually keep it simple and last night was no different. I really wanted a beer (there is a great new American gluten-free beer) and wings. We couldn't find Buffalo wings in Belgium, so John and I are on a mission to find the best wings in St. Paul.

Our afternoon and evening had been about driving the carpool to ballet, making sure homework was done, feeding Grandma and the crew and herding everyone through baths and showers. Then it was time to grab the keys and get out the door without looking back. I had a lipstick in my purse and I swiped it over my lips in the car. I am in desperate need of a haircut, and I'm always cold, those two factors combined mean I haven't taken my winter hat off my head since we arrived in Minnesota in December. In other words, we weren't exactly all decked out. I wasn't worried.

We found our way to a local pub. It specializes in a variety of beer and their menu is more European than most around here, but I assumed they still had wings. Of course they did, it's America.

Their sophisticated beer selection and "European" menu (as well as their location on the edge of downtown) attracts young professionals, like corporate climbers and attorneys. We bellied-up to the bar and ordered.

The bar was crowded, but thinned out as the night went on. There was a young couple near us at the bar and they were obviously on a date. He was dressed uber-cool and had thick, dark, stuck-his-finger-in-an-electrical-socket-type-hair and black-rimmed glasses. If I had to guess? He was a new lawyer. There is no judgment intended, it's just that I used to be one myself once. The palpable self-confidence emanating from his being was easy for me to recognize. His date was a petite blond, and she was wearing a sweater vest. She had a look of sweet innocence, that made me think she might be a kindergarten teacher. She seemed to hang on his every word and acted as if she was the luckiest girl in the world to be out with him.

Whenever we sit at the bar, my extroverted, salesman-husband looks for any opportunity to talk to everyone around us. When the waitress delivered an amazing chocolate dessert to the date-couple, John leaned over to ask, "What is that? Is it ice cream? It looks really good." Uber-cool-guy answered in the most pretentious, arrogant voice I've heard in a while, "No, it's a chocolate torte." I think his nose turned up in the air a bit as he said it too. The judgment in his eyes was emphasized by the tone in his voice. We clearly weren't worth talking to.

John nodded his head slightly, smiled politely and said, "Thanks." Then John turned to me and we laughed. I laughed so hard, I cried.

In those moments of laughter, I realized what we must look like to the uber-cool guy. Me in my black stocking hat, drinking local beer from the bottle and eating a messy plate of wings. I certainly didn't look like the lawyer I once was.

He certainly wouldn't know by looking at us that we had just moved to Minnesota from Central Europe. We looked as Minnesotan as anyone else there that night. How could he possibly know that of course I know what a chocolate torte is! Last spring, I took a cooking class taught by my friend from the kids' school who had trained as a French chef. In that class, I learned how to make a chocolate torte from scratch by melting butter and dark Belgian chocolate. In that class, I had to learn by only listening to and speaking French.

I think it is safe to say that John and I have mastered the art of blending in. After years of living and traveling abroad in a post-9/11 world, we have learned to fit into whatever scene surrounds us, in the moment. It's a skill that I am rather proud of, as I would rather not stand out in a crowd. At this point in my life, I am much more comfortable blending in…like chameleons. Last night, I was happy to let the spotlight shine on the lawyers and young professionals who were excited to be out, enjoying the more exotic choices on the menu and drinking fancier drinks. We looked exactly how we wanted to look…like two cold Midwesterners, with a chance to sneak out for a quick beer and a plate of wings. If that means we don't deserve Mr. Uber-Cool's approval, so be it…we will probably just laugh it off.

But I have this message for Mr. Uber-Cool, and a reminder for all of us, myself included: Be careful not to judge. For you never know, the person sitting next to you might just be a chameleon.

About the Author

Natalie Fowler is an author and freelance editor. Her paranormal mystery series and young adult trilogy are represented by literary agent Terrie Wolf, of AKA Literary, LLC. Natalie is also a staff editor and regular contributor for FATE Magazine, the longest running paranormal magazine featuring true stories of the strange and unknown.

Fascinated by ghost stories from an early age, Natalie is also a member of Ghost Stories Ink, a group of authors and illustrators who go on paranormal investigations in search of creative inspiration. Natalie serves as the group's researcher and historian. In her free time, Natalie can often be found in dusty old attics, creepy dark basements or amidst the stacks of old books at the history libraries. Her book, MONSTERS OF THE MIDWEST co-authored with Jessica Freeburg, was released in October 2015 by Adventure Publications.

Find out more about Natalie's projects and books by visiting her website www.NatalieFowler.com

Follow her on Twitter @NCTFowler or find her on Facebook, www.facebook.com/NCTFowler

Natalie and her husband, John, are excited for their children to have an American high school experience. But they hope that one day, life will offer them another adventure overseas.

Made in the USA
Middletown, DE
11 January 2024

47649071R00165